Jamming
the
MEDIA

jamming
the media

A

[by GARETH BRANWYN]

Citizen's
GUIDE

RECLAIMING THE TOOLS
of COMMUNICATION)

CHRONICLE BOOKS
SAN FRANCISCO

© 1997 by Gareth Branwyn.
All rights reserved. No part of this book may be reproduced in any form without written permission from the Publisher.

Page 354 constitutes a continuation of the copyright page.

Printed in the United States of America.

Library of Congress Cataloging-in-Publication Data available.

ISBN 0-8118-1795-4

Book and cover design by Post Tool

Distributed in Canada by
Raincoast Books 8680 Cambie Street Vancouver, BC V6P 6M9

10 9 8 7 6 5 4 3 2 1

Chronicle Books 85 Second Street San Francisco, CA 94105

Web Site: www.chronbooks.com

Contents)

Jamming
MEDIA

Clients From Hell Fuel Career Launch] It started out like any other day in the life of a freelance graphic artist. I'd been propped up at my drawing board most of the weekend working on a "corporate identity program" for a new client. With a hired illustrator, I had created mock-ups for a presentation folder, brochure, letterhead, business cards, and an envelope. We were both giddy with enthusiasm over the results. I was sure it was one of the snappiest little packages I'd ever put together and was anxious to show the clients. Properly stoked on coffee, I waited in my home studio for their arrival, nervously shuffling papers and picking bits of eraser and spray mount off of the presentation boards. The clients soon arrived and I, confidently, went through my usual routine, going through the presentation in that slightly obtuse and snobby language that designers learn in school and design journals. I took them through each piece and then showed them ink and paper swatches. They said little, betraying few emotions. After I'd finished, they hovered over the layouts, silently passing them back and forth. The coffee in my stomach turned on me as their little frowns and lip-biting started to do the talking for them. Over the next few minutes, they turned my "best work" into my biggest nightmare. They hated everything about it, down to the typestyles and the text formatting ("Why on Earth would you want to center the text?" "Shouldn't this headline be *really big?*") They even disliked the illustrators' rough sketches, which I found beyond belief. As I lay emotionally twitching and moaning on the floor, they left with that dreaded "back to the drawing board" request on their lips. As I watched them get into their car from my living room window, I heard myself drone: "That's it. I quit!" And I did.

Luckily, at the time, I was in a living situation where I didn't have to make a lot of money to sustain myself. I continued working for a few well-paying clients that liked what I did, but took on no new work. Since being a graphic artist still felt like a fundamental part of my cosmic job description, I immediately began thinking of what I could do creatively with my newfound "free time." I had just started a regular monthly art and culture club called Cafe Gaga and I decided that I'd produce an amateur magazine (or a "zine") to

augment these monthly discussions. I figured I'd make it non-specific to the
group so that I could send it to other friends and acquaintances. The first
issue of *Going Gaga* (subtitled "Art, Information, and Noise") was a modest
six pages with a few graphics and several articles hijacked from other
sources (like Luis Buñuel's recipe for making a surrealist martini). Besides
a few "ohhs" and "ahhs," the first issue received little fanfare. The second
issue was larger and had a theme: "Dead Dadaist Defiled." It explored the
bizarre paradox of an anti-establishment art movement like Dada becoming
the subject of academic debate, art history and preservation. I sent a copy of
the issue to Lloyd Dunn, then editor of the "machine art" zine *Photostatic*.
He responded with encouragement and suggested I send a copy to *Factsheet
Five,* a quarterly review of zines that listed hundreds of basement-produced
pubs like mine. When *Factsheet Five* printed a favorable review, I began getting orders from all over the world and people asking me about annual subscription rates and upcoming themes. It was this response, this hungry
audience, that prompted me to get serious. "They think this is an actual
magazine," I chuckled to myself. "Maybe I should try and give them one."
Firing up the ol' Mac SE and laser printer, I quickly churned out a subscription card and a schedule of upcoming issues. Suddenly . . . totally unex-
pectedly . . . I was in the publishing business.

And, people liked what I did! Setting out to please only myself, covering
things I found interesting, designing something that I found visually
provocative, I began to attract attention. The icing on the cake was when
well-known people started to respond. One morning I got an email message
from Julian Dibbell of the *Village Voice. "Going Gaga* rocks!" he enthused.
Kevin Kelly (who's since gone on to become the editor of *Wired* magazine)
called *Gaga* one of his favorite zines in *Whole Earth Review*. Steward Brand,
Howard Rheingold *(Whole Earth Review),* Erik Davis *(Village Voice),* R.U. Sirius
(Mondo 2000). The list goes on. People who I'd admired for years, people I
never imagined having an opportunity to interact with, were suddenly paying attention to me. If I'd tried to get these people's attention, to be clever and
hip and relevant, it undoubtedly would have backfired. I would have labored

too hard and the panting would've given me away. That's what was so deeply gratifying. I wasn't trying to be anything special. I was basically talking to myself . . . and I had attracted a roomful of brilliant conversationalists.

Every step I've taken from that point on leads down a path that ends in the present—to the book you're holding in your hands. From *Going Gaga,* I was asked by R.U. Sirius to work on *Mondo 2000.* Another fan of *Going Gaga,* fellow zine publisher Mark Frauenfelder, was producing a surprisingly similar photocopied zine called *bOING bOING.* He and I began working on each other's publications and I eventually rolled *Going Gaga* into *bOING bOING.* The *Mondo* and *bOING bOING* work led to my writing for *Wired,* and the *Wired* exposure has led me into the book writing business. Without *Going Gaga,* a little digest-sized zine, printed on a laser printer and copier in my basement, none of this is likely to have happened.

The Electronic Cottage: A Flashforward] My four-year-old, Blake, and I had just finished a father and son project. He'd created a picture on our Macintosh, using a paint program that he already knew better than I. We printed the art out on our laser printer and he decided that he wanted to make some additions to it. He didn't want to make the changes in the paint program, he announced, he wanted to make multiple copies of the art at various sizes and then collage them. With my permission, he fired up the desktop copier and waited patiently for the green ready light. After reducing and enlarging the image several times and cutting and pasting, he presented the finished art to me. After my obligatory parental praises and pats, he announced, "I want to fax it to someone." I wracked my brain trying to think of a suitable recipient who knew Blake and had a fax machine. I scribbled down a number on a piece of paper and handed it to him as he confidently padded towards the fax machine. He fed the paper in properly, dialed the number and sent the fax as he obnoxiously mimicked the high-pitched fax tones. Later, when I was tucking him into bed and telling him how much fun I'd had, I casually added: "By the way, did you know that all that stuff we used tonight—the computer, the printer, the copier, and the fax machine—didn't even exist a few years before you were born? All that stuff is new." He looked genuinely stunned, as his eyes began darting back and forth, trying to grasp this thought. He managed a simple and distant "Really?" as he rolled over, his eyes still wide and blinking. "My God, I think I just blew his mind," I thought as I turned off the light and left the room.

The central image of James Dreyden's 1981 book *The Electronic Cottage* is of a home wired into a global interactive data environment. In the antiquated Apple II and TRS-80 world of the time, these projections seemed fantastic, verging on sci-fi. I now live in such an electronic cottage, one that is far beyond the technology explored in Dreyden's book. The back bedroom of our small brick colonial house, built right after World War II, is now crammed with digital technology. Two computers (one with a built-in TV) are wired into the Internet with high-speed modems. Laser printers, a copier, a fax machine, a headset telephone, a digital camera, three CD players (one audio, two computer), a professional portable tape recorder, a shortwave receiver, and other devices clutter tables that skirt the room. Cast-off and forgotten old tech gathers dust in corners and on shelves. Hundreds of floppy disks and CDs, offering libraries worth of information and entertainment, are everywhere stacked into twisting towers of plastic.

The rest of our house is similarly choked with '80s and '90s "personal tech": more computers, a portable phone, a personal data assistant, sound mixing equipment, TVs, VCRs, etc. While my work as a technology writer and my insatiable techno-lust makes our house somewhat of an exception, a survey of middle class American homes would probably find a similar cache of high techery, albeit in less obscene quantities.

Sometimes, in the middle of the night, when I get up to go to the bathroom, I stop in the doorway of my office and peer in. The cosmic screen-savers are cruising along at warp speed and the green, red, and yellow lights on all the hardware twinkle in the darkness, making the room look like the cockpit of a work-a-day spaceship. I wonder what the original owners of the house would think if they had a similar vision in the night . . . a flashforward on their way to the bathroom. For them it would be science fiction.

Let's take their hands for a moment, pull them into the Twilight Zone, and show them what we've done with the back bedroom.

Our Media Hack Shack] Over the years, my wife and I have built up this little home media studio. Living on a rather tight budget (being flaky artist types), we've built our global media shack with mainly mid-priced and used techno-toys. Using this cobbled-together tech, and lots of sweat equity, we've so far produced:

> two highly-regarded print zines
> two software packages
> seven professional recordings on tape, vinyl, and CD
> the text for seven books
> countless magazine and newspaper articles
> the print materials for dozens of art and cultural events
> four World Wide Web sites and other Net-based publications

And, that's not counting our work for years as freelance graphic artists, cranking out other people's newsletters, annual reports, stationery, ads, logos, and signage. It also does not count the daily global communication that goes on over the Internet to make all the above happen. Between my wife's self-managed career as a jazz singer and my octopus-like existence as a do-it-yourself (DIY) publisher and freelance writer, our house hums all day long like a tiny CNN newsroom.

All of this personal profiling is not meant to be a brag, but simply to show what an "average human intelligent unit" (to paraphrase Buckminster Fuller) can accomplish, given these available technologies, a passion to communicate, and . . . oh yeah . . . no sleep! And, all of it was done on less money than most yuppies spend on the family Voyager. If these media hacking stories appeal to you, read on, there's plenty more in the pages to come . . .

Closing the Loop] Decentralized, fringe media, of the kind outlined in this book, begs participation . . . feedback. And so did I. If you're currently involved in an amateur media project or are inspired to start one because of this book, I'd love to hear from you. My email address is garethb2@earthlink.net. Also, check out the Jamming the Media site on the World Wide Web at home.earthlink.net/~garethb2/jamming/.

Gareth Branwyn
Arlington, VA

**MEDIA,
by altering the
ENVIRONMENT, evoke in
us unique ratios of sense
PERCEPTIONS.
The extension of any
one sense ALTERS the way
we think
and act—
the way we perceive
the WORLD. When these
ratios change,
MEN CHANGE.**
—Marshall McLuhan,
The Medium Is the Massage

**HELLO big eye in the sky.
Please DON'T BLINK
while I'm on.**
—Firesign Theater

We live in a televisual, wired world. We stare like possum caught in headlights at a mind-numbing parade of talk shows, game shows, summer film blockbusters, infomercials, celebrity murder trials, and news programs scripted to juice ratings. We've waded deep up to our eyeballs into a media spew of TV, film, video, print, radio, CD-ROMs, and online services. Until recently, most of this media was "read-only," strictly for passive consumption. An individual or group could do little to contribute to or contradict the official big media feed. Producing and broadcasting quality media rested in the hands of megacorporations, governments, and individuals with deep pockets.

In the past decade, things have changed, thanks in part to new media technologies in which hardware has dramatically shrunk in size and cost. Desktop publishing was the first advance on the new media front, offering small organizations and individuals the ability to circumvent established printing and publishing channels. What once took days, several people, and expensive equipment to produce could suddenly be done by one industrious individual on a PC in an afternoon.

In the 1990s, all forms of media have been experiencing a similar migration from equipment-choked studios and publishing houses to individual desktops. The creative and democratizing potential of this is staggering. A personal computer, bought at your local Akbar and Jeff's Computer Hut, can now be wired up to act as a full-color publishing house, a broadcast-quality TV studio, a sound recording studio, or an island in the digital oceans of cyberspace. Any adventuresome geek with cheap retail parts and some electronics aptitude can kluge together a micro radio station that can broadcast to a neighborhood. Musicians, once dependent on major record labels, can now do an entire record's production at home and either self-distribute it or plug it into a growing number of independent distribution channels. Internet-based music services are springing up like mushrooms in a moist meadow, offering unsigned bands the opportunity to hawk their wares to an increasingly wired global audience. Street-level music technologies (synthesizers, samplers, mixers, tape decks, turntables) have spawned whole new musical genres such as rap, industrial, and the many flavors of techno. In the realm of video, cheap, portable camcorders have turned regular citizens into roving cyborg eyes of the media, constantly on the lookout for the next Rodney King incident, hurricane, or Hollywood actor caught with a hooker. Camcorders are also being used by no-budget artists and filmmakers to create innovative work, unburdened by a commercial studio's bottom line.

In repressive countries where the government is the broadcaster, portable video cameras have become high-powered weapons in a war of truth versus propaganda. Videotapes contradicting official government spins are circulated through alternative distribution channels called *bicycle networks*. This type of clandestine networking was instrumental in eroding communism in the Eastern bloc and during China's student uprisings. Fax machines linked into worldwide networks have also been pressed into service, churning out non-status-quo political, cultural, and artistic messages.

The tradition among repressive governments of controlling the use of communication technology is a testament to how subversive it can be.

FROM PASSIVE
to ACTIVE MEDIA)

As technology travels along its inevitable trajectory towards "cheaper, faster, better," it's putting powerful communication technologies into the hands of greater numbers of people. While the media continues to go hog-wild hyping the Internet, panting over it as the ultimate consumer marketplace where you can mainline "interactive" TV, video on demand, and virtual shopping, there's a growing number of people who are discovering the many-to-many media potential of the Net. A new form of media is growing up in cyberspace, a global do-it-yourself newsroom and cultural salon where individuals simultaneously create and consume news and information, blurring the distinction between publisher, reporter, and reader. *Sociomedia* is a term that's been suggested to describe this new type of media born out of online social interaction. Participants on bulletin board systems (BBSes), Usenet newsgroups, Internet virtual worlds, and online services like AOL and CompuServe trade news, information, ideas, experiences (along with lots of rumors, flames, and utter nonsense). When a disaster or other big news event occurs, netizens immediately log on to share news, argue, offer assistance, and to publicly piss and moan. With the explosion of the World Wide Web, individuals, students, and corporations large and small are trying to cobble together their own little media empires in cyberspace.

And, while the Internet gets most of the media ink and electrons—and is unquestionably in the vanguard of widely distributed participatory media—

pirate radio, audiocassette publishing, and disk-based multimedia are also available to amateur medianauts. The big bottleneck in do-it-yourself media production has always been promotion and distribution. Now, anyone with an Internet connection can reach a potentially huge audience at a reasonable cost. If you've got something to say, modest resources, and a healthy measure of pioneering grit, chances are you can find a media channel on which to broadcast.

ENTER *the*
MEDIA HACKER) Producing your own media can be both a lot

of fun and a way of tossing a mote into the big unblinking eye of the media. Amateur media hackers run the gamut, from politicos—left, right, and over-the-wall—to Internet denizens, Gen X-ers, kooks, media pranksters, and plain ol' vanilla citizens. Many of these people may be ignorant of (or uninterested in) the larger implications of what they're doing, but they are part of a communications revolution that is radically changing the way media are created, delivered, and consumed.

GOING GAGA N°.1 *by* Gareth Branwyn ^

The term *hacker* became popular in the 1970s, defining any pocket-protected geek who could program computers and overcome imposed limitations in working with machines. In its early usage, it also implied someone who embraced a "hacker ethic," or a general belief in free and open sharing of information and the questioning of authority structures that might limit access to information. The term took on more ominous connotations in the late '80s and early '90s, when overzealous, often clueless, journalists struggled to convincingly report on a new era of computer intrusions, data heists, and digital viruses. (The hacker community uses the term *cracker* to refer to hackers with malicious or criminal intent.) In their most flattering light, hackers are often presented as the postmodern equivalent of frontier trailblazers and eccentric visionaries. We certainly have them to thank for the personal computer and the Internet, both made possible by their ingenious, obsessive efforts.

In this book, I've cooked up the term *media hackers* to describe those who enjoy tinkering with various forms of media and who believe in a similar hacker ethic. Media hackers are to big media what independent computer hackers are to big computer corporations. They share the hacker's mistrust of imposed limitations, the challenge of doing more with less, and the joy of finding creative solutions to systemic problems. Media hackers are not satisfied with the mainstream media's long-standing monopoly on news, information, and entertainment. Like most computer hackers, media hackers are proud of their pioneering spirit and technological prowess in spite of limited resources and their vigilance against the forces that would seek to restrict knowledge and free inquiry.

SAME *as it*

EVER WAS?) DIY media is nothing new. The history of the twentieth century is filled with stories of hobbyists and amateurs who cobbled together low-cost radios, hand printed and bound books, and cranked out newsletters and handbills on mimeograph machines. **New media technolo**gies have always attracted amateurs who help forge each new medium. The radio, the television, the computer, and the Internet are prime examples. It's easy, when considering these new technologies and the potential they promise, to come down with a techno-utopian fever dream of limitless, universally available technology, independent production, and a crowded marketplace of enlightened content. It's sobering to remind ourselves of the

< "BODY READER" < Going GaGa
K. Gekker,

hype that precedes new technologies and how few of the loftier human goals are fulfilled through these technologies.

Todd Lappin, in an article in the May '95 issue of *Wired*, compares the similarities between the early days of radio with today's burgeoning Internet. He finds shocking similarities between the two, with radio pioneers also blathering on about the political, educational, artistic, and even spiritual fulfillment that radio promised to the plugged-in masses. This vision of unbound information riches over the airwaves took a dramatic downturn as soon as radio went commercial. Soon, the amateurs who helped pave the way were cast aside, and those who couldn't afford to pay the advertising piper lost their voice. Lappin concludes, "Maybe things will be different this time. Online media enables us to be both consumers and suppliers of electronic content. Today, we have a second chance to 'develop the material that is transmitted into that which is really worthwhile,' as Hoover put it in 1924. Perhaps radio wasn't the right technology. But the Web and the Net may well be. Our job is to make sure that glorious potential doesn't get stuffed into yet another tired, old media box."

There are other sobering thoughts, not the least of which is how these Goliath-size corporations are going to respond to threats to their domination of the mediascape by lots of puny media-hacking Davids. Book and magazine publishers, the record industry, and other media and entertainment providers are extremely nervous about the growth of decentralized media and the grand divergence that's rapidly morphing the mediascape beyond their control. The phone companies, the TV and cable networks, the online services, and the print industry are all fighting a war on multiple fronts. They're trying to figure out where the future is going to land so that they can build the landing facilities, but the future seems to be threatening to touch down everywhere at once. There are too many new digital technologies, delivery systems, and divergent theories about their impact. Companies are frantically forming and reforming alliances and schizophrenically retooling themselves in anticipation of the next big trend. Add to this the fear that they may be losing control to smaller, leaner independents and pesky media hackers, and you've got a lot of panicked dinosaurs lumbering around in circles. One can only wonder how all this will shake out (and who's gonna get stepped on in the process). It's obvious that these companies are not going to just lie down and die. A few of them will dart off in the wrong direction and end up as fossils, but most of them are likely to mutate into something new to remain viable. Hopefully, this Darwinian process will happen without them attempting to block the decentralized media channels that are rapidly growing.

John Gilmore, a cryptographer and founding member of the Electronic Frontier Foundation, is reported to have said, "The Net reads censorship as damage and routes around it." If this is true, and true in the broader sense where censorship can mean any attempt to impose central control, how will these media giants reclaim the commercial high ground without spoiling the party? It is possible that big and little media can peacefully co-exist in the new mediascape? If so, consumers who want passive "on-demand" entertainment and information will get it, while those who want to continue to build alternative media networks will be able to use the same cyberspace and cheap media tech to do so. If the majors get greedy and insist on being the gatekeepers of all media, things could get ugly.

And, last but not least of the issues to dampen our techno-enthusiasm concerns access. Listening to the news, watching the growing crop of breathless computer-related TV shows, and surfing the Net, one could naively conclude that most everyone in America (and a big chunk of the rest of the world) is hot doggin' on the big Internet tsunami. In truth, only an estimated 23 percent of American households have access to the Internet.

Widespread debate rages on Capitol Hill and in cyberspace over issues of universal access (where everyone would have free Net access) and the growing chasm between information "haves" and "have-nots." The Internet (and most realms of DIY media) is still largely populated by white, middle-class males. The Net has grown out of a culture of scientists, academics, and students who've been able to use this new technology to mine its riches. They have become very familiar with its eccentricities. For those un-wired masses who haven't learned how to use an ATM or program a VCR, the Net will present a real challenge, even as the technology becomes more user-friendly. So, even given universal access, there would need to be a massive investment in education and training to get everyone up to speed. There will also be a need to convince people that the Net is worth the effort. In a world where the common belief is still that the Net is a place where students, perverts, and brainiacs hang out, we have a long way to go before Uncle Morty and the corner grocer find a practical reason to log on (if, in fact, they can). Acces issues will continue to be vigorously debated as the future of the medium unfolds.

PIRATES

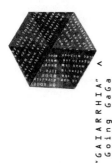

of the MEDIASCAPE **)** Appropriation. Recuperation. Plagiarism. Copying. Cutting. Pasting. Sampling. These could very well be the mantras of our age. The coupling of cheap, ubiquitous media technologies with the ability to sample the world around us has had a Promethean effect on our art, culture, and legal system. Sounds, images, text, and everything else have become stored bits of light that can be endlessly replicated, morphed, and mutated. This development has called into question old notions of property, theft, place, and the ownership of ideas. Artists and cultural activists, especially those on the fringes, have been grappling with the implications of all this throughout the twentieth century, most vehemently in the last few decades. The rapid cultural migration into cyberspace has greatly accelerated the debate.

"GAIARRHIA," Going GaGa
P. Adams, Media

Is it theft, in the traditional sense of the word, when you're only peeling off a copy and not disturbing the original? Is it plagiarism when you use sounds, images, and text from the mediascape as source materials in your artwork? When does the original work dissolve into something that no longer maintains its originality? This is highly debated in rap and other sampler-intensive forms of music where there are varying degrees of recognizing the original material. The copying of commercial music and software is almost a universal practice, yet it is clearly illegal. Should *all* the copy pirates (which probably includes most everyone reading this book) be hauled off to jail, or should more realistic laws and commercial practices be adopted that accept new digital realities? And where exactly are electronic media located anyway? If someone in Peoria, Illinois, downloads hard-core porno from a BBS in Southern California, should that BBS be accountable to the community standards of Peoria or the more open standards of its hometown?

Media hackers have always been keenly aware of these issues and in many ways have helped accelerate their debate. Zine publishers, amateur video-graphers, computer hackers, and audio collage artists have always played fast and loose with copyright laws. Some are convinced that because they're small-time and noncommercial, the owners of the material will not find out. For others, skirting copyright law is an intentional antago-nism towards "pre-electronic" laws and outdated mainstream values. Performance-art band and cultural provocateurs Negativland, who were sued by U2's label Island Records for sampling without permission, have taken up a crusade to bring public attention to the complexities sur-rounding current copyright and fair use laws. And they are going about it with a great deal of humor. One of their projects, a book/CD combo called *Fair Use*, sports a sticker that says "Copyright infringement is your best entertainment value."

Of course, not everyone engaged in media piracy is either lazy or crusading for new laws and attitudes surrounding intellectual property. Some are in it for purely destructive, criminal purposes and naked financial gain. It is these rip-off artists and con men who help clearly define the difference between those who care about the media—and therefore want to change the law to reflect current realities—and those who simply want to pillage for fun and profit.

Why Jamming?)

In William Gibson's visionary 1985 short story "Burning Chrome," the main character declares, "The street finds its own uses for things." Like so many aspects of Gibson's future, the idea of "street tech"—trickle-down high technology used in ways unimagined by its designers—has increasingly become a '90s reality. The early developers of desktop publishing and the original architects of the Internet would undoubtedly be shocked by today's personal media technologies and the wild diversity of their uses. And what would the developers of the record turntable make of an art form like rap that builds its sound (and an entire musical subculture) around the apparent misuse of the device?

This book is about people using media in new and creative ways, "jamming" like musicians jam, making it up as they go along. *Jamming* also refers to the scrambling of broadcast signals, as in the interruption of a radio signal by electronic means. We will explore this literally, in our coverage of pirate media, but more generally we'll explore the breaking up of the mainstream media's monopoly on ideas through the introduction of new voices. The whole point of alternative media is to jam the status quo with ideas and viewpoints not found in conventional media and not subject to the tidal influences of commercial sponsorship and demographics. In its purest form, DIY media is simply the unfettered opportunity for people to say what's on their minds, regardless of the unpopularity of their viewpoints or the anticipation of an audience.

Subsequent chapters of this book will include a section on piracy related to the medium being discussed. We will look at "piracy" as it falls into an interzone between old and new value systems, and piracy as out-and-out theft.

THE NEW MEDIA HACKER'S STARTER KIT

RUBBER RAT < from Cafe GaGa "bagazine"

Getting Started) DIY media is for doers, not pontificators. (You won't find too many media hackers sitting around watching *Geraldo* reruns or QVC.) When media moguls and software company press releases use the term *interactive*, they really mean "randomly accessible static content," such as a CD-ROM that has lots of links between its multimedia files or a movie with several plot paths. In truth, interactivity is something that *people* do. Most DIY media are interactive in the sense that they grow out of conversation and are highly responsive to feedback. Zines, both print and Net-based, are often nodes in a network as much as they are publications, with lively letters columns (or chat areas), reviews of other zines, and large amounts of the content contributed by readers. Electronic mailing lists and BBSes are mostly, or entirely, composed of participant responses. Mail art, collaborative collage, and other forms of so-called networking art use art, cultural detritus, and screeds to build a conversation among participants. In audiocassette networking, poetry, rants, homegrown music and found sounds, and personal audio documentaries are exchanged.

If you really want to get involved in interactive entertainment and participatory media, don't wait for your cable company to wire up that set-top box. It's only going to offer you such piquant choices as whether Stallone decapitates the terrorist, blows him up, or runs off with the babe. Make your own media . . . now! It's infinitely more fun and stimulating, and it disengages us, at least for a moment, from the monoculture that big media offers.

The Starter Kit sections of this book will provide ideas and resources to get you started in each medium under discussion (zines, multimedia, cable access, web publishing, etc.). For this introductory chapter, I've provided a short survey of ideas that have shaped our perception of media in the twentieth century, a list of books that explain these ideas in greater detail, and other resources that may be useful to budding media hackers.

The Lowdown Guide to High-Brow Media Theories)

What follows is an attempt at a plain English translation of a number of influential media theories relevant to media hackers. If after looking into them you still conclude they're nonsense, at least knowing basic media theory will make you sound cooler at parties and art openings. (For instance, did you know that Marshall McLuhan's famous book is actually called *The Medium Is the Massage?* Try tossing that often overlooked detail into your next cocktail party.)

THE SOCIETY OF THE SPECTACLE

In 1967, a book called *Society of the Spectacle* appeared in France, penned by Guy Debord, chief theorist for a group of grumpy French anarchists called Situationist International. In this slim volume of ponderous aphorisms, Debord attempted to outline a new theory of media that updated Marxism for an increasingly media-dominated twentieth century. Debord and the Situationists have had a tremendous impact on subsequent radical theories of media and culture, influencing everyone from postmodernists such as Baudrillard and Foucault to early punk rock and the zine publishing movement.

K e y P O I N T S

: The Situationists believed that our media-dominated capitalist society ("The Spectacle") has replaced the industrial age's state control of the masses through pain and hard labor with control through pleasure and the promise of a perpetually illusive "good life." The main means of this control is the creation and manipulation of spectacles and commodities, a kind of virtual reality, that creates the illusion of free choice without any of the messy noncomformity and free thinking that come with actual freedom. (Remember the 7-11 campaign in the 1980s that hyped America's freedom of choice as the freedom to choose between Coke and Pepsi?)

: To the Situationists, people are duped through the media into cross-wiring true human desires (for such things as pleasure, love, creativity, and liberty) with products and spectacles that promise to fulfill these desires. Human power is voluntarily exiled to a world beyond —the world that television offers but never delivers. Debord wrote, "All that once was directly lived has become mere representation."

: The Situationists also believed that The Spectacle had become so sophisticated that it could successfully recuperate rebellion, strip it of its threatening content, and re-sell it as pure image. So-called alternative rock is a consummate case in point.

: One of the main Situationist tactics for fighting The Spectacle was *detournement,* or the altering of ads, news items, cartoons, etc., to render them meaningless or to point out their subtle manipulation. Detournement has since become a common tactic in all forms of media hacking.

THE MEDIUM IS THE MESSAGE

Marshall McLuhan is arguably the most influential media philosopher of the twentieth century. In the late '60s, his ideas about media, culture, and technology, as presented in *Understanding Media,* sparked controversy and debate that echoes to the present. Clearly a product of the times, when the Vietnam War and student protests were nightly televised into the world's living rooms, McLuhan's theory of an electronic global village offered an optimistic view of how electronic media could bring people back together. He spoke of "retribalization," the idea that the linearity and fragmentation resulting from the dominance of print media would be overtaken by the liquid, sensual, multimedia worlds of TV, video, and other electronic media.

K e y P O I N T S

: McLuhan's central thesis and oft-quoted statement "The medium is the message" (which he changed to "massage" on the book title because "no part of us is untouched" by it) concerns the way our tools shape us and how "we become what we behold." In other words, the technology that carries the message shapes the nature of the message. Text, presented in a linear, fragmented, and static form, led to an overemphasis on reductionist thinking, logic, facts, and a mechanical worldview. On the other hand, McLuhan believed that the advent of an electronic global village would lead us back to more nonlinear, preliterate, and mythic forms of thinking and behaving.

: While the medium of print had helped to isolate nationalities, factions, and generations of humankind, the electronic commons would reunite us into a global community of "commitment and participation."

: Contrary to one criticism of him, McLuhan was not completely naive about the power of electronic media. He argued that, if media were a physical extension of the human body, like an exterior nervous system, that extension came at a loss of some kind, an "amputation." One doesn't have to think very hard to generate a list of what some of these losses might be (the loss of flesh and blood community, for instance).

: Given the common reading of McLuhan and his vision of a retribalized humanity, it's not surprising that he's become a patron saint of cyberculture. Certainly the Internet, even with all its shortcomings, is an obvious manifestation of an electronic global village. Ironically, the Net is still very much like a print medium (with text and static images), whereas McLuhan saw his electronic village as awakening us from the "typographic trance" of Gutenberg.

MANUFACTURED CONSENT

American linguist and political activist Noam Chomsky has also had a tremendous influence on contemporary media theory. In his 1988 book *Manufacturing Consent*, coauthored with Edward S. Herman, he attempted to systematically outline and describe the mechanisms by which corporations, politicians, academics, and the media work in chorus to shade the truth and to manipulate public opinion in an effort to maintain the status quo.

K e y POINTS

: Conservative journalist Walter Lippmann coined the term *manufactured consent*. He used it to defend the government's mistrust of the public's ability to make intelligent decisions, arguing that real power had to remain in the hands of a learned elite (which is more capable of making informed decisions). Lippmann went on to insist that the illusion of public consensus must be maintained. He believed that this was a necessary evil for the progress of democracy.

: Chomsky countered this, saying that if manufactured consent is a function of democracy, it must be resisted. In a democracy, what people think is critical, because when people think, they have the capacity to act. Chomsky sees many of our modern democratic institutions as filters that indoctrinate compliant members (those who support the status quo) while filtering out undesirable freethinkers.

: As the "political economics" of media manipulation have become more sophisticated, politicians and the rest of the power elite (including members of the mainstream media) have acquired an uncanny ability to use media to control public opinion. Knowing the mechanics of this manipulation is the first step to counteracting it.

CYBERNETICS AND MEDIA ECOLOGIES

In the late twentieth century, an evolving family of sciences has emerged that offer insights into how complex, dynamic systems work. The accelerated technological developments necessitated by World War II led to the dawning of a science called cybernetics. Cybernetics is the study of feedback (communication and control) within systems, first applied in developing guided missiles that could self-correct their courses during flight. A guided missile constantly compares its current course and the location of its target and self-corrects for any course deviations. A companion discipline, systems theory, an outgrowth of military operations planning, uses mathematics, engineering, and the behavioral sciences to predict how complex systems (battlefields, corporations, economies, governments, etc.) might behave as certain conditions change. In the 1980s, a new theory about systems, called chaos, created a small revolution within the sciences. Chaos science examines the edges of systems where order dissolves into apparent disorder. By using computer modeling, scientists have discovered higher levels of order operating within this seeming chaos. In Kevin Kelly's book *Out of Control: The New Biology of Machines, Social Systems, and the Economic World*, he explores how our machines are becoming so complex that they are starting to exhibit lifelike behavior, while at the same time, machines are becoming sophisticated enough to accurately model various aspects of nature.

And how are these new ideas about cybernetics and chaos relevant to media?

K e y POINTS

: The distinctions between the born (the biological) and the made (the mechanical, the artificial) are becoming blurred. Human-made things are becoming more lifelike and life is becoming increasingly engineered. Human-made systems have become so complex and chaotic (out of control) that they exhibit lifelike behaviors, such as self-sustainability, self-improvement, and self-expansion. Kelly calls these "vivisystems." Today's globally interconnected web of telephones and computer networks, cable systems, satellites, and their human operators can be thought of as a vivisystem.

: If this complex network of human media is becoming some sort of hive-like bionic organism, it thrives on complexity, diversity, wildness, and works best when it's slightly off-kilter, or "out of control."

: A media vivisystem this large and complex cannot be controlled by any one entity. A wide variety of feedback loops affect the overall performance of the system. Just as a rain forest, a mountain range, or any biological ecosystem maintains a dynamic balance between its staggering number of nested ecosystems and individual life-forms, a media ecology, seen in this light, could self-correct damage done to it.

: Seeing the media as an ecology switches one's focus from black-and-white issues of commercial versus noncommercial, sidestream versus mainstream, top-down versus bottom-up to a more fluid and permeable model. It all becomes one big interpenetrating organism where small niches can be exploited to produce disproportionally larger impacts, where amateurs can exploit the tools and images of commercial media in ways unintended by their creators, and commercial media can do the same by appropriating amateur efforts. It's all a dynamic Gordian tangle of feedback loops, information spews, and chaotic eddies. The decentralized and anarchic Internet is often offered as a model for this type of emerging media vivisystem.

MEDIA VIRUS!

In his book *Media Virus!*, journalist and cultural critic Douglas Rushkoff runs with the idea that the media is a living organism, and like all living things, is therefore susceptible to viral "infections." He calls these attacking agents "media viruses."

Key POINTS

: According to Rushkoff, "Media viruses spread through the datasphere the same way biological ones spread through the body or a community. But instead of traveling along an organic circulatory system, a media virus travels through the networks of the mediascape. The 'protein shell' of a media virus might be an event, invention, technology, system of thought, musical riff, visual image, scientific theory, sex scandal, clothing style, or even a pop hero—as long as it can catch our attention. Any one of these media virus shells will search out the receptive nooks and crannies in popular culture and stick on anywhere it is noticed. Once attached, the virus injects its more hidden agendas into the datastreams in the form of ideological code— not genes, but a conceptual equivalent we now call 'memes.' Like real genetic material, these memes infiltrate the way we do business, educate ourselves, interact with one another—even the way we perceive "reality." Examples of media viruses include the subversive content imbedded in *The Simpsons* TV show, the much-publicized antics of AIDS activists ACT UP!, and the media hype factory created around the early days of virtual reality technology.

: Rushkoff believes that the post–baby boom generation is the first generation to have grown up completely immersed in the datasphere of TV, MTV, video games, and cyberspace. Therefore, he contends, they are more sophisticated critics of media than previous generations and are better suited to effectively hack its technology and its signals.

: This new generation of media hackers, claims Rushkoff, are also well-versed in how to construct potent media viruses and how to plant them in the appropriate areas of the media host body. DIY media is seen as being part of this bottom-up media hack.

TEMPORARY AUTONOMOUS ZONES

Crazed anarchist rantmeister Hakim Bey clearly hit a resonant chord when he published his essay "The Temporary Autonomous Zone" in the 1991 book *T.A.Z. The Temporary Autonomous Zone, Ontological Anarchy, Poetic Terrorism.* Bey was fascinated by eighteenth-century pirate societies, late-'80s BBS culture, and the fictional pirate data havens described in Bruce Sterling's cyberpunk novel *Islands in the Net.* Bey's TAZ concept has since become very influential among media hackers, coffeehouse bohemians, and the denizens of the computer underground.

K e y p o i n t s

: Bey writes, "The sea-rovers and corsairs of the eighteenth century created an "information network" that spanned the globe: primitive and devoted primarily to grim business, the net nevertheless functioned admirably. Scattered throughout the net were islands, remote hide-outs where ships could be watered and provisioned, booty traded for luxuries and necessities. Some of these islands supported 'intentional communities,' whole mini-societies living consciously outside the law and determined to keep it up, even if only for a short but merry life."

: Bey proposed that the growing planetary "Net" (defined as "the totality of all information and communication transfer" and *not* synonymous with the Internet) can be used to create a "counter-Net" or a "web" of human connections out of which can emerge temporary anarchist free zones, islands that rise out of the fabric of the Net and then disappear when they've fulfilled their purpose. (Note: Bey proposed the terms *Net* and *Web* long before the Internet became a household term and the World Wide Web was born.)

: The purpose of these zones is up to the participating individuals. A TAZ can coalesce into a media prank, a global event, a virtual commune, or an illegal pirate action.

: TAZs are different than real-world communities or established virtual communities in that they are temporary and free arising. One example of a TAZ would be the grass-roots campaigns that pop up on the Net to counter threats of government intrusions, such as the notorious Clipper Chip and the Communications Decency Act. When one of these proposed programs hits the wires, a loose-knit TAZ of civil libertarian groups, individual computers hackers, and average net.citizens band together to strategize appropriate responses. The Internet, fax networks, phone trees, zines, and other communication resources are all pressed into service. Once the issue at hand is resolved, the TAZ collapses back into the Net. This ability to appear within the Net, act quickly, and then disappear is a hallmark of a TAZ.

: Although the TAZ concept has been embraced most enthusiastically by the computer underground, Bey did not intend it to be restricted to cyberspace or to be completely virtual. Bey, a sensualist, strongly resists the drift into virtuality, holding flesh and blood encounters above all others. Ultimately, he sees the Internet (and the greater sphere of communications technologies) as a powerful tool for the construction of TAZs, not the TAZ's true home.

THE CONSPIRANOIDS

In the smoke and debris that settled after the Oklahoma City bombing, a previously hidden feature of the American landscape was revealed. Little did most Americans know, but since the FBI fiasco at the Branch Davidian complex in Waco, Texas, a growing underground of extreme anti-government factions had been organizing and arming for a fight. They had formed militias, "patriot" and survival groups, and had begun circulating zines, videos, audiotapes, self-published books and pamphlets on their conspiratorial and paranoid worldview. This worldview is not new, having existed among populist groups, Constitutional absolutists, and fundamentalists for decades, out on the fringes of reason and beyond more mainstream beliefs. A number of these fears about government conspiracy and a thinly veiled police state thread their way through many politically oriented zines, both far left and far right. For a time, there was even a zine devoted to people's accounts of how the government had planted chips in their heads that were controlling them. Timothy McVeigh, the man charged in the Oklahoma bombing, believed that the U.S. military had planted an experimental computer chip in his butt while he was in the service.

K e y **POINTS**

Anti-government factions believe…

: The U.S. federal government has become a tyrannical force seeking to use law enforcement agencies to take away American citizens' constitutional rights, especially their rights to bear arms and to protect their property.

: The shadowy evil force behind all this is the international Jewish banking system, the Tri-Lateral Commission, and the United Nations.

: The goal of these forces is the eventual takeover of the United States and the installment of a new world order led by the U.N. The first step in this invasion is getting weapons out of the hands of the American citizens (e.g., gun control).

: The mainstream media is simply a puppet in this invasion plan and therefore refuses to report on such things as the unmarked black helicopters that constantly surveil those in the resistance, the existence of tracking devices embedded in money to monitor citizens' movements, the hidden surveillance cameras in street signs, and the training of foreign troops on U.S. soil.

: The bombing in Oklahoma City and the Arizona train derailment were orchestrated by the federal government (or rogue elements within it) to provide an excuse to crack down further on extremist groups.

These patriot groups make extensive use of DIY communications to create their own alternative media networks. They've created computer bulletin boards, Internet newsgroups, zines, cable access shows, shortwave and pirate radio broadcasts, and have circulated lots of videotapes and printed propaganda. While many of these groups are rather cagey in public about their core beliefs and motives, tapping into their media quickly reveals what they are thinking. The mainstream media, struggling to dig deeper into the Oklahoma story, found a gold mine in this media underground. Militia/patriot zines, books, radio broadcasts, and videos such as *Waco: The Big Lie* suddenly found their way onto nightly newscasts. Overnight, this fringe culture had gone from almost complete obscurity to being a runaway media virus. The sales of conspiranoid media skyrocketed . . . at least for fifteen minutes.

Words of Wisdom)

For each Starter Kit, I asked a number of media hackers to put together some useful tips and shiny pearls of wisdom to share with budding media hackers. For this introduction, I'll start with some thoughts of my own.

: Save yourself a lot of money spent on books and magazines (like the ones listed below) by cajoling your local library into ordering the materials for their collection so you can use them for free. Technical and trade books and magazines can be very expensive. You probably wouldn't even think of shelling out big bucks for *EMedia Professional* (see the Multimedia Hacker's Starter Kit in Chapter 3), but your library might. Also, don't be afraid to make use of your library's research personnel and resources. Sometimes, you'll find these researchers will bend over backwards to help you. It never hurts to ask.

: In fact, "It never hurts to ask" should be its own piece of advice. "Hacking" is about being resourceful and curious. Don't hesitate to call people on the phone and ask them questions. Be bold. You can always hide behind the anonymity of the phone. The worst they can do is bark at you and hang up. I was always phone-shy until I started writing for magazines and needed to interview people quickly, without a lot of song and dance. Now I'm fearless on the phone. You should be, too. The advent of email is also a boon to media makers on a budget. You can track down almost anyone's phone number and email address using search engines and Internet white pages (which often link to all phone directories). Email is a great way to approach people you may fear are unapproachable through other means. And you'll be surprised how often they respond.

: You can get lots of free stuff if you're set up as a business. If you don't already have one, make one up. If you're doing a zine, make up a letterhead with the zine's name or a "parent company." Same for a cable access TV show, e-zine, multimedia project, etc. If you do several of these activities, make up a general company name: "Dog Boy Media," "Breakdown Communications," or whatever. Paper Direct (see Catalogs below) has all kinds of stationery that you can use in your laser printer (or at a copy shop). With a little creativity (very little, actually), you can rival the big guys in the "corporate identity" department. It's astounding what sorts of stuff you can get with a letterhead and a business card. One of the editors of the cyberculture zine *.tiff* got the use of a brand new motorcycle for a week because he told the manufacturer he was writing an article on it. Which he was. The article was all about how one can get super-cool stuff (like a motorcycle) simply by having a zine and a letterhead. When I was writing for *Mondo 2000*, a Mondo business card that I made on my Mac in about fifteen minutes got me into every trendy nightclub and media event in D.C. Sometimes I even got free drinks, T-shirts, and was taken around to meet owners, DJs, producers, etc. It was totally on the up-and-up. I actually did write several of these clubs into my articles.

: When trying to get a handle on something, a new medium, a new idea to cover in your publication, or when doing investigative reporting, try to target the "apex" resources. These are the books, magazines, persons, organizations, and Net sites that are at the top of the information pyramid. By obtaining that one book, or tracking down that one person, or downloading that one FAQ (Frequently Asked Question), you are gaining access to a motherload of information and resources that flow from it. There is so much information swirling around these days that we need to become well-trained data surfers to stay on top of the wave. Knowing how to pinpoint the apex resources is a key to timely and effective media hacking. The resources in this book are far from exhaustive. I tried to target those resources that would be of interest to newcomers. The apex resources in each Starter Kit are marked with an asterisk(*).

Resources)

The more studious media hackers may want to bone up further on contemporary media theory and add some general media guides and directories to their libraries. Tweaking one's Bullshit Detector is always advised in a media environment brimming with shameless hype and commercial hustle. Also, knowing how to successfully surf the gnarly info waves is a key to staying on the edge while maintaining your sanity.

BOOKS
[M e d i a T h e o r y]

Manufacturing Consent:
The Political Economy of the Mass Media
EDWARD S. HERMAN & NOAM CHOMSKY
RANDOM HOUSE, 1988, 412 PAGES, $17

A worthy attempt at cataloging the mechanisms by which politicians, corporations, and the media engineer public opinion.

Manufacturing Consent:
Noam Chomsky and the Media
MARK ACHBAR, EDITOR, BLACK ROSE BOOKS
CP1258 SUCC., PLACE DU PARC, MONTEAL QU H2W 2RS
1994, 272 PAGES, 18 TRADING CARDS, $22

The companion book to the award-winning film of the same name (see Videos below). This book includes a complete transcript along with excerpts from the writings, interviews, and correspondence of Chomsky, coauthor Edward S. Herman, and others. Also included are exchanges between Chomsky and his critics, additional historical and biographical material, filmmakers' notes, a resource guide, and 300 stills from the film. A set of eighteen Philosopher All-Stars trading cards are included.

Media Virus!
Hidden Agendas in Popular Culture
DOUGLAS RUSHKOFF
BALLANTINE BOOKS, 1994, 338 PAGES, $12

Rushkoff has penned a number of rather reckless books on pop culture, and this is one of them. His naive optimism about media (blathering on about the radical impact that Pee Wee Herman and Ren & Stimpy are having on mainstream society), and his apparent ignorance of media critiques like those of the Situationists, makes this book laughable in parts. There are numerous factual errors and an overall lack of rigor and research. Though there are some thought-provoking ideas here (such as the media virus concept), the explanations and conclusions that are offered hold little water.

Out of Control: The New Biology of Machines, Social Systems, and the Economic World
KEVIN KELLY
ADDISON–WESLEY, 1994, 521 PAGES, $28

Out of Control is in many ways an answer to the question "Whatever happened to cybernetics?" In an extremely readable, even poetic, writing style, Kevin Kelly examines cutting-edge research and developments in the sciences, technology, economics, and culture from the approach of self-organizing systems. The ideas pioneered by cyberneticists like Norbert Weiner, Gregory Bateson, Warren McCulloch, Heinz Van Forester, and others have made their way into artificial life research, the Gaia theory, chaos science, and other new ways of looking at complex organic and nonorganic systems. Because this systems view is increasingly used as a way to explain the behavior of distributed networks like the Internet, it's important to understand its basic tenets.

Situationist International Anthology
KEN KNABB, EDITOR AND TRANSLATOR
BUREAU OF PUBLIC SECRETS, 1991, 406 PAGES, $15

The Situationist International Anthology is an extensive collection of Situationist essays, newsletters, tracts, and internal texts. Also includes pre-S.I. documents from Lettrist International and Imaginist Bauhaus, two groups that came together to form the S.I. in 1957.

Society of the Spectacle
GUY DEBORD
ZONE BOOKS, 1994, 154 PAGES, $10.95

Not for the faint of heart, Debord's *Society of the Spectacle* is the *Das Kapital* of the modern mediascape. The book is a series of aphorisms, and each aphorism can be chewed (or gagged) on for days. If you're interested in basic media literacy, you should at least have a working understanding of Situationist theory.

T.A.Z. The Temporary Autonomous Zone, Ontological Anarchy, Poetic Terrorism

HAKIM BEY
AUTONOMEDIA BOOKS, 1991, 144 PAGES, $7

Bey is a prolific essayist and poet. This book is a collection of his rants and communiqués, most of which were previously published in various underground journals and as broadsides. The most potent piece here is the "Temporary Autonomous Zone (or T.A.Z.)" essay.

Understanding Media: The Extensions of Man

MARSHALL McLUHAN
M.I.T. PRESS, 1994, 365 PAGES, $14.95

Yet another media book that you'll need stamina and fortitude to slog through. Most of what I've ever gotten out of McLuhan has been through other people's interpretations. Lewis Lapham's introduction to this new M.I.T. edition lays good groundwork. From there, you can peek and ponder your way nonlinearly through the rest of the text. McLuhan would have appreciated such an approach.

[P r a x i s]

Covert Culture Sourcebook, Vols. 1 & 2*

RICHARD KADREY
ST. MARTIN'S, 1993 & 1994, 216 PAGES EACH, $12.95 EACH

Richard Kadrey is a tireless encyclopedist of fringe art, culture, music, and science. This two-volume set catalogs fringe books, software, zines, and other cultural artifacts being cranked out from below. These sourcebooks are a great way to get an overview of fringe and DIY media and to find entry points to the areas that interest you. Highly recommended.

The Millennium Whole Earth Catalog*

HOWARD RHEINGOLD, EDITOR
HARPERSANFRANCISCO, 1994, 384 PAGES, $30

The Whole Earth Catalog of the late '60s and '70s became synonymous with hippie DIY culture. The Woodstock Generation wanted to fashion their own lifestyles, build their own homes, educate their children, and grow their own dope. *The Whole Earth Catalog* was an inspirational guidebook for its time. The new catalog contains the perennial wisdom of previous editions, along with lots of new material relevant to today's so-called digital generation. There's lots of material on all facets of DIY media and communications.

PAMPHLETS

Culture Jamming:
Hacking, Slashing, and Sniping in the Empire of Signs
MARK DERY
OPEN MAGAZINE PAMPHLET SERIES
P.O. BOX 2726, WESTFIELD, NJ 07091 ($4 PLUS $1 SHIPPING)

Cultural critic Mark Dery pens a concise, lucid, and entertaining survey of today's more noteworthy media hoaxters, "subvertisers," billboard bandits, posterers, and fringe media makers on the Net. As with all Dery's work, he puts these culture jammers into a broader historical and cultural context. This pamphlet has become a culture jammer's manifesto.

Seizing the Media
Immediast Underground
OPEN MAGAZINE PAMPHLET SERIES
P.O. BOX 2726, WESTFIELD, NJ 07091 ($4 PLUS $1 SHIPPING)

In this well-argued little pamphlet, the Immediast Underground outline their scheme for the liberation of the public airwaves and the establishment of a national public media network. Plans are in the works for an expanded "back pocket" version of *Seizing*. *Open Magazine* also has a number of other excellent pamphlets related to media, cultural criticism, and related topics, such as Mike Davis's *Urban Control: The Ecology of Fear* and Noam Chomsky's *Media Control*. Ask for a catalog.

VIDEOS

Manufacturing Consent:
Noam Chomsky and the Media
PETER WINTONICK AND MARK ACHBAR
ZEITGEIST FILMS
247 CENTER STREET, 2ND FLOOR, NEW YORK, NY 10013, 800-343-5540
1994, VHS, 187 MINUTES, $39.95 (PLUS $6.96 SHIPPING)

This award-winning documentary by Peter Wintonick and Mark Achbar examines the life of Noam Chomsky, one of America's preeminent media critics. The two-volume film covers Chomsky's life from his New York City childhood, working in his uncle's newsstand, to his controversial career as a linguist, a media analyst, and a tireless dissident.

Also see *The Culture Jammer's Video* in chapter 6, Media Pranks and Art Hacks.

CATALOGS

J&R Music and Computer World

59-50 QUEENS-MIDTOWN EXPRESSWAY, MASPETH, NY 11378-9896
800-221-8180
(free catalog)

> This New York superstore has everything related to consumer-grade media: stereo components, tape recorders, computers, printers, telephones, TVs, and fax machines. If you're looking for reasonably priced new equipment and supplies, J&R is worth a look.

Paper Direct*

100 PLAZA DRIVE, SECAUCUS, NJ 07094-3606
1-800-A-PAPERS

> This catalog can be incredibly useful to zine makers, book publishers, posterists, media pranksters, and other media hackers in need of professional-looking print materials. Paper Direct sells a huge line of laser-friendly fancy papers, cover stocks, color dummies, low-end desktop bindery equipment, laser-printable signage, and sticker paper. The prices are not cheap, but they have fast service, lots of cool stuff, and most importantly, they sell in small quantities.

Radio Shack*

Catalogs are available at local Radio Shack outlets.

> This consumer electronics mega-chain has equipped more media hackers and street techies than any other supplier. They have everything from inexpensive consumer-grade systems (audio, video, computer, radio) to the parts and manuals to hack everything together yourself. Unfortunately, as little Radio Shacks have popped up in every strip mall and street corner in America, they don't carry as much DIY stuff as they used to, but you can order anything from their catalog and have it delivered in a few days.

NET SITES

For more detailed information about getting online, see chapter 7.

CTHEORY

WEB: www.ctheory.com

> Run by Arthur and Marilouise Kroker, *CTHEORY* is an international online journal devoted to the critical examination of culture and technology. The site contains academic papers, book reviews, and interviews with key figures from art, culture, technology, and science.

Disinformation

WEB: www.disinfo.com

Think of Disinformation as the Yahoo! of the fringe/underground culture. They review and link to hundreds of sites covering conspiracy theories, paranoids, psychic tomfoolery, Nazism, UFOs, narcopolitics (illegal drugs, Prozac, tobacco, the CIA/cocaine connection), brainwashing, end-of-the-world news, kook sciences, and just about anything else that's off the radar of the mainstream. Disinformation is also a stunning example of a noncommercial website that rivals, in beauty and quality of content, anything that a big-bucks commercial site can offer.

DIY Search

WEB: www.diysearch.com

This relatively new site is an attempt at building a search index for the DIY community. It includes sections on art, humanities, zines, music, web resources, and small businesses.

Journalism and Media Criticism Page

WEB: www.shss.montclair.edu/english/furr/media.html

A very useful link list that includes the Noam Chomsky Archive, *FAIR* (Fairness and Accuracy in Reporting), *Covert Action Quarterly*, M.I.T.'s Media Watchdog Page, Project Censored, the Media History Project, and links to other media resources.

The Militia Watchdog Page

WEB: www.sff.net/people/pitman/militia.htm

A huge list of links to militia groups, militia media, and anti-militia organizations.

Pirate Utopias Project

WEB: www.actlab.utexas.edu/~vreed/PU_shock/

A hypermedia document done in Shockwave format that examines the idea of Hakim Bey's TAZ alongside the "psychic nomadism" of hacker culture. The graphics are rather hokey and the naive utopian view of both pirates and hackers is silly, but if you want to see how this cybernetic subculture relates to the TAZ concept, this animated document is a good starting point.

Society of the Spectacle

GUY DeBORD
WEB: www.cs.oberlin.edu/students/pjaques/etext/debgsociespec/index.html

The complete electronic text of Guy Debord's hugely influential book (see Books above).

.

T.A.Z. The Temporary Autonomous Zone, Ontological Anarchy,
Poetic Terrorism

HAKIM BEY
WEB: www.hok.no/marius/bey/taz/

The full electronic text of Hakim Bey's book (see Books above).

WEB SEARCH ENGINES

As the Net and the Web grow like hungry bread molds, it's becoming increasingly difficult to find material of value. It's out there, but it's buried in an avalanche of gunk. The "anyone can play" ethos of much of the Internet, a hallmark of most DIY media, leads to a glut of bad content and total nonsense all mixed in with the good stuff. Internet engineers talk about artificial intelligence (AI) agents as a solution to this needle-in-a-haystack dilemma. While the Net has yet to see any full-blown commercial AI agents, there are a number of excellent search sites (called "search engines") and experimental retrieval systems you can use. Using these is an excellent way to cut through a lot of the deadwood. Now, whenever I read about a new media entity, person, or group that sounds interesting, I fire up my Internet connection and initiate a search.

Useful Search Engines *and* Directories

www.yahoo.com   [*a navigable directory with subject and category listings and keyword searching*

www.altavista.com   [*the grandparent of comprehensive search engines*

www.search.com   [*a meta-search site that lets you access all of the major search engines from a single Web page*

www.dejanews.com   [*a searchable archive of Usenet newsgroup postings*

www.switchboard.com   [*a "white pages" with a reported 90 million listings*

www.bigbook.com   [*a national online "yellow pages" listing business contact information and even street maps!*

It's impossible to stay current by perusing the Web in a linear fashion (i.e., visiting each new site), but by using a search engine, you
can scoop up links to anything the search site has indexed on the
keywords you enter. To get the most out of a search engine, it's
important that you know how to best set up your search strings, so
read the help file! Unfortunately, different search engines use different search string modifiers, so it's a good idea to find a couple
that you're comfortable with and stick to them.

Information Filtering Resources

WEB: www.enee.umd.edu//medlab/filter/filter.html

> A listing of currently available information-filtering services (both free and commercial) as well as links to papers, organizations, and media coverage related to information filtering.

Stanford News Filter Service*

EMAIL: netnews@db.stanford.edu

> This unique service allows you to subscribe to keyword searches that the program will carry out for you on Usenet newsgroups. This is a great way of keeping track of a subject that might be discussed beyond the confines of one or a few select newsgroups. I use this filtering service for fishing out all references to "jargon" and "slang" (used in my monthly *Wired* Jargon Watch column). To get more information on this service, send the message "help" to the email address above. A guide to the service will be sent by return email.

The Well BBS

1750 BRIDGEWAY, SAUSALITO, CA 94965-1900
VOICE: 415-332-4335, BBS: 415-332-6106
EMAIL: Info@well.com
WEB: www.well.com

> The Well has been my virtual home since 1987. In many ways, the ideas and resources in this book have grown from the discussions and information-sharing that goes on there. If you're interested in being a part of a virtual community and a "think tank" on late-twentieth-century art, politics, culture, science (and just about everything else), I can't recommend the Well highly enough. For further discussions related to the topics of this book, check out these Well conferences: Media, Factsheet Five, bOING bOING, FringeWare, Mirrorshades, Film, Music, Radio, Muchomedia, Internet, Web, and Wired. When you get on, send me an email message. My Well name is: gareth.

Jamming
[GLOSSARY] the
MEDIA

"Language is a virus from outer space," at least in the alien mind of
the late William Burroughs. Language certainly feels viral, as it's carried from speaker
to speaker, learning, mutating, and altering its environment. Out on the fringes of
language lives slang, jargon, techspeak, subcultural utterances that have not yet infected
the host body of established speech. The following glossary cuts across many
subcultures involved in media hacking—from zinesters to billboard bandits to
Internet websters. Rather than put them in separate compartments for each medium,
I thought it would be more fun to stew them all in the same pot.
Ahh . . . the aroma. Enjoy!

ADSL: [Asymmetrical Digital Subscriber Line] ADSL is an up-and-coming modem and compression technology that will allow much faster transfer of data over conventional copper phone lines. *See also* ISDN.

Anonymous remailer: A forwarding system on the Internet that sends anonymous messages to newsgroups and over email (and receives responses), all without revealing the sender's identity.

Anti-copyright: A number of zines use an anti-copyright symbol and statement on their materials. The anti-copyright symbol is the copyright symbol with a diagonal line through it. Some of these publishers are ideologically opposed to all forms of copyright, others are just offering their readers the right to reproduce the materials without permission. *See also* Shareright.

APA zine: [Amateur Press Association] A zine that's created when each individual of a group contributes multiple copies of their submissions to an APA editor (called a "Central Mailer"). Each participant duplicates and sends a set number of copies of their writing and/or artwork to the Central Mailer, who collates all the submissions, binds the APA, and then sends a completed copy to each contributor.

Appropriation: Lifting pre-existing media (audio, print, video) and using it in a new context. This cutting and pasting of media—often used in art and political satire—is one of the aesthetic hallmarks of postmodern culture. Also referred to as "reappropriation," "recontextualization," and "detournement." *See also* detournement.

Artificial intelligence: The area of computer science concerned with creating machines that successfully mimic human intelligence. In the '70s and '80s, the governing approach was to create "expert systems," massive databases of information and a set of rules to access and manipulate that data. In the '90s, the governing models have been inspired by the structure and processes of the human brain and other biological systems, and the idea of "growing" intelligence from simple subsystems that can learn and adapt.

ASCII: [American Standard Code for Information Interchange] The standard character set used on a computer keyboard. ASCII text does not include special fonts, styles, proportional spacing, or other typographical goodies you get with other fonts. Email and Usenet newsgroup postings usually are in ASCII text, although some mail programs and newsreaders allow individual users to convert their incoming mail to a desired font. Because they have to be sent to many different types of computers across the Internet, text-based zines are usually created using only ASCII characters.

ASCII art: Graphics made out of ASCII characters, sometimes used by e-zine publishers and posters to Net discussions to embellish their words. The nauseatingly popular "smiley" (sideways smile) is one example: :-)

Audio collage: A technique of cutting up existing audio material, either mechanically or electronically, and using it to create audio art. TV commercials, films, news, pop songs, industrial propaganda, motivational training tapes, and other bits of popular culture are often collaged to create caustic cultural and political commentary.

Authoring: The process of creating a multimedia presentation on a computer. The software in which all the media parts (text, sounds, graphics, video, animation) are scripted together is called "authoring software."

Baby pirate: An adolescent pirate radio operation. The term has negative connotations due to the antics common for such stations (crude, objectionable content; bad signal; stepping on other broadcasts; etc.).

Bagazine: A publication comprised of objects stored in a paper or plastic bag. A typical bagazine might contain flyers and/or booklets, a mini-comic or two, a cassette tape, stickers, and some kitsch culture ephemera. It is most common in mail art circles and among practitioners of experimental literature.

BBS: [Bulletin Board System] A computer conferencing and information storage and retrieval system. A BBS usually offers discussion groups, email, and file transfer. It is usually housed inside an individual's computer and often not connected to the Internet (although this is changing). There are a reported 65,000 BBSes in the United States. Usenet is often thought of as a global BBS. *See also* Usenet.

Betamax, or Beta: Half-inch video format. Betamax VCR technology was eventually overtaken by VHS in the home market. "Betamaxed" is humorous techie slang referring to any technology that's been eclipsed by another, believed inferior, technology. For example, "The Mac was betamaxed by Windows."

Bicycle network: A practice common among cable-access TV shows whereby tapes of shows are circulated (ah . . . through the mail, not by bicycle) from one cable-access station to another.

Billboard hacking: The act of clandestinely altering a commercial billboard, from slightly changing the text and images to deploying an entirely new image and message. It is also called "billboard banditry" and "billboard alteration."

Bitnik: Someone who uses a public, coin-operated computer terminal to log into cyberspace. "He's one of those bitniks who hangs out at the Cyber Cafe."

Bitraking: [electronic muckraking] Used to describe the act of journalists trolling the Net looking for story ideas. Bitraking is also a great way of finding material and contacts for zines, radio and TV shows, and other DIY media endeavors.

Bit-spit: Any form of digital correspondence (text, bit-mapped images, email, fax) or the act of sending same. "Yeah, bit-spit me those names and I'll send them a promo pack."

Blendo: Combining lots of different media (type, computer graphics, scanned imagery, animation, video) in a computer-based document or presentation to create a dense, psychedelic look. It can also refer to computer-generated print images that have these combined elements.

Blue Book: A set of standards that define the data formats that can be contained on an enhanced CD (or ECD) that mixes CD-ROM with CD-Audio. *See also* Red Book.

Bon bons: Paint bombs used to vandalize billboards. A bon bon is made from a Christmas tree ornament filled with paint and then capped. It is then tossed or launched at the billboard where it explodes on contact. Most billboard alterers look down on such destructive and uncreative practices.

Bookazine: A perfect-bound zine, often one that comes out as a large annual.

Box: Techno-slang for any digital device, especially a computer. "I just got a new box, a screamin' Pentium 100 MHz." It can also refer to a device that's used by phone phreaks to make free phone calls. The function of these boxes are indicated by their color (a red box mimics the sounds of coins, for instance). *See also* phone phreaks.

Boxing: Using a phone phreakers' box to make free phone calls. *See also* box.

Break-in: The pirate radio practice of intentionally broadcasting on top of a commercial radio station. Many pirate broadcasters frown on this practice, which furthers ill will from commercial broadcasters towards pirates. Most pirates take pains to stay away from licensed broadcast signals. Break-ins are also possible over the audio portion of TV broadcasts. *See also* zipping.

Browser: A software program that's used to access the hypertext/hypermedia documents on the Internet's World Wide Web. Browsers can be text-only, such as Lynx, or offer full multimedia browsing, as is the case with Internet Explorer and Netscape Navigator.

CD-R: [Compact Disc-Recordable] One-off compact discs that can be made using a CD-R deck, commonly used for making archival CDs and for making test CDs for CD-Audio. CD-R discs are usually gold in color (CD-Audios and CD-ROMs are silver). *See also* one-off.

Clandestine radio: Unlicensed radio broadcasts that are overtly political and propagandistic in nature, and often broadcast outside the target country by a political opposition. Clandestine stations sometimes become official broadcasters in the target country after a successful revolution has taken place. *See also* pirate radio.

Client: A computer (and its relevant software) that can access computers over the Internet. The computer being accessed is known as a server. Once connected, the client computers can access services such as FTP (file transfer protocol), gopher, and the World Wide Web. *See also* server.

Computer underground: The loose-knit network of people involved (or at least intensely interested) in hacking, phone phreaking, and other fringe activities in cyberspace.

Cracker: A computer hacker with malicious or criminal intent. The mainstream media refuses to differentiate between benign hackers and malicious crackers, despite the computer community's attempts to clarify the difference. Crackers are also sometimes referred to as "dark-side hackers."

Crash edit: A low-tech video edit achieved by editing from a camcorder onto a video deck. It is the most common form of editing used by amateurs who can't afford editing equipment. *See also* in-camera editing.

Culture jamming: Any form of media sabotage (e.g., postering, billboard hacking, media hoaxing, guerrilla art) designed to call attention to the media environment and how it's used to manipulate us. The original term *cultural jamming* was coined by the media hacker band Negativland to refer to billboard alteration. *See also* media hacker, poetic terrorism.

Cyberspace: Word coined by sci-fi writer William Gibson to refer to a near-future computer network where users can mentally travel through a three-dimensional matrix representing the world's data. The term has now become synonymous with today's Internet.

Cyborg: [shortened form of "cybernetic organism"] A term originally coined to refer to the futuristic marriage of flesh and machines. But such a marriage has already taken place in ways that aren't as obvious as a bionic arm or a chip implant. For those of us who work and recreate on a computer and on the Internet, much of the day is spent connected to a mouse and keyboard and the world's computer networks. Our lives have become so interdependent with technology that we are already cyborgs.

Dead media: Extinct and near-extinct forms of media, everything from pneumatic transfer tubes and the Edison wax cylinder to the Pixelvision camera and 8mm film. Cyberpunk authors and technology journalists Bruce Sterling and Richard Kadrey maintain an Internet mailing list dedicated to research on dead media. Those who research and collect dead media have been dubbed "dead media necronauts" by Sterling.

Desktop video, or DTV: The convergence of video and computer technologies, whereby video can be digitized and then edited on a home computer.

Detournement: A technique used by the French Situationist International (S.I.) for waking people out of their media-induced slumber. The S.I. altered and recombined images from popular culture (ads, comics, news stories) to make stinging cultural and political satire. This technique has now become a hallmark of collage art and music, zines, mail art, and other forms of media hacking. Situationist Raoul Vaneigem wrote: ". . . we have to defend ourselves against the poetry of the bards of conditioning—to jam their messages, to turn their songs inside out."

Digizine: An electronic zine distributed on floppy disk, CD-ROM, or downloaded from an online software archive. Sometimes *digizine* is used synonymously with *e-zine*, although that term is usually reserved for electronic publications delivered by email or over the World Wide Web. A digizine is infrequently called a "micro-zine."

Dingbats: A set of fonts comprised of symbols and graphics. By pressing a key with the dingbat font selected, a symbol or graphic corresponding to that key appears on-screen. Dingbats are commonly used to spice up printed communications.

DIY: [Do-It-Yourself] DIY has become a commonly used slogan among punks, zine publishers, and media hackers of other stripes. There is often an anti-commercial, anti-mainstream agenda behind DIY media projects.

Dumpster-diving: Searching through dumpster bins and trash cans for cool stuff that other people consider to be garbage. Any veteran dumpster-diver will bend your ear with stories of all their great finds.

DXing: In radio hobbies, DXing refers to long distance radio listening (i.e., shortwave). DX is radio geek-speak for "distance." A "DXer" is a DX enthusiast. If you want to listen to lots of pirate radio broadcasts, you'll have to become a DXer to do so. DXers are more seasoned SWLers who also listen to strange codes and signals. *See also* SWL.

E-book: [electronic book] A book, either an existing print book or an original work, that is readable on computer. E-books usually have some multimedia (a few images and sounds), but are mostly text. The Voyager Company, probably the largest e-book publisher, calls their line "Expanded Books."

8mm: A film gauge or videotape format where the tape is 8mm in width. 8mm and Super 8 film cameras were the first consumer-grade point-and-shoot cameras. Today, 8mm video is used in standard and Hi-8 camcorders. "Regular 8" and "Normal 8" are both synonymous with the basic 8mm film gauge.

E-list: [electronic mailing list] E-lists are Internet mailings, part publication/part discussion group, that are sent out to a list of subscribers. The content of an e-list is either assembled automatically (as subscribers submit emailed material) or is overseen by a moderator.

Eternal network: *See* mail art.

E-zine: [electronic zine] E-zines are small-circulation publications distributed over computer networks. The word *zine* comes from the print world, where it's used to describe small, do-it-yourself publications. Unfortunately, *e-zine* (and even *zine*) is now used to refer to any publication on the Internet, even commercial ones.

F2F: Hacker acronym for "face-to-face" (meaning "in person," as opposed to over the Net).

Fanfic: [short for "fan fiction"] A subculture within science fiction fandom where fans write fiction centered around their favorite sci-fi universe and circulate it through dedicated fanfic zines or general sci-fi zines. *See also* slash.

FAQ: [Frequently Asked Questions] A text file on the Internet or on a bulletin board system (BBS) that answers commonly asked questions on a given subject. FAQs are a major source of Net knowledge and wisdom.

Faxback: A system for automatically returning requested information to a fax machine. The person requesting the information calls the fax server and types in access information about what information they're interested in. The fax server faxes back the requested file.

Faxzine: A zine that's delivered exclusively by fax machine. Faxzines appear to be most popular among right-wing grassroots groups.

FidoNet: A system of interlinking bulletin board systems (BBSes) so that information and email can be sent back and forth electronically.

Flame: An angry over-the-top outburst or rant in cyberspace. A flame that incites a series of equally angry and venomous responses is called a "flame war."

Fourwalling: Renting, or otherwise securing, a venue yourself to show your independent film/video, hoping that the ensuing press and attention will convince a venue to schedule more screenings. DIY booking.

FreeNet: Large community bulletin board systems that provide free accounts to local residents. Many FreeNets provide full Internet access. FreeNets are supported by the National Public Telecommunications Network (NPTN).

Freeware: Software that's distributed free of charge. Freeware, some of it quite good, can be found in profusion on services like AOL and CompuServe, on the Internet at large, and on bulletin board systems (BBSes). Before you buy software, check out the freeware and shareware that's available. *See also* shareware.

Fringe culture: A subculture that's obsessed with anything new, bizarre, creepy, and outside mainstream cultural norms. A whole fringe media has arisen to feed the interest of these "fringoids."

FTP: [File transfer protocol] A commonly used means of transferring files from one computer to another. Also, the act of transferring files ("I just FTPed some back issues of *F5-Electric*").

Glass-roots campaign: Grassroots campaigning over the Internet. The recent fervent online campaigns against Internet censorship are a perfect example of glass-roots campaigning.

GMT: [Greenwich Mean Time] The global time standard that's used in radio hobbies to verify broadcast times. It is also called "UTC" (Coordinated Universal Time), "World Time," and "Zulu Time." You need to convert local time into GMT when requesting QSL cards from a pirate radio broadcaster.

Gomi: The Japanese word for junk. The concept of gomi was highlighted in William Gibson's cyberpunk novels where a high-tech future has become so choked with last week's techno-junk that it has trickled down to street level. *See also* street tech; gutter tech.

Grunge fonts, or grunge typography: An unfortunately named school of typography that's grown out of several design and pop culture mags. *Emigre* and *Ray Gun* are two of the best-known examples. Grunge fonts are usually heavily decayed and distorted, calling to mind the kind of image degradation that comes with multiple generation photocopying. This now-popular style was innovated in the underground of the '80s in such copy culture art zines as *Photostatic/Retrofuturism* and various punk publications.

Gutter tech: Word used to indicate extreme street tech: super crude and super low budget, or a particularly brilliant no-budget techhack. *See also* street tech; gomi.

Hacker: Originally used to describe an obsessive computer enthusiast. It can also be used more generally to mean "one who enjoys the intellectual challenge of overcoming or circumventing limitations" [*The New Hacker's Dictionary*]. *See also* cracker.

Hi-8: [high-band 8mm] An improved version of 8mm video that is more compact/lightweight and delivers a sharper picture. *See also* 8mm.

High-tech paperweight: Derogatory term for an obsolete piece of desktop hardware. "I paid almost $6K for my LaserWriter II and now it's nothing but a high-tech paperweight."

Homepage: The document displayed when you first open up a World Wide Web browser. It is also used to refer to the first document (the front page) in any collection of documents on a Web site.

H/P: Computer underground abbreviation for "computer hacking and phone phreaking." Sometimes written as H/P/A, with an added "A" for anarchy.

HTML: [Hypertext Markup Language] A system for marking up or "tagging" Web documents that tells the Web browser how to format and present a document's text, sounds, graphics, and linked media.

Hypermedia: The hypertext concept extended to include linked media such as graphics, movies, and audio.

Hypertext: Documents that are cross-linked in such a way that the reader can explore nonlinear information trails through them (e.g., clicking on a word might link to a definition of that word or to another document related to it).

Identity hacking: Posting on the Internet or a BBS anonymously, pseudonymously, or by giving a completely false name, address, phone with the intent to deceive. All these forms of identity hacking are controversial in cyberspace. *See also* anonymous remailer.

In-camera editing: The lowest low-budget film/video technique where the camera shooting sequence is the same sequence as in the final film, i.e., a 1:1 shooting ratio.

Intel: [from Neil Stephenson's novel *Snow Crash*] Used to describe any useful information found in cyberspace. "Got me some cool intel from the FAQ site." It is taken from the shortened form of "intelligence."

IRC: [Internet Relay Chat] A system for real-time chatting over the Internet. Think of it as Net-based CB radio.

ISDN: [Integrated Services Digital Network] A digital telecommunications standard that allows for the transfer of multiple channels of voice, video, and data over standard phone lines. *See also* ADSL.

ISP: [Internet Service Provider] A company that provides Internet access and other Net-related services. *See also* Presence Provider.

J-card: The print cover of an audio cassette. It is called a "J-card" because, after being folded to fit inside the plastic tape box, it makes the shape of a "J" when viewed from the side.

Jewel box: The hard plastic case that houses an audio CD or a CD-ROM.

Juice a brick: To recharge the big and heavy nickel-cadmium batteries used in portable video cameras. "You better start juicin' those bricks, we got a long shoot tomorrow."

Kludge, or kluge: [pronounced "klooj"] Used by hackers (but with a much older origin) to mean something that's been jerry-rigged, a makeshift fix. "I had to do a total kludge to make this thing work."

Knowbot: An "intelligent" program that can search out information on the Net. Although the term is used in general, it is actually a registered trademark of the Corporation for National Research Initiatives.

Kode kidz, or codez kidz: Derogatory hackerspeak for phone-phreaking kids who steal, buy, sell, and trade credit card and phone card numbers. One of the common methods used for nabbing the numbers is "shoulder surfing."

Letterzine: A zine that is comprised entirely of correspondence.

Low-fi filmmaking: A technique of combining video formats (VHS, 8mm), film gauges (8mm, 16mm, Pixelvision, found footage), computer images/digital effects, low-fi sound, toy cameras, and whatever else to create a hybrid visual medium.

Low/no-budget filmmaking: Filmmaking on a shoestring. Generally, "no-budget" films are produced on a day-to-day basis, whenever sufficient resources exist. No formal budget is made. Credit cards often finance these films. Low-budget filmmaking usually has some sort of budget and initial capitalization (generally less than $1 million), but not from a studio.

Magalog: A mail-order catalog that's disguised as a magazine. Most magalogs are more catalog than magazine, but there are exceptions.

Mail art: A form of noncommercial art distributed through the postal system. The emphasis here is on openness (anyone can participate), clever forms of communication, and stretching the limits of the postal service (e.g., mailing a 3-D object without packaging to see if it will reach its destination). Mail art is also called "correspondence art," "postal art," "networking art," or "The Eternal Network." *See also* networking arts.

M2M: [Many-to-Many] Medium that involves numerous participants communicating with one another. *See also* APA zine.

Meatspace: One of the many online slang terms for the real world (as opposed to cyberspace). Other terms are "F2F" (face-to-face) and "RL" (real life).

Media hacker: The term used in this book to refer to amateurs experimenting with various forms of media production, making use of readily available technologies in an effort to "hack" the often bland monoculture sold through commercial media. Basically, a media hacker is the same as a culture jammer, although one could argue that a media hacker has an overtly political agenda. *See also* culture jamming; poetic terrorism.

Medianauts: A term used to describe those who interact in the electronic global village, floating through a universe of media and information.

Mediascape: One of the many terms that's been coined to describe the entire global media feed. Other synonyms include *datasphere,* or even *cyberspace.*

Media virus: Concept put forward in Douglas Rushkoff's book of the same name. A media virus is a clandestine media "meme" (or idea) that invades a host media body, revealing its viral nature once inside. One of Rushkoff's examples is *Pee Wee's Playhouse,* which masqueraded as regular children's programming but actually delivered lots of progressive messages about homosexuality, gender bending, media overload, and psychedelia.

Meltomedia, or muchomedia: Playful perversion of the term *multimedia.*

Memes: Memes are self-replicating patterns of information that, like genes or a virus in the body, can leap from mind to mind. The term was coined by biologist Richard Dawkins in his famous book *The Selfish Gene.*

Micro-zine: *See* digizine.

MIDI: [Musical Instrument Digital Interface] An audio standard for the connection of synthesizers, digital instruments, and computers. The term *MIDI* applies to the computer interface, the instruments, and all software and hardware used. MIDI-controlled devices can send and receive MIDI "events" to a computer for storage and manipulation.

Mini-comic: A comic book of any size smaller than digest (5 $^1/_2$ by 8 $^1/_2$). Mini-comics are very common in the zine and amateur comic circles.

Mixed mode: A CD that has both CD-Audio and CD-ROM information on the same disc. Some mixed mode discs have the CD-ROM info on track 1 and the audio on all subsequent tracks. This causes problems because you can damage a CD-Audio system if you play track 1 by mistake. A new CD-plus format puts CD-ROM info on track 0, making it safe for CD-Audio systems. There is currently a standards war going on about which mixed-mode technology the industry should adopt.

Mod: [short for "modification"] In radio hobbies, refers to changes made in radio listening or broadcasting equipment. Mods are done to today's radio scanners to allow them to receive cell phone frequencies that, by law, can no longer be manufactured into commercial models.

Netizen, or net.citizen: [Short for "net citizen"] A member of the Internet community, especially one who is involved in activism to keep the Net as free and democratic as possible.

Networking arts: Refers to noncommercial art that grows out of interactions over a network, be it the postal system, a fax network, or the Internet. Examples of networking arts include mail art, fax jams, and art-related net "happenings." The term originated with mail art, which is also sometimes referred to as the Eternal Network. *See also* mail art.

Newbie: Net-slang for a new user. Often used derogatorily.

NTSC: [National Television Standards Committee] The video standard used in the United States and Japan. PAL [Phase Alteration by Line] is used in the U.K., Germany, China, and Australia. SECAM (Systeme Electronique pour Coleur Avec Memorie) is used in France and the Soviet republics. The three technologies are not interchangeable, making it a big hassle to produce video for an international audience.

Offset: The most common method of printing. An image developed onto a paper or metal plate is passed through water and ink. The ink sticks to the image on the plate and then transfers the image onto a rubber drum. Paper passing over the drum receives the image.

One-shot: A zine (or other DIY production) that's done as a one-time project, with no plans for subsequent issues.

One-off: A single copy made of a CD-Audio or CD-ROM. One-offs are popular for vanity projects and for using CD-ROM to archive large amounts of data.

Perzine: [Short for "Personal Zine"] A zine that is exclusively or predominately focused on the life of its editor/publisher. Some perzine publishers even go so far as to create a one-of-a-kind copy of their zine for each person that orders one.

Phone phreaks: Hackers and crackers of telephone systems. The practice of telephone hacking is called "phreaking."

Pirate radio: Unlicensed radio. Pirate radio broadcasters can be anyone from kids wanting to pull pranks over the air to serious media hackers who believe that the airwaves should be free. Radio pirates contend that the FCC's licensing requirements make it impossible for local communities and non-corporate entities to have access to radio. Pirate broadcasts are usually free-form, with music, political commentary, comedy, ranting, whatever the pirate has in mind. There is a long list of other terms for, or related to, pirate radio, such as "clandestine radio," "free radio," "low-power radio," "micro-radio," "people's radio," "homebrew radio," "microcasting," and even "peanut whistle radio" (for very low power stations). Unlicensed ham (amateur) radio is called "bootlegging." *See also* clandestine radio.

Poetic terrorism: The media hacker's art of shaking up the status quo through usually nondestructive, absurdist acts of "terrorism." In an essay on the subject, anarchist Hakim Bey suggests things like dancing naked in a bank lobby, creating mock UFO landing sites in state parks, and kidnapping people and doing kind and wonderful things to them. Years ago, anarchist writer Robert Anton Wilson proposed a similar activity he called "Operation Mindfuck" (or "OM"). *See also* TAZ.

Poster zine: A zine where the entire contents fit on one side or both sides of a large sheet of paper. If the zine is meant to be posted, it is often blank on one side. Some posters zines are offset printed, others are screen printed.

Posterist: An artist or activist who pastes up posters. Sometimes the posters are art for art's sake, other times they are political in nature.

Presence provider: A company that provides World Wide Web services only (as opposed to full Internet services). *See also* ISP.

Pro-sumer: [professional + consumer] Refers to a spectrum of Goldilocks technology ("not too hot, not too cold") that's a little too expensive to be consumer grade, but not quite professional grade either. Hi-8 is often called a "pro-sumer" technology.

Prozine: A publication that falls someplace between a zine and a commercial magazine. Prozines usually have higher circulation than zines (in the thousands), slick production values, color covers, and numerous ads from record labels, book publishers, etc.

QSLing: In radio, a QSL card is sent from a radio station (or ham) to a listener (or fellow ham) to verify that the listener tuned in to a broadcast. The listener sends a note (called a "reception report") to the broadcaster's address—usually given during the broadcast—stating the date, time, and frequency of the broadcast. The station responds with a QSL card verifying the information. Hams, DXers, SWLs, and other radio hobbyists collect these cards. Many pirate radio broadcasters also issue QSL cards. *See also* DXing; pirate radio; SWL.

RAM: [Random Access Memory] A computer's short-term memory. When buying a computer, you should choose a model with as much RAM as possible. It will allow you to open a number of programs at once and allow your computer to perform multiple tasks.

Rant: Named for a 17th-century sect of British preachers (the Ranters), rants became popular in the 1970s post-punk scene, in live poetry performances and in zines. The rant tradition continues in today's zines, both online and offline.

Rasterbation: The far too common practice of compulsive digital manipulation with Adobe Photoshop or some other graphics program. Practitioners are called "rasterbators."

Raves: Illegal dance parties where techno music is played. Raves became popular in Britain in the late '80s and subsequently spread throughout Europe, the United States, and much of the rest of the world. Rave culture is still going strong, but like all subcultural movements, it has become highly commercial and devoid of much of its early spirit.

Red Book: The standard, developed by Philips and Sony, for CD-Audio technology. All other CD standards spring from the Red Book. The CD-ROM standards are contained in the Yellow Book and the Green Book.

Reel: A sample of one's work on film and video. "I'll send you my reel" is what you're likely to hear if you call up a film or video maker and ask for examples of their work. A film/video maker's portfolio.

Riot grrrl: A young woman with an attitude. Riot grrrls are usually postfeminist, politically active, sex positive, and into fringe pop culture (such as zines and punk rock).

Riot nrrrd: A nerd with an attitude. A nerd who celebrates his/her nerdiness.

RL: Online shorthand for "Real Life" (as opposed to your time spent in cyberspace).

Samizdat: Term coined in the late '50s by a Russian poet who called his hand-bound, typewritten poems *Samsebyaizdat* or "publishing house for oneself." The same unknown poet coined the word *samizdat,* which roughly translates to "self-publication." *Samizdat* quickly became an unofficial Russian word to describe all forms of subversive publishing. In the West, it is often used to refer to any documents that are distributed through "underground" or sidestream channels.

Sampler: A digital device to capture sounds and manipulate them electronically.

Scanning: Using a scanner to monitor the VHF/UHF radio bands in search of interesting police, military, emergency, and private communications. Scanning can be used to watchdog law enforcement and military activities. The scanner moves through the VHF/UHF spectrum until it hears a communication in progress. When the communication stops, the scanner moves on.

Scouting: In film and video production, "scouting" refers to checking out possible locations before setting up a shoot. The more you know about a site (human/vehicle traffic conditions, lighting, power access, etc.), the better use you can make of it during shooting. Scouting is also a good idea when planning an act of poetic terrorism, altering a billboard, or other clandestine media hack.

Sequencer: A digital device, either software- or hardware-based, that records and plays back MIDI information. *See also* MIDI.

Server: A computer that offers various services (document viewing, file transfer, etc.) to other computers. *See also* client.

Shareright: A scheme for sharing non-copyright information. A Shareright document includes a statement saying it can be freely distributed as long as the Shareright statement remains attached. The statement also includes the date and the author's name. Sci-fi author Bruce Sterling has a similar arrangement he calls Literary Freeware. *See also* anti-copyright.

Shareware: Software that's distributed free with the understanding that if the user likes the program, they'll send the creator a shareware fee. Registering shareware usually gets you documentation, tips, updates, or some other "extras" that are offered as incentive for sending money.

Shoulder surfing: Looking over someone's shoulder to get their credit card, phone card, or access passwords.

Shovelware: A kitchen sink approach to multimedia in which content (text, images, sound) is tossed onto a CD-ROM or Web site with little regard for its usefulness to the consumer.

Slash: A fanfic subculture of individuals (mainly women) who write homoerotic stories based on their favorite TV shows and characters. The term arose from "Kirk/Spock" (later shortened to K/S), stars of the original *Star Trek* who were the first subjects of slash. All of the *Star Trek* shows have been "slashed" along with *Babylon Five; The X-Files; Space, Above and Beyond;* and non-sci-fi shows such as *Man from U.N.C.L.E., The Professionals,* and *C.H.I.P.S. See also* fanfic.

SneakerNet: Hacker euphemism for delivering something by hand (as opposed to over the Net). "The system was down, so we delivered the backups by SneakerNet." Also known as "Armpit Net."

Sniping: Clandestine postering, billboard altering, and leafleting.

Social engineering: The hacker art of conning people out of information, usually by posing as someone else (a computer technician, fellow employee, janitor, etc.) in person or by phone. Social engineering is a common way that hackers get passwords, credit card and social security information, and other personal data that they can use to exploit a computer system or to intimidate their enemies. Social engineering can also be used to gain info for various forms of media hacking and pranking.

Sociomedia: Computer media used for social purposes, as a means of exchange, collaboration, and the social construction of knowledge. Computer conferencing is a perfect example of sociomedia. The term was introduced by hypermedia theorist Edward Barrett in his book of the same name (M.I.T. Press, 1992).

SoHo: [Acronym for "Small Office, Home office"] Used in marketing desktop products and services.

Spaghetti processing: A hand-developing process used in no/low-budget filmmaking. The film is simply stuffed into big buckets filled with the developing chemicals. It produces a funky, mottled image, one that can be used to interesting effect.

Spamming: Flooding Usenet newsgroups or email with obnoxious commercial messages. Usenet netiquette dictates that the newsgroups are for conversation and information exchange, not advertising.

Spew: Net slang for the global media feed of TV, radio, adverts, cyberspace, and all the rest of it.

Splatter: A radio signal that bleeds outside its intended frequency.

Squirt the bird: TV production slang for transmitting a signal up to a satellite (or "bird").

Stampoid: A "phony" postage stamp. Mail artists use stampoids to decorate their envelopes and correspondence. Many stampoids contain mail art slogans ("Plagiarism saves time," "This is not art!," "Read and Destroy") and celebrate well-known mail artists and mail art events. Also called "postoids."

Stink pipe antenna: A pirate radio antenna masquerading as a bathroom ventilator pipe on a building's roof. The antenna is hidden inside a mounted length of PVC pipe.

Streaming audio/video: Audio and video data that is delivered over the Internet with no download time.

Street tech: Taken from a quote in William Gibson's short story "Burning Chrome": "The street finds its own uses for things"; later used in Bruce Sterling's preface to the 1986 cyberpunk anthology *Mirrorshades*. It's a term that perfectly typifies the idea that high technology—much of it originally developed for military purposes—eventually makes its ways into the hands of the masses. The "street" part of it also implies attitude, an edge. *See also* gutter tech.

Subvertising: Anti-ads that are used to subvert or ridicule the messages put forth in conventional commercial advertising. *See also* detournement.

Swag: Trinkets and freebees (demos, T-shirts stickers, mini-comics) that are given away at trade shows and to potential customers. Having a cool collection of swag to toss in with your media products is a great way to get people's attention. Everyone loves getting free stuff.

SWL: [Shortwave Listening] The hobby of scanning the shortwave radio spectrum to hear broadcasts from around the world. Pirate broadcasts can also be heard via shortwave. It is basically synonymous with "DXing," although that term is usual reserved for the more serious shortwave listener. *See also* DXing.

Tagger: Another name for a graffiti artist. The act of making graffiti art is called "tagging."

Talent: In film, video, or television, anyone who is in front of the camera is talent. Everyone else is crew.

TAZ: [Temporary Autonomous Zone] A spontaneous enclave that arises with the aid of interconnected computers, phones, fax machines, etc. Unlike a virtual community, which has a history, a TAZ pops up for a specific purpose, only to disappear when its task is complete. The term was coined by the anarchist Hakim Bey.

TCP/IP: [Transmission Control Protocol/ Internet Protocol] A system of network protocols that govern how packets of information are constructed and transferred over a computer network. The Internet is a network that uses TCP/IP.

Toasternet: The use of old PCs and other cobbled-together hardware and software to create cheap Internet servers. The origin of the term is unknown. It may have been inspired by NuTek's Video Toaster desktop editing device for the Amiga, or by the common household appliance for burning bread.

Trashing: The hacker practice of rummaging through wastepaper baskets and dumpsters looking for computer passwords, credit card info, and other valuable "intel." *See also* social engineering.

Tray card: The printed card that constitutes the back cover of a CD or CD-ROM jewel box. The tray card covers the back and the two spines of the box. The other printed part of the CD package is the front cover booklet.

TX: Radio geek shorthand for "transmitter."

URL: [Uniform Resource Locator] The standardized addressing system used on the Internet. A URL address contains information about what part of the Internet is being accessed (the Web, a file library, etc.), the computer being accessed, and the path to the files. For instance, a Web address always starts with: http://.

Usenet: A large bulletin board system that forms a large chunk of the Internet. It is home to more than 10,000 "newsgroups," ongoing global discussions on almost every conceivable topic.

Vanity tape: An audio or video tape that is made to give to friends and family members and not intended for commercial release.

Video vigilantis, or eyewitness video: The use of consumer-grade video equipment by private citizens to capture newsworthy events.

Wares, or warez: Techno-weenie shorthand for "software." Computer hackers, especially the young turks, usually use "warez."

Wax: Hip-hop slang for a vinyl record.

White paper: A detailed or authoritative report on a subject. White papers are often issued in research and industry to introduce a new product or process. One example is the original "Java White Paper" from Sun Microsystems that introduced this new Internet technology to the Net community.

World wide web: A hypermedia document presentation system that can be accessed over the Internet using a browser. *See also* browser.

Xerox subsidy: Euphemism for swiping free photocopies from a workplace. Many people believe that the '80s zine explosion was heavily fueled by temporary office drones who worked on their zines at work and duplicated them on the office copy machine when no one was watching.

Zine: A zine (rhymes with "scene") is any small-circulation amateur publication. Circulation can be anywhere from a few copies to thousands. Zines are almost always noncommercial in nature, often lose money, and are driven by the passions of their creators (often just one individual). Although there are zines on every conceivable subject, produced by people of all ages, the majority of zines cover music, pop and fringe culture, science fiction, experimental art and literature, and other subjects geared toward a youth audience. *See also* e-zine.

Zipping: A short interruption of a TV broadcast by a pirate, usually an image or text that flashes on-screen for a few seconds.

[C H A P T E R O N E] The Passion PRESS

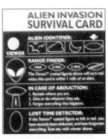

A ALIEN SURVIVAL CARD,
B. Barker

WE DON'T get laid,
WE DON'T
get paid, but boy
DO WE
work hard!

—Zine publisher's motto
MAXIMUMROCKNROLL

One publishes to find comrades! Or so declared the irascible surrealist André Breton in the 1920s. Such a statement would certainly tilt the heads of today's commercial publishers like dogs responding to a high-pitched squeal. Obviously, the mainstream publishing world strives to make money, to win awards, and to fill marketing niches. Finding new friends and revolutionary co-conspirators is unlikely to appear on a commercial publisher's list of objectives. Breton was obviously talking about an entirely different realm of publishing.

That world can still be found today, in the basements of group houses, in the corners of old garages, in paper-strewn loft apartments, on kitchen tables, and on the layout boards of all-night copy shops. This is the realm of the homemade, noncommercial publication, or "zine" (pronounced "zeen"), as it's commonly referred to. Zines are amateur desktop publications fueled by passion rather than profit and by a desire to connect with people of like minds. They are forums for the exchange of new and controversial ideas and a soapbox for non-mainstream opinions. Enthusiastically exchanged among fellow

52]

zine makers as much as sold to a public, zines are a kind of intellectual and artistic calling card and trading bead, letting other creative and thoughtful people know where you stand and what your interests are. Zines come in all shapes and sizes, greatly varying in quality, frequency, circulation (from dozens to thousands), and cover a staggering variety of subjects. Besides the well-known fanzines that obsessively fawn over rock bands, movie stars, and other common objects of cultural worship, there are zines on politics, sex, technology, hobbies, literature, art, music, and much more. Given their noncommercial means of exchange (usually via the mail rather than the newsstand), many taboo subjects also find a voice in the zine pipeline. Zines about serial killers, illicit drugs, outré forms of sexuality, Nazism, Satanism, and other icky and marginalized interests have active zine subcultures. And, increasingly, regular folks are crankin' out zines. There are zines for housewives, zines by blue-collar workers, and zines by kids who want to connect with other kids. Zines are no longer just a vehicle for bohemians, radicals, groupies, and *Star Trek* geeks . . . anyone who has access to today's almost ubiquitous desktop publishing and copying technology can jump on the bandwagon. And they are.

 **ZINE HISTORY 101**) Amateur publishing has been around since Gutenberg invented the printing press in the sixteenth century. In the twentieth century, it has steadily grown in popularity alongside ever-cheapening print technology. In the teens and '20s, marginalized art movements such as the Dadaists, the Surrealists, and the Futurists published their own material working with small sympathetic printers who donated or discounted their services. Writers like D. H. Lawrence and Anaïs Nin, unable to find a forum for their controversial works, bought old printing presses and produced their own publications. In the '30s and '40s, fans of

the growing literary genre of science fiction used mimeograph machines to create fanzines for their clubs and societies to trade. These sci-fi zines are often acknowledged as a direct descendant of today's zine. In the '50s and '60s, the Beats started the small press movement to give voice to authors and poets who couldn't swim in the mainstream. Allen Ginsberg's now-classic *Howl* was one of these first efforts.

The late '60s and '70s saw a boom in underground publishing as youth culture came into its own and every aspect of Western culture came under its scrutiny. There was a giddy cannabis-fueled enthusiasm in the air, as youth culture sought to unmoor itself from history and convention. A cultural revolution was declared—one that needed a new politics, economics, religion, art, and lifestyle. Alternative-minded print shops and publishers arose to crank out the publications that would carry this youth movement to the masses.

These underground publications flourished for as long as the youthful enthusiasm (and the pot) held out, but producing and distributing them was expensive and time consuming. The affordable printing technology of the era was still industrial age: obscenely heavy cast-iron presses, finicky and maintenance-intensive folders and cutters, giant carbon arc platemakers, room-size copy cameras and darkrooms that guzzled expensive and noxious chemicals, typesetters, and addressing machines that required little tin address plates for each addressee. The printing process itself was hard and took days to complete. While the resourcefulness and dedication of these underground publishers created an impressive alternative publishing network, some of which still survives today, the effort and expense involved put significant limits on who could undertake such publishing.

By the time punk rock broke in the late 1970s, with its "return to the garage" ethos of earlier rock, advances in media technologies were there to meet it. Punk revolved around a do-it-yourself/anti-commercial approach to music. Cheap tape duplication and vinyl record pressing technology allowed bands, unsigned to commercial labels, to record and distribute their own work. Music fanzines arose to promote the punk scene and to celebrate the anti-art, anti-fashion, and anti-establishment expressions of a burgeoning subculture. The art of punk emphasized the reappropriation of words and images from print, TV, film, and other media. It was aggressive, negationist, and demonstrative of the chaos and "no-future" attitude of the youth of that time. Like punk music, which emphasized passion over talent and praxis over theory, punk publishing was about being raw, immediate, experimental, and uncensored. Much of the attitude and aesthetic of punk DIY zines continues to influence the zines of today.

THE MOTHER

of All Zines) One cannot talk about the modern zine without giving *Factsheet Five* a lot of credit. This "zine of zines" is the highly regarded (even worshiped in some circles) directory of the scene. Peek into the past of any zine publisher and you're likely to find them thumbing through their first issue of *Factsheet Five*, overwhelmed by the anarchic beauty of it all and filled with inspiration to join the party. For over ten years, this quarterly guide has served as the connective tissue holding together a mutant media beast.

FACTSHEET FIVE COVER, ISSUE #11

Factsheet Five was started in 1982 by Mike Gunderloy, then a student at Rennsaeler Polytechnic Institute in upstate New York. Gunderloy was already well known in geek circles for his writing in *Alarums & Excursions*, a fantasy role-playing fanzine. *Factsheet Five* began as a listing of science fiction and gaming fanzines. Mike put the first issue together on the kitchen table of his apartment "before the roaches drove us to seek other lodgings." The first issue, cranked out on a ditto machine, was two sheets, mailed out to twenty-five people. Each issue found the zine expanding in scope and size. Gunderloy's compulsive nature began to get the best of him as the zines started clogging up his living room and his brain. He was perhaps the first real victim of the full-blown zine virus that now gobbles up the lives of thousands of other obsessive zine creators and collectors. Zines can be habit forming, and Mike undoubtedly had the monkey on his back. For Mike, as is often the case with zinesters, the pleasures of zines (and in Mike's case, he was also a sort of air traffic controller for the scene) kept him at it even as the work and the emotional stresses mounted. *Factsheet Five* was more than a dry, exhaustive listing of zines and other DIY media. Gunderloy was an excellent, unaffected writer whose insightful views, personal revelations, rivalries, and humor permeated the magazine. The intensity and chaos that seemed to swirl around him was almost palpable. There was a reckless edge, a sense of danger, a missionary zeal. One couldn't read *Factsheet Five* without being at least fascinated by the world that seemed to swirl around Mr. Gunderloy.

In 1990, after nine years and forty-four life-sucking issues, Mike ran out of blood. He was working as much as ninety hours a week and drinking a reported twenty-five cups of coffee a day; the guru's alternative media heaven had become a flaming hell. Attempts to avert the inevitable crash and burn by hiring a co-editor, Cari Goldberg Janice, proved to be too little, too late. Mike was coming unglued. One morning in July of 1990, he posted a message on the *Factsheet Five* conference at the Well BBS in Sausalito, California, announcing that it was all over. Zinesters there and elsewhere were horrified as the news spread. It was as if the guru of a religious sect had gotten up one morning and told his followers to beat it. Gunderloy also made it clear that his decision was final, that he didn't want to talk about it, and that he was going away for awhile. One Well member, Hudson Hayes Luce, was not content with giving up so easily. Hudson, a long-term supporter of *Factsheet Five*, called Mike and began to talk to him about what could be done. Meanwhile, calls and email messages began ping-ponging across the United States, as other zine publishers heard the news. It was clear to everyone that *Factsheet Five* (or something like it) was vitally important to link together the zine network. Without such a zine review, the attrition rate would be huge. As different strategies were being discussed (such as the forming of a Zine Press Association), another bomb was dropped: Mike Gunderloy had given *Factsheet Five* to Hudson Hayes Luce. Who was this guy? What experience did he have? What resources? "None. And none are required," came a terse message from Gunderloy on the Well. "I didn't have any experience when I started, and look what I was able to do." But, many zine publishers wondered (including myself), did we want to go back to the crude ol' days of the early *Factsheet Five* . . . back to square one? Hadn't we all come too far? Apparently not. *Factsheet Five* was now under new management. The zine community held its collective breath as Hudson disappeared into his secret laboratory with plans to fashion a better monster.

After much personal and professional struggle (and several moves), Hudson's issue, the infamous number 45, appeared in mailboxes in early 1991. Luce had obviously put his heart and soul into it, but he was just not equipped to handle such a herculean task. The stillborn results were ghastly. Looking through it was almost painful, like watching someone freeze in front of live TV cameras. Things seemed hopeless. With *Factsheet Five* in shambles, the future of zines didn't look so bright. A new zine review would have to be started and laboriously built up, taking years of slugging away before it could rival the old *Factsheet*. But then, something totally unexpected happened.

The negative response to Hudson's editorship was swift and brutal. Battles began to break out over various editorial policies, the least bizarre of which was his refusal to review anyone's publication if they said bad things about him or *Factsheet Five*. Already paranoid and conspiratorial by nature, the flak exploding around Luce was too much. Shell-shocked, he did the admirable thing and gave up. Once again, *Factsheet Five* was without an editor. And again, fans and dependents began to cast about for a replacement. Seth Friedman, an unemployed computer programmer who'd recently relocated to San Francisco from New York City, began asking friends if they'd take on the job. "At first, I wasn't interested in editing it myself, I just wanted to write for it," chuckles Friedman. He already had his own zine called *Food for Thought*, a "recipe and rant zine" where cultural and political diatribes were intermixed with cooking tips. Like other zine makers, Seth had been inspired by *Factsheet Five* and couldn't bear to see it die. He'd started *Food for Thought* mainly so that he would have something to trade for other zines. When no one else stepped forward to claim the title of chief zine kahuna, Friedman whipped on the mantle himself. Everyone held their breath again, not wanting to get their expectations dashed a second time.

Issue number 46 of *Factsheet Five*, Seth's first, was cause for celebration. It met, and in many ways surpassed, the high standards of the Gunderloy era. Unlike the old *Factsheet Five*, which was poorly designed and choked to the margins with tiny eye-straining type, Friedman's version was well laid out and easy to navigate. And it included a sorely needed index. Friedman had used his considerable computer programming skills to automate the gnarly process of assembling reviews, categorizing them, indexing, etc. His keen business sense and general can-do attitude (aptly symbolized by number 46's cover photo of a hammer bearing down on a nail) did wonders for

Factsheet Five's complexion. Critics often lament that the new *Factsheet Five* doesn't have the same edge as Mike's—that sense of volatility—but that's perhaps just the sign of a maturing movement and the fact that Seth seems to be more on top of the zine's operations. The new *Factsheet Five*, with its well-designed covers, fastidious layout, and automated review system may be too together to be a zine, but in its role as the yeast that makes the DIY print culture rise, it's more active than ever. Friedman even claims that the magazine is financially healthy.

FACTSHEET FIVE

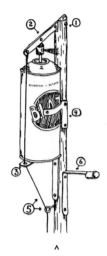

in CYBERSPACE) Jerod Pore is another player in the *Factsheet Five* story. A veteran of the punk zine scene and someone who knew Mike Gunderloy from the *Alarums & Excursions* days, Pore was instrumental in getting *Factsheet Five* online and in promoting electronic zines in general. When Mike walked out on *Factsheet Five*, Pore kept the ball rolling by starting *F5-Electric* to exist alongside Hudson's print edition. Today's *Factsheet Five* takes many different forms. Besides the print version, you can access *F5-Electric* on the Well, on the Internet, via the Well's Gopher (FTP) system, on the alt.zines newsgroup, and on the *Factsheet Five* page of the World Wide Web.

A MAP *of* ZINEDOM) Remember the game of croquet in *Alice in Wonderland* played with flamingoes as mallets and hedgehogs as balls? Trying to get a handle on the zine scene is like playing such a game. Zines pop into existence in one issue of *Factsheet Five* only to disappear one or two issues later. Attrition is so bad that the editors of *Factsheet Five* caution readers about sending off for zines listed in previous issues. They also carry a lengthy "Change of Address" listing and a "Dead Zines" column to track the lost and the dead. The best way to "map" zinedom is by air, looking at the basic terrain rather than individual features. Let's look at some basic zine types.

Arts, Literature, Poetry: This has always been a very active area of zinedom, serving as the radical fringe of the small press movement. Many of the art zines follow in the traditions of Dadaism, Surrealism, the Situationists, and punk collage art. Poetry zines multiply like spawning salmon, but unfortunately you can't grill and eat them. Maybe it's just me and my general distaste for poetry, but I haven't found many inspiring works in the general poetry zines. The literature zines fare a little better, with lots of bad-to-mediocre writing periodically offset by something truly inspirational.

Bottom Feeders: One of the motivations of zine publishing is the simple unadulterated freedom to say whatever you damn well please. Some publishers like to push the envelope of taste, decency, and constitutional protections. This desire to shock and disgust has led to zines like *ANSWER Me!*, *The Brutarian*, and *Boiled Angel*. They cover just about everything taboo: serial killers, incest, racism, Satanism, death, and destruction. Some take a dispassionate "we're just showing you what others will not" approach, while others are downright celebratory. Some of these zines have run into problems with the law and have sparked fierce debates about the freedom to express and publish anything in our society.

Comics: If you think breaking into the world of commercial writing is hard, try being a successful comic artist. Comics zines (often spelled "comix") are a cheap way of getting your work out to the masses. A number of rising comic artists such as Julie Doucet and Shannon Wheeler got their start this way.

Cyberculture: Cyberpunk science fiction and the computer hacker subculture of the mid- to late 1980s spawned a number of zines related to the burgeoning computer networks and the fringe cultures that were emerging around them. These cyberculture zines helped build an aesthetic that eventually fed into magazines such as *Mondo 2000* and *Wired*. Today's cyberculture zines include hacker publications such as *2600* and more culturally oriented *FringeWare Review*.

Fanzines: When most people think of zines, they think of fanzines, publications devoted to rock bands and other celebs. These types of fanzines do exist, but there are also zines devoted to more obscure hobbies and bizarre pastimes. Regardless of how obscure your obsession, if you look hard enough, you're likely to find a fanzine.

Fringe Culture: Some people are obsessed with everything new, strange, and out of the ordinary. Stewart Brand, creator of the *Whole Earth Catalog*, once said, "You have to look at the fringes to find out where the middle is going." Fringe culture zines regularly chart the activity on the cultural outlands. Strange new pop trends, the more surrealist dimensions of mainstream culture, media pranks, practical jokes, and subcultural curiosities are all fodder for these zines.

Fringe Science and Kookdom: From nano-technology to cryonics, to little green men and hollow Earth theories, you'll find it in fringe science and "fortean" (study of unexplained phenomena) zines.

Humor: The best humor zines, such as *Baby Sue* and *Funny Pages*, cover the kind of tasteless humor that mainstream publications won't touch.

Medley: *Factsheet Five* uses the term *Medley* to describe general interest zines. Like mainstream publications, they can cover art, science, culture, and anything else that strikes the editors' fancy.

Music: Since music provides the soundtrack to youth culture, it's not surprising that it would also play a huge role in zinedom. The punk mega-zine *Maximumrocknroll*, like *Factsheet Five*, has inspired many a zine publisher and punk rock band. Music zines cover everything from mainstream rock to specific subcultures gothic music and rave.

Perzines: Personal zines (or perzines) shamelessly flaunt their makers. They detail the lives of their publishers through intimate stories, anecdotes, comics, photos, and pieces about them written by others. A perzine is like an elaborate letter from a friend (that you happen not to know).

Political Zine: Publishers like to hail eighteenth-century pamphleteer Thomas Paine as a father of the political zine. There is a libertarian and populist thread that runs through much of zinedom, but it's most obvious in outright political publications. Many of the political zines cover extreme views that cannot find a voice in even the fringiest commercial magazines.

Punk/Riot Grrls: Punk zines are alive and well, covering what they've always covered: music and heated opinions about society and what it means to be a punk. From within this culture has arisen a postfeminist offshoot that mixes women's liberation with open sexuality, political action, and punk.

Science Fiction: The world of science fiction has always been a bastion for DIY media. Sci-fi fans create all types of media and culture around their favorite fictional worlds. Their fanzines cover everything from debates on existing stories to fan fiction and art. Zines are also a main mechanism for organizing the all-important fan conventions.

Sex and Relationships: If you want to get a sense of just how diverse human sexuality is, don't bother looking at *Playboy* and *Playgirl*. It's in zines such as *Blue Blood*, *ApaEros*, *Eidos*, and *Libido* that the astonishing diversity of human sexuality is revealed. *ApaEros* is an apazine (amateur press association), which means that individuals send multiple copies of their stories to a central mailer who then collates them and re-distributes the results.

Now that you have a bird's-eye view of zinedom, you're ready to zero in on those that interest you. *Factsheet Five* is undoubtedly the best place to look. Seth Friedman claims that they only see an estimated 20-25 percent of the zines published (and they review 1,200-1,500 zines per issue!). By getting zines in the areas that interest you and ordering the zines they review, you can collect most of the zines in a given genre.

ZINES: FARM LEAGUE
for the HIP MAINSTREAM?)

Few zinesters go into publishing with designs on becoming rich and famous. Sure, there's an ego boost in being your own media mogul and having people recognizing your name and your work, but it's on a very small scale. Mainly, zinesters just wanna have fun. And, it's a good thing, too. Zines are interesting because they're not trying to compete in the marketplace and they're done by amateurs who choose not to play by the rules. From this murky pool of struggling zines, new talents eventually coalesce and rise to the surface. Inevitably, hip commercial magazines take notice and want to siphon off this new talent. *bOING bOING* was a favorite among *Wired* editors when they were putting together their first few issues. They ended up hiring *bOING bOING* publisher Mark Frauenfelder as their associate editor. His wife, *bb* copublisher Carla Sinclair, is also a frequent contributor to *Wired*, along with numerous *bOING bOING* regulars. Darby Romeo of the Los Angeles zine *Ben Is Dead* was catapulted into the media spotlight when she started an anti-Shannen Doherty zine called *I Hate Brenda* that became an overnight sensation. *Details*, *Sassy*, *Spin*, and other magazines regularly use zine writers. Chris Gore, editor/publisher of the B-movie zine *Film Threat*, eventually sold himself and his publication to *Hustler*'s Larry Flynt. (He has since bought the magazine back.)

Artists who start out in zines also catch the attention of the mainstream. John Bergin, who published the art and music zine *Brain Dead* in the late '80s, has gone on to do graphic novels for Tundra and Kitchen Sink Press and album art for a number of established indie labels. Shannon Wheeler, creator of the Austin comic *Too Much Coffee Man*, recently did a commercial for Converse tennis shoes. And Claudia Newell, a frequent zine illustrator, now contributes to numerous computer publications. Julie Doucet, who's been called the female R. Crumb, started out photocopying her own mini-comics. Now she's very successful doing work for established independent comic publishers.

While the zine scene as a whole often turns its collective nose up and screams "commercial sell out," it is a fact of life. Publishers and artists who make the jump to the mainstream don't necessarily leave their zine roots behind. In fact, many of them justify their commercial work by pointing out that it allows them the financial security to be able to continue zine publishing.

DO-IT-*Yourself*
BOOK PUBLISHING)

ENLARGE
200% & TRIM OUT.
GLUE ONTO CARDBOARD
AND STAPLE ON A STICK.
ALIEN IMPOSTOR MASK
Apply to face as needed. Caution: inhale eyeholes.

∧ ∀ ℥ H ∪ S · S R E K R A B · ⅃ ⅃ I B

Desktop publishing has been a boon to newsletters and magazines, but what about books? Most people seem to be unaware of the potential for producing high-quality professionally bound books on their desktop.

Don Lancaster, an early guru of microcomputers and desktop publishing, has been printing, binding, and marketing his basement books for years. Lancaster runs Synergy Press, which offers bound volumes of his street-tech wisdom and computer hardware manuals. He uses a high-speed duplex laser printer that prints on two sides of a sheet at a time. He keeps little inventory, which saves money at tax time, and prints and binds books on demand. Lancaster has become an evangelist for DIY bookmaking and has written a number of how-to articles and books on the subject. By keeping costs down and offering valuable hard-to-get information, he's managed to make a living as a DIY book publisher.

When artist Darick Chamberlin began taking notes for an intended sci-fi novel, he noticed something interesting. The notes themselves, a run-on list of fictional products, places, and characters, looked strangely compelling by themselves. He continued writing in this shorthand style, mixing in an ever expanding laundry list of techno jargon, pseudo-computer code, and other fragments of uniquely postmodern language. The result is the mock-epic *Cigarette Boy*. Once the book was finished, knowing it was far too strange to interest a conventional publisher, Chamberlin decided to self-publish it. He typeset it himself and had the inside pages printed at a local Seattle copy shop. The color covers were done at a conventional printer. For bindery, Darick used the simple GBC binding available at copy shops. The result is a beautiful and bizarre piece of book art that is perfectly served by its low production values. The GBC binding makes it look like a computer manual, which fits with its "machine gone mad" contents. While *Cigarette Boy* has only sold 500 copies, it's gotten rave reviews in a number of sci-fi publications and gained Chamberlin much admiration.

With the recent introduction of professional-quality inexpensive bindery, self-published books are a viable option for authors who have something to say that the mainstream press may not care to hear.

PIRATES *of*
PRINT)

The advent of inexpensive copiers, scanners, and laser printers has instigated an all-out war over copyright of intellectual and cultural property. These technologies, which can instantly reproduce printed materials and translate them for transport through cyberspace, have opened a

Pandora's box of issues and debates over intellectual property and the reappropriation of cultural iconography.

The Situationists strategy of detournement is everywhere evident in zinedom. An ad for The Gap, depicting an emaciated model in jeans and a T-shirt, is turned back on itself by changing the "P" to a "G" in the logo. "GAG" is a statement against choking commercialism, uniformity stuffed down our throats as hipness, and anorexia as a fashion statement.

One of the first zines to fully understand the implications of how modern desktop machines (copiers, computers, etc.) would raise the stakes on intellectual property was Lloyd Dunn's *Photostatic*, which appeared, in its first incarnation, from 1983 to 1993. Lloyd and his Iowa City cohorts published several zines under the name of The Drawing Legion and produced reality-bending audio collage as the infamous band Tape-Beatles. The loose-knit collective of artists and writers that orbited *Photostatic* were hell-bent on pushing the limits of copyright and the conversation about art as commodity. They called themselves "art plagiarists" and even trademarked the term *Plagiarism*, always following it with a ® symbol. Unlike the criminal act of stealing someone else's work and claiming it as their own, they sought to create a kind of anti-commercial anti-art that flaunted the original sources and revealed the true desires hidden beneath them. To the Plagiarists, mainstream commercial art and media was like the great and powerful Oz, and their mission was to reveal the shriveled old man cowering behind the curtain. The Tape-Beatles logo was the AT&T globe with a pair of Mickey Mouse ears on it—two of the most recognizable logos on the planet. The various slogans of the group showed not only their desire for a more open intellectual and cultural commons but also their great sense of humor. "Plagiarism: It was our idea," "Plagiarism: A Collective Vision," and "Plagiarism Saves Time" were a few of their bumper-sticker manifestoes. Sadly, the Drawing Legion/Tape-Beatles went away in 1993 when Lloyd Dunn moved to France. As I write this, he has recently returned and is working on a new *Photostatic* and a new recording.

Although many zines make liberal use of previously published art and text without seeking permission, there are surprisingly few cases of these copy pirates getting into trouble over infringement. Part of this is due to the tiny circulation of these zines and their noncommercial nature. The bigger a zine gets, the larger its circulation, the more cautious its editor becomes over this issue. A zine with a print run of 100 copies is little threat to AT&T or Condé Nast. If a zine does get in trouble with the law, the publisher can simply stop selling the offending issue without losing their shirts financially. Most of the infringement cases I've heard of have not involved major corporations, but rather other small publishers whose work has been used without attribution. In these situations, a credit in a future issue, a free T-shirt, or a few bucks has usually been agreeable to all parties involved.

Given the noncommercial, anti-authority attitude found in much of zinedom, people might get the impression that zinesters have no qualms about outright piracy. This is generally untrue. A large segment of the zine community frowns on outright theft of material (calling it your own and making money on someone's work). It is their belief, however, that for noncommercial purposes, or for making political and social commentary, intellectual and cultural property should be more open for public use. The rationale goes like this: "If all this media is going to be beamed into us constantly, we have a right to deflect it and feed it back on itself in creative and self-serving ways. We didn't ask to live inside a 24/7 media feed. We need a way of shouting back."

There is a radical fringe of zinedom that believes that ideas and artistic expressions should not be owned and that the desire for such ownership is pathological and needs to be destroyed (or at least drastically modified). To this end, they will appropriate all media as they see fit.

The loose-knit global network of zines is wildly diverse, so there's no agreed-upon position on plagiarism (or anything else). The most fascinating thing about zines is the phenomenon itself and the part it is playing in a more general debate over intellectual property, appropriation, and media making.

: I don't **NEED** to take a **SHOWER** just yet.

: The table of contents is really just an **APPROXIMATION.**

: Of course the **CHECK is** in the **MAIL.**

: It's a **GOOD IDEA** to call in sick in order to finish my zine.

: The folks at the **POST OFFICE** are **MY FRIENDS.**

: **SOMEDAY** I'll look back on all this and **LAUGH.**

THE ZINE HACKER'S STARTER KIT

Getting Started **)** First rule of zines (the first rule of all DIY media making, in fact): **There are no stinkin' rules!**

Everything I say in this book is simply based on my own experiences and the other media hackers I spoke to. As the hacker saying goes, "Your mileage may vary." Use what you find valuable and—by all means—toss out the rest. Don't be content with what others have done. Push the envelope. Thanks to today's information glut, getting people's attention is increasingly difficult, so be anything but boring.

The really cool thing about zines is that anyone can play. You don't need lots of cash, a fancy printing press, advertisers, or a publicity budget. I've seen handwritten zines, as well as zines produced on carbon paper, ditto, mimeograph, or other ancient forms of printing. Zines have arrived in my mailbox as miscellany stuffed in plastic bags, on home-duplicated cassettes, in lunch bags, on sheets of poster stock, on index cards, and on sticky-back paper. Especially if you don't plan on messing with store sales and distributors, there are no limits to what form your dispatches can take. The important thing is content. Seth Friedman of *Factsheet Five*, who undoubtedly eyeballs more zines than anyone, says he gets calls from people saying, "I want to start a zine, but I don't know what it should cover." " They ask me what their zine should be about!" he says with slight exasperation. "How the hell should I know? I tell them they should wait 'til they have something they can be passionate about, then they'll be ready to make a zine." Friedman is convinced that the zines that are good, the ones that gain a loyal audience and sustain themselves over time, are the ones that speak from the heart. Sure, there are really slick design-intensive zines, but for many of them, the art is the main point. One of my favorite zines from the late '80s was called *Eulipian*, an oversized, multicolored extravaganza created by graphic artist Don Baker. To be honest, I never found much of its fiction and poetry inspiring, but the production and artwork was captivating. Baker used a Minolta copy machine and changed color cartridges to achieve multicolored pages. I anticipated each issue more than just about any other publication. On the other end of the production spectrum (but still highly anticipated) was the *Eraser Carver's Quarterly*, a modest little zine for people who like to carve their own "rubber stamps" out of art gum erasers. Another favorite, *Interesting!*, was a low-tech affair, filled with Harper's Index-like nuggets of news and statistics. I could list dozens of other examples of zines spanning a wide spectrum of production values that have one thing in common: They communicate something worth paying attention to.

Since passion often eclipses moderation, there may be a temptation, in starting your zine, to go overboard. There may be something to be said for the crash-and-burn approach, but if you want to sustain your zine over time (and not get an ulcer in the process), you might want to start small and work your way up. If longevity is of no concern, and you want to jump in on all fours, go for it! You may get something spectacular that never would have been produced with moderation. Whatever you decide, remember, it's not a "real" magazine, so it doesn't have to act like one.

One of the first things you might want to do before taking the big leap into publishing is to find out what others are up to. Get a current issue of *Factsheet Five* and send off for a number of zines, especially ones in the subject area you're interested in. If you're in an urban area, go to a trendy bookstore, record store, or large newsstand and peruse their zines. By looking at existing publications, you'll get some idea of the variety of editorial and design approaches and the different production values (size, quality of paper, number of colors, etc.). If you find a couple of zines that you really like, write to the publisher and strike up a correspondence. Most publishers are more than happy to talk to fledgling zinemakers. Keep in mind that they're likely to be overworked—doing the zine in their spare time—so don't ask too many stupid questions. While there is infighting in various quarters of zinedom, most zine producers are surprisingly open and cooperative. You can help perpetuate this ideal by not taking advantage of people's generosity, and by reciprocating when you're asked for help or to trade your zine with others.

Once you've dealt with your motivations, decided what type of zine you want to create, and gotten an idea of what others are doing, you're ready to roll.

Design and Layout)

One of the most intimidating things for an amateur publisher is the prospect of having to do design and layout. Believe me, it can be intimidating to anyone, even a trained graphic artist—staring at a bunch of articles and a few art scraps—trying to create something that's graphically interesting. The first thing to do is remind yourself that if the content is strong, the graphic design will not be quite as important. Of course, you'll want to make it look great, but you can make improvements in the quality through successive issues. In fact, your readers will enjoy seeing the zine grow and expand with each issue.

Since the content is paramount, you'll want to invest in a good dictionary and a spellchecker (if you're using a computer). Just because zinedom is a lawless frontier doesn't mean that people aren't going to be bothered by bad grammar and typos. Snag a couple of style and grammar guides in paperback and keep them on hand for reference (I got mine at a used book-store for pennies). Once you've assembled all the pithy prose that you and your friends have written, take the time to spellcheck and edit everything carefully. Try to get another person to read the material and give you crit-ical feedback and editorial suggestions. The more you work on something, the less objective about it you become. Borrowing another person's critical eye can be extremely useful.

Finding suitable artwork can be nerve-wracking, especially in the begin-ning. Once you get rolling, you're likely to attract a group of sympathetic artists. There's a ready pool of up-and-coming artists out there who want to see their work in print. To connect with them, look over other zines and check out the artists that they use. Sometimes, their addresses will even be provided. Contact them about your zine and ask them to send you some art clips. I've even written to zine publishers asking for artists' addresses and numbers and I've never been turned down. A lot of zine artists are used to broadcasting their work freely, so they'll often have a package of photocopied art ready to send for free. Since it's rare for anyone to be paid in zinedom, writers and artists who submit material don't usually expect payment, but they do expect to get a copy of the issue in which their work appears. Unfortunately, you can't expect that the work they submit to your zine is exclusive and hasn't be sent around to lots of other zines. Exclusive rights are rare in zinedom. Just be thankful if you're able to latch onto a few cool artists. They'll save you a lot of headaches when layout time rolls around. If it's a more established artist, he or she may ask you to run a display ad in exchange for their work. The display ad "payment" is a great way to get an established artist to do something original for your cover. I've always made it a policy to be very generous with ads, connections, and other trades with the artists in my zines. They have reciprocated by giving me original work, designing and illustrating covers, and connecting me up with other artists. Design and layout doesn't have to be a big headache. If you've taken the time and energy to get good, well-edited material, and you've found some kickin' artwork, the battle is half over.

Because there are so many production options available, it doesn't make sense to go into too much detail here, but if you're using a computer and a page layout program, there are a number of free design templates available. If you have Internet access or are a member of AOL, Prodigy, or CompuServe, check design and layout sites and you're likely to find templates, clip art, and layout and design tips. You can look through a number of the newsletter and magazine templates and find something that fits your needs. Most of the stuff available online is likely to be dull and business-oriented, but you may be able to tweak it by changing the fonts and loosening up the design. Cool artwork will go a long way towards covering up any design and layout shortcomings. You can quickly become design literate just by studying existing media. Start deconstructing the design world around you. Look at books, magazines, ads, CD covers, TV, architecture, and ask yourself how it was done. What is it trying to say?

How are the elements working together to communicate their message? What fonts were used? What were the production methods? Cultivating this type of awareness will not only make you a better zine designer, it'll make you more design literate in general, increasing your aesthetic and critical awareness.

There are oodles of books out there on everything from design philosophy to typography to quick and dirty layout tricks. Don't bother buying them (they can be very expensive), check them out of the library and photocopy the relevant pages. To keep my design senses stimulated, I have a series of file folders filled with pages I've clipped out of magazines and other print materials. If I'm feeling particularly uncreative, I go to these files and hunt for inspiration. I also have a little pocket notebook where I jot down ideas and sketch out layouts. If you get really desperate, you can always swipe a design wholesale from a magazine. Don't worry about being hauled away by the copyright police, by the time you pour in your text, artwork, photos, and graphic embellishments (lines, boxes, fancy borders, dingbats, etc.), your zine is unlikely to look like the publication where you got your inspiration. If it does end up looking too similar, play around with it until it has your creative signature on it.

What layout and design equipment you'll need is dependent on the print technology you'll be using (typewriter, computer printer, offset). Regardless of the tech, you'll need paper (duh), glue, a metal ruler, masking tape, an X-acto knife, a non-reproducing blue pencil or pen, white-out, and a well-lit layout area. All of these basic supplies can be found in an office or art supply store. As you develop your own work style, you'll want to add other supplies that fit your needs.

Your imagination is the limit in terms of what form your communiqués can take, but you'll most likely opt for a printed or photocopied paper zine. The cheapest and simplest way of generating copy is with a typewriter. If you don't already have one, you can buy a good used model for next-to-nothing. Even electronic typewriters, with a memory and the ability to justify text into neat columns, can be bought super cheap. Undoubtedly, the most versatile design and layout system is a computer with desktop publishing software. If you already have a computer and a decent printer, you're in business. You can even get by without the page layout and graphics programs if you need to. I've seen very handsome zines that have been created entirely within word processing programs such as Microsoft Word and Word Perfect. If you need to buy computer equipment, you can get a low-end used system for as little as a few hundred dollars. Prices for swiftly obsolescing systems are always plummeting. If you're willing to buy a used system that's several tech generations old, you can get wired on just about any budget. In thinking about what layout system you're going to use, don't underestimate how much time the system you buy will save (or add) or how much it will affect your options. Sure, you can get an old electronic typewriter for fifty bucks, but that's going to mean a lot more manual layout time and you'll be limited to a few type fonts. A computer system will allow you great flexibility, not only in fonts and layout possibilities but in your ability to expand into bigger and better programs and capabilities (like adding a scanner to digitize artwork). Even an "expensive" system, with a decent computer, a laser printer, scanner, and basic software can be bought new for less than two thousand dollars. And obviously, you can use this machine for lots of other things (including most of the other types of media hacking covered in this book).

Printing and Binding)

Once your layout is all done, it's time to "go to press." This can range from printing out multiple copies on your laser printer, going to the corner copy shop, or taking it to a full-blown offset printer. Multiple laser printing only makes sense if your entire zine is computer-based (no paste up) and your print run is very small. There are super-fast laser printers that print both sides at once (called "duplex printing"), but they're very expensive. A good copy shop is your best bet for print runs in the hundreds. Once you get into the thousands, compare prices and you may find offset to be the same price or even cheaper. Offset is definitely preferred for its higher print quality, especially in reproducing graphics and photos.

There are a number of ways of getting photocopying and printing for free, or at least discounted. *Xerox subsidy* is the zine slang for swiping copies from the copy machine where you work. If you're only printing a few copies, you can probably get away with this (if you go in for this sort of thing). For an art project I helped organize years ago, an employee at Kinko's awarded us a xerox subsidy until she got fired. It wasn't our association that got her into hot water—she was discovered making photocopied love with her boyfriend on top of one of the machines! (Fill in your own joke about Kinko's here).

Buying your own copy machine is not out of the question. Desktop models, or used floor models, can be found at very reasonable prices. If you're handy with tech, you can quickly learn how to repair and maintain your own machine. I've had a Canon PC-24 for over seven years and it still makes great copies. I do all my own work on the machine, so my repair bills are nil. Whichever type of machine you opt for (new or used), make sure you get one that has enlargement and reduction capabilities. This will allow you to resize artwork, giving you a lot more design versatility.

Buying your own print shop probably is out of the question. You can get old presses for cheap, but getting them up and running, and keeping them running, is a different story. They are big, obscenely heavy, and immensely temperamental. Working with this type of predigital printing technology only makes sense if you want to make a full-time hobby out of printing. If not, you're better off leaving the headaches to the local quick copy or mom-and-pop print shop.

While it pays to shop around and to have more than one offset printer to call on, it's also a good idea to establish a close relationship with your printers. I've used the same family-owned and -operated printer for over ten years. There are many advantages to having this type of long-term relationship with a vendor. They've been extremely good to me over the years, providing excellent service at shockingly low prices. And because we're friends and longtime associates, if they screw up a job, they're more than happy to re-do it. When my zine *Going Gaga* got too large for me to photocopy myself, I had them take over printing, folding, stapling, and trimming. I got all this for half price in exchange for a small ad in the zine. One issue I got for free in exchange for the ad and a couple of *Gaga* T-shirts. Besides finding a cheap printer and bartering for ads, another way of saving big on offset printing costs is to have a school print your zine. Many high schools, vocational schools, and colleges have printing classes. They are often on the lookout for real-world printing challenges. I've heard of zine publishers getting excellent work done through a school and paying only for the cost of supplies and materials. Call around to local schools and see what you can find. And again, other zinesters can be an invaluable resource. Contact local zinesters and get their recommendations (and warnings) about printers and copy shops.

Distribution)

Once your zines are printed and ready to go . . . the question may arise: Who the hell do I mail this thing to and how? If you've taken my advice about starting slowly and building a readership, you'll probably only have a small initial printing. Send the zine to friends, enemies (to show them how clever

COMMON ZINE SIZES AND FORMATS

DIGEST
5 ½" x 8-½"

STANDARD
8 ½" x 11"

STANDARD (EURO)
8 ¼" x 11-½"

COMIC BOOK
6 ¾" x 10-¼"

HALF-LEGAL
7" x 8-½"

LEGAL
8 ½" x 14"

TABLOID
11" x 15"

POSTER ZINE
14" x 17", 17" x 22"

(OR OTHER LARGE-SHEET SIZE)

MINI
smaller than digest
(COMMON FORMAT FOR COMICS)

BAGAZINE
zine inside paper or plastic bag

CASSETTE ZINE
zine on audio cassette

DIGIZINE
zine on floppy disc or CD-ROM
(ALSO CALLED A MICROZINE)

E-ZINE
online electronic zine
(OR WEB ZINE ON THE WWW)

FAXZINE
zine delivered via fax machine

BOOKAZINE
perfect-bound zine

CHAPBOOK
literary booklet, various sizes

you really are), and to other zine publishers. If you're publishing on a computer, start a mailing list in a database program. There are a number of basic mailing list programs you can get for free on the Net and with services such as AOL and CompuServe. You can print the list directly onto mailing labels.

When you're designing your zine, don't forget to think about how it will be mailed. Will it go in an envelope? Will it be folded over and addressed on one side? Will it be mailed flat, as is? If you have a large enough mailing to use bulk mail (over 200 copies), whatever you do, don't forget to print your bulk mail permit box on the mailing area. In my career as an amateur publisher, I've forgotten this imprint several times and it's been a disaster. And don't forget about weight! Your bright idea for a *Flintstones* fanzine chiseled in granite might look snazzy, but the mailing costs will make you scream for Wilma!

Another uncodified rule of zine publishing is: "Do unto your postmaster as you would have him/her do unto you." After years of mailing (and receiving) the most outrageous stuff, I have great respect for my local post office employees. I treat them well and they usually do likewise. If you get to know the postal service and its rules and regulations, you can make the best of them . . . and exploit them, when necessary. Go to your local post office and get all of their booklets on mailing services and rates. You'll probably start out sending things first class. Being informed about postal services will allow you to take advantage of different mailing options, such as bulk mail, as you grow.

When you're ready to hit the big time and get your zine into stores, you'll need a distributor. Luckily, there are a number of reliable small press/zine distributors who are set up to handle small fry publications like yours (see Resources below). Tower Records also distributes zines. How they deal with all of these odd-sized, erratically published, wildly varied zines is a mystery. They obviously don't make any money on them, and probably carry them only to increase their hip cachet. I personally don't have any trouble with Tower being in the zine business, but many publishers do. They feel as though it cuts into the business of local small record and book stores who also carry zines and deal with zine publishers on a more one-to-one basis. It is a good idea to patronize these stores whenever possible for buying zines, and if you're peddling a zine, you definitely want to target local stores, cafés, and other places where your audience might hang out. You'll find many of them prefer going through a distributor, but it doesn't hurt to ask. The smaller, more noncommercial the store, the more likely they are to distribute your publication.

Promotion and Advertising)

The best promotion and advertising for your zine is to make it so gosh-darn wonderful that it promotes itself. This is no joke. In the zine network, word of mouth is a major source of promotion. Almost every zine has a zine review section. If your zine gets into the big pipeline and enjoys favorable reviews in other zines, the orders will start rollin' in. *Factsheet Five*, other review zines, and online zine forums (such as alt.zines) are your first lines of attack.

You can also set up ad exchanges with other zines where they print your ad if you agree to reciprocate. You should also put together an ad/promo kit. This can be as simple as a copy of your zine, a sheet of different size display ads (called an "ad slick"), an ad rate card (for people who want to buy ads in your zine), and a press release describing your publication. Put some energy into making this kit spiffy. It doesn't need to be overly fancy or expensive, but it should be creative and well put together. Even zine publishers are overstimulated, with a dizzying flow of DIY media constantly pouring into their mailboxes. Make sure that what you send looks like it's worth paying attention to. A decent-looking promo kit (and zine) can also get you press in the local, and even national, media. Regional magazines, newspapers, radio, and cable TV are always on the prowl for local people and projects that will make good copy. Your erotic *Star Trek* zine or your philosophical musings about being an elevator operator (or whatever) might just be the thing they're looking for.

And, once you've developed a readership, make sure you keep it by maintaining your mailing and promotions lists. Send a copy of each issue of the zine and a press release to your promo list. Send review copies to magazines and newspapers that might review it. If you do a special issue on something—let's say, art-decorated automobiles—you'll want to contact all the media sources in your area that deal with automobiles and art. And if you're really creative and ambitious, you can organize an event around the theme of your zine (or a special issue). In the above case, you could sponsor a parade of these goofy-looking cars. You'd almost be guaranteed a spot on the evening news.

Pricing)

Another perennial truth about zines: They rarely make money. Zines are a hobby, pure and simple. This is not to belittle your passion for publishing, but only to acknowledge the noncommercial nature of what you're doing. Producing a zine might even cost you money. The lucky ones break even. The first line of defense for your pocketbook is to price your zine correctly. You'll need to figure out your actual expenses and then add something on top of that. Make sure you consider everything: basic overhead, printing (not only your zine, but all the support materials), mailing costs, phone bills, etc. And also think of the value of your zine to its readers. If you're producing one of several hundred zines on alternative music, you'll want to be price-competitive with them. If your zine is the only one out there that covers tiki collecting (and you know there's a demand among tiki fandom), you can charge more. The production value is also a factor. If your zine is a ten-page hand-lettered jobbie printed on a geriatric office copier, you won't find many takers at $3 an issue. An artfully designed, typeset zine with a color photocopied cover can sell for $5 or $6, especially if word gets around about how cool it is. And if you're going to use a distributor, keep in mind when pricing your zine that the distributor will require a discount (sometimes 50 to 60 percent off the cover price). If you sell direct to stores, they'll usually want 40 percent off the cover price. If you've decided to sell your publication for a dollar, there won't be much left over for you.

Words of Wisdom)

Jerod Pore (*Poppin' Zits!, Factsheet Five-Electric*):
: Always stay passionate about your subject, even if it means changing subjects every third issue.

Mark Frauenfelder (*bOING bOING*):

1) If you don't love a story or piece of art, don't use it.

2) Don't promise that you'll publish your zine on a regular schedule, because you won't. Every issue will be late.

3) Before you start using a distributor, ask them for references from other zinesters and talk to them!

4) If your zine becomes popular, it'll take over your life. You'd better make sure that's what you want.

5) A clean, easy-to-read layout means people will read your zine.

6) The purpose of a zine is to communicate. Don't assume that your audience knows the background behind the articles and stories. Explain it to them.

7) There are already thousands of music zines. If you want to do a music zine, it better be flat-out amazing, or nobody will care.

8) When producing an issue, decide on a page count that you can afford in terms of time and money, and stick to it. Three 32-page issues over a year are better than one 100-pager once a year.

9) Become friends with the people who work behind the counter at your local copy shop. They'll usually give you deep discounts.

10) You'll become successful if you always try to make your next issue better than the previous one.

Darby Romeo (*Ben Is Dead*) :
:   To stay on the ball, you have to be really organized, from file cabinets to an inner self-control and focus. You've got information coming at you every second. You have to learn how to keep what you need and how to filter out the rest.

Jim Romenesko (*Obscure Publications*) :
:   When you think your zine is finished, put it away for a few days, and then look at it again. You'll probably find areas to improve. Maybe you'll simply want to tweak it or you'll want to rip the whole thing apart. Your ultimate goal should be to end up with a zine you can really be proud of.

Resources)

_____**BOOKS**

Zines!

V/SEARCH PUBLICATIONS
20 ROMOLO #B, SAN FRANCISCO, CA 94133
415-362-1465
1996, 184 PAGES, $18.99

V. Vale, former copublisher with Andrea Juno of the popular Re/Search publications (*Modern Primitives, Angry Women, Incredibly Strange Music*), has now ventured out on his own as V/Search. His first offering is *Zines! Vol. 1*, a collection of interviews with the publishers of eleven different zines including *Bunnyhop, Mystery Date, Crap Hound, Fat Girl*, and *Out Punk*. There's also a history of zines and a large zine directory. A second volume is in the works.

'Zine

PAGAN KENNEDY
ST. MARTI
N'S/GRIFFIN, 1995, 184 PAGES, $15.95

For six years, zine queen Pagan Kennedy published a perzine called *Pagan's Head* (among other names). This book collects the eight issues of her zine along with Pagan's reminiscences and how doing a zine changed her life.

GUIDES AND DIRECTORIES

Crap Hound
Encyclopedia of Clip Art
SEAN TEJARATCHI
P.O. BOX 40373, PORTLAND, OR 97240-0373
$5/ISSUE

In just five issues of *Crap Hound*, Sean has become a true hero of zinedom. If you've ever turned to commercial clip art to spice up a tired layout, you know how depressing that exercise can be. There just aren't a lot of cool and unusual graphics available, unless you hunt each one down yourself. That's the dilemma that inspired *Crap Hound*. Each issue includes art collected around several different themes. The juxtapositions, and Sean's visual playfulness and commentary, are just as interesting as the images themselves. So far, issues have covered themes of death, telephones, scissors, clowns, devils, bait, hearts, and hands. Future issues will include graphics of sharks, bones, insects, and eyes. Even if you don't plan to use *Crap Hound* as an alternative image source, its bizarre spelunk through images from advertising, catalogs, book art, and other graphic icons makes it a treat to peruse.

Dustbooks
P.O. BOX 100, PARADISE, CA 95967-9999
800-477-6110
(free brochure)

Publishers of several directories relevant to zine publishers, small presses, and independent book publishers. These include the *International Directory of Little Magazines and Small Presses*, the *Small Press Record of Books in Print*, and the *Directory of Small Magazine/Press Editors & Publishers*. Dustbooks also carries a number of excellent books such as *The Complete Guide to Self-Publishing* and *The Publish-It-Yourself Handbook*.

Factsheet Five*:
The Definitive Guide to the Zine Revolution
SETH FRIEDMAN, EDITOR
P.O. BOX 170099, SAN FRANCISCO, CA 94117-0099
$20/6 ISSUES; $6 SAMPLE ISSUE
EMAIL: seth@factsheet5.com

The keys to the kingdom of zines. Invaluable to zine readers, publishers, and anyone else who wants a current map to this constantly morphing cultural terrain. Also includes ads for zine-friendly distributors and printers. Now published two times a year.

Obscure Publications
JIM ROMENESKO, EDITOR
45 SOUTH ALBERT STREET, #1, ST. PAUL, MN 55105
$5/5 ISSUES; $1 SAMPLE ISSUE
WEB: www.pr.menet.com/~obscure/

Obscure is another valuable link point to zinedom. *Obscure* includes discussion of various aspects of zine culture, along with the zine reviews.

Outposts
RUSS KICK
CARROL & GRAF, 1995, 259 PAGES, $18.95

Kick, who has written reviews for *Factsheet Five* and *Gauntlet*, has put together a catalog of zines, books, newsletters, and catalogs from fringe/DIY publishers. It covers freedom, conspiracy theories, sex, drugs, comix, the unexplained, cyberculture, and underground art with lengthy reviews and contact information.

The World of Zines
A GUIDE TO THE INDEPENDENT MAGAZINE REVOLUTION
MIKE GUNDERLOY AND CARI GOLDBERG JANICE, EDITORS
PENGUIN BOOKS, 1992, 181 PAGES, $14.00

Gunderloy's swan song to zinedom. The zines listings are hopelessly out-of-date, but the book gives a decent overview of zine publishing circa 1991. Sadly, because of the controversy and disappointments surrounding the death of Mike's *Factsheet Five* and his nervous breakdown at the time, the book suffered and was not well received. This book is out of print but still worth hunting down.

Zine Publisher's Resource Guide
BY THE EDITORS OF *FACTSHEET FIVE*
FREE (*F5* SUBSCRIBERS); $4 (NONSUBSCRIBERS)
AVAILABLE FROM *FACTSHEET FIVE* (*see address above*)

A 36-page guide listing over 250 print shops, magazine stores, and distributors that deal with zines. Invaluable to those just getting starting or those looking to increase their zine's circulation.

CATALOGS

Atomic Books
"LITERARY FINDS FOR MUTATED MINDS"
1018 NORTH CHARLES STREET, BALTIMORE, MD 21201
410-625-7955, FAX: 410-625-7945
EMAIL: atomicbk@atomicbooks.com
WEB: www.atomicbooks.com
CATALOG $2.95 (*Adults only*)

A thick catalog, in both print and online formats, that has tons of books, zines, trading cards, and other paraphernalia related to underground publishing, high weirdness, sex, drugs, and any other taboo subject that has found its way into print. A major watering hole for outré culture. You can order anything from the catalog over the Net.

See Hear

59 EAST 7TH ST., NEW YORK, NEW YORK 10003
WEB: www.zinemart.com
CATALOG $3.00

See Hear is a well-known zine and book store located on St. Mark's Place in New York City's Lower East Side. Zinemart is the online version of their catalog. You can search the catalog by category or do keyword searches. Each month, they also provide excerpts from the featured zine of the month.

Wow Cool

48 SHATTUCK SQ. #149, BERKELEY, CA 94704
WEB: www.wowcool.com

A small catalog of zines and underground comics put together by Josh Petrin and Marc Arsenault, "two guys in a room." They have no storefront, but you can order by mail or through their Web site.

ZINE-FRIENDLY PRINTERS

Arena Press

P.O. BOX 5, POINT ARENA, CA 95468
707-882-2833

A printing press owned and operated by zinesters. They offer full printing, bindery, shipping, and mailing services for zines from 200 copies to 5,000 or more.

Market Hill Printing

216 MARKET ST., AMSTERDAM, NY 12010
518-421-1064
EMAIL: markethill@aol.com

Printing of saddle-stitched zines, tabloids, booklets, and catalogs.

Morgan Publishing

402 HILL AVE., GRAFTON, MD 58237
701-352-0640

A full-service comic book and zine printer. Morgan's prices are reasonable and their quality is reportedly good.

Small Publishing Co-Op

2579 CLEMATIS ST., SARASOTA, FL 34239
941-922-0844
EMAIL: spcoop@netline.net

An independent publisher that caters to small commercial magazines, zines, and comic books.

Thomson-Shore

7300 WEST JOY ROAD, DEXTER, MI 48130-9701
313-426-3939, FAX: 313-426-6219
WEB: www.tshore.com

Printer for small-run saddle-stitched booklets, hardcover books, and paperbacks. They also put out a free monthly newsletter filled with surprisingly useful tips and how-to instructions for small publishers (how to get printing quotes, what papers to use, what is a good halftone, shipping considerations, etc.). They also have a web page that includes a plant tour, library, new updated info, and quote request forms.

ZINE DISTRIBUTORS

There are a number of regional and national distributors that carry zines. These are just two of the larger national ones that carry zines. Be careful with distributors. Before you set up a deal, make sure you talk to other zinesters (on alt.zines, for instance) to hear their recommendations (and horror stories).

Desert Moon Periodicals

1226-A CALLE DE COMERCIO, SANTA FE, NM 87505
EMAIL: xines@desert-moon.com
WEB: www.xines.com

Desert Moon also maintains a great online zine catalog (at above Web address).

Fine Print Distributors, Inc.

500 PAMPA DR., AUSTIN, TX 78752-3028
800-874-7082, 512-452-8709
WEB: www.fineprint.com

NET SITES

alt.zines Newsgroup*

If you have access to Usenet newsgroups, you'll want to subscribe to the group alt.zines. It's where all the Net-connected zine publishers hang out. Lots of zine news and announcements, pointers to electronic and print zines, and information sharing (and arguing) on all the aspects of zines covered in this chapter.

Factsheet Five-Electric*

JEROD PORE, EDITOR
Available on the Internet:
FTP: etext.archive.umich.edu/pub/FactsheetFive
GOPHER: gopher.well.com
WEB: www.well.com/conf/f5/f5index2.html
INFO/EMAIL REQUESTS: jerod23@aol.com

> This electronic version of *Factsheet Five* contains the entire contents of the print issues, along with additional reviews, links to zine-related Web sites, FAQs, and other e-zines.

The How-To Guide to Comics

WEB: www.teleport.com/~ennead/ampersand/how_to.html

> A basic page of links useful to artists, writers, and self-publishers.

rec.arts.comics.alternative *and* rec.arts.comics.misc Newsgroups

> The places to go to discuss the issues of the small comics press and to announce new releases. Many of the articles are cross-posted between the two groups.

The Small Press Comics FAQ*

WEB: www.sentex.net/~sardine/spfaq.html

> Maintained by indie comic artist John MacLeod, this excellent Web site includes how-to info on making comics, getting your comics into print, and other aspects of the fringe comics scene. Includes a bookshelf of recommended reading on small press comics and the comics biz in general. Lots of related links.

Small Press Zone*

WEB: www.cloudnet.com/~hamlinck/faq.htm

> A Web site dedicated to small press/underground comics and zines. The site's main features include a publishers list, a zine and comics review page, and a news section. There's also the Big Mini-Comics List, a list of mini-comics put together by Scott Dutton and posted to various newsgroups. There's also a large Links page that will take you to other cool sites.

Zine Distributors List

EMAIL: sarootabaker@mail.utexas.edu
WEB: www.well.com/conf/f5/distro

> A regularly updated (that's the plan, anyway) listing of zine-friendly distributors. If you'd like to receive this list via email, send your email address and specify that you want the "zine distros list."

> (*See the Resources section of chapter 7 for more zine-related Net sites.*)

Never Mind the MUSIC BIZ!

∧ THE BRAIN

In the **DIGITAL ERA,**
with the ability
TO TRANSMIT
at the CD level of
quality down the pipe
without a public
PERFORMANCE
right . . . we stand
vulnerable and naked
TO THE WORLD.

—Al Teller,
Former MCA chairman

"I spent years shopping my demo tapes around until one day I realized I could just make the damn records myself." In the 1980s, this became a common discovery among unsigned musicians. These musicians-cum-indie labels usually go on to say that it was well worth all the hair-pulling and headaches. They may not have gotten rich and famous on their self-publishing, but most of them feel it was ultimately more productive than chasing the treadmill of success. And for some, their homemade efforts ended up attracting the attention of established labels.

The decade between the mid-'70s and mid-'80s saw a number of structural shifts occur in the music industry that proved advantages to small-fry record makers. As bloated stadium rock and disco collapsed under their own excesses, they sent out spores that pollinated punk, new wave, house, and numerous other musical subgenres. These new and smaller niches compelled record-pressing plants and tape duplicators to begin catering to smaller clients. Recording technology, the biggest cost-prohibiting factor in self-publishing, was also starting to become affordable, thanks to cheaper equipment and an increasing market demand for quick-and-dirty production. The introduction of 4- and 8-track tape recorders made home recording a reality. Depending on how frugal and improvisational you were, by the early '80s you could get a professional-sounding album recorded and several hundred copies pressed for a few thousand dollars. If you wanted to go super low budget, you could record on a high-quality consumer tape deck and have a master tape made from that. My wife did such a recording on a Sony TC-158SD in 1981 and sold the tape at gigs for years. She only duplicated 100 copies at a time and continued doing so until the master tape became too worn and the original recording turned up damaged.

Punk, house, and rap, three vastly different subculture music genres, all had a major decentralizing impact on the music industry. Punk was a return to the garage of early rock 'n' roll, reanimating the pop culture myth that a group of teens with pawnshop guitars and a few weekends of practice could gel into a band. Punk's disdain for the establishment and the record industry dictated that "doing-it-yourself" was the only way to get the music out with one's integrity intact. Hundreds of tiny independent labels sprung up in the United States, Britain, Europe, and elsewhere. Bands, punk record shops, and clubs pooled their resources and purchased their own vinyl pressing machines. Band members and fans cranked out zines, handbills, posters, and even album jackets. This cobbled-together culture circulated itself through a network of clubs, stores, the mail, and word of mouth. The common punk practice of suturing holes in one's clothes with safety pins is a fitting glyph, symbolizing much of the early punk aesthetic.

In the mid-'80s, as disco was gagging on its own success, DJs such as Chicago's Frankie Knuckles and Ron Hardy and New York's Larry Levan began to get more creative with the dance mixes they spun, using tracks with dub elements and breaks that allowed other records to be mixed in. "House" music was born, a postdisco phenomenon that de-emphasized big-name artists over the club scene and the DJs unique mixes. DJs began to record "white label" 12-inch records of their mixes to conveniently carry around from gig to gig. These were basically one-off mix recordings. As DJs became more popular, they started doing small press runs of these mixes, circulating them through other DJs and clubs. Eventually, DJs began to go commercial, leading to today's DJ superstars such as Sven Vath and the Chemical Brothers.

Rap is perhaps the ultimate expression of the DIY impulse. Its roots stretch back to the early '70s when Jamaican DJ Kool Herc moved from Kingston to the West Bronx of New York City. Herc began to "toast" (create impro-vised rhymes) over the percussion sections of the music he played. Since the R&B music he was playing was not the reggae dub he was used to, he would extend these percussion sections by spinning two identical discs so he could continuously play the same segment. Similar toasting and rapping caught on at hip-hop parties as DJs improvised rhymes on the names of people "in the house" and various aspects of street culture. Eventually, DJs wanted to focus on the record playing and the growing popularity of "cutting and scratching" (spinning the records backwards and forwards to create percussion), so they brought in "emcees" to handle the mike. Like punk, rap relied on a strong subculture (hip-hop) to support it and spread its message. Like House, Rap DJs soon became superstars in the hip-hop uni-verse and by the mid-'80s began to cross over into mainstream pop success.

Although all three of these genres have gone on to mainstream success, there is still an underground for each of them that continues to hold onto its

DIY roots. Threads of this ideal run all through today's zine, hacker, and Internet underground cultures.

DIRECT CONNECT) The price of all manner of audio equipment has continued to plummet in the last two decades. Compact Disc technology was, for a brief moment, the record industry's best hope for maintaining master control over the music distribution pipeline. After some initial stumbling, the industry did an impressive job of re-grooving us all to accept the CD format, eventually sweeping vinyl LPs—and in many instances, even cassette tapes—out of record stores. But hot on the heels of the CD's takeover, the price of CD pressing soon dipped low enough that any musician with a day job could afford to finance his or her own CD. And, of course, tape-duplicating technology has long been ubiquitous. With a consumer-grade dual cassette deck, bought for a few hundred bucks, you can do your own recording and duplicating (at least until the deck or the master tape poops out).

And now there's the Internet. Distribution has always been the weak link in the chain of self-publishing, but the Net is changing that. Internet music sites such as Independant Artists' Services, IndiSonic, and Rabid Underground are popping up everywhere, offering slots on their virtual jukeboxes and promotional spaces for unsigned bands. At this point, modem speed is still a serious limiting factor for transferring audio over the wire. Downloading an entire song can take hours with today's modems. Music sites often work around this by storing small low-fidelity clips that don't take up much space. This format is funky, but you can at least hear what *type* of music a band plays. If you're interested in checking them out further, you can download a higher-quality sample. Music pages on the

Web usually include background information on the bands, photos, reviews, chat areas, and links to related sites. "Streaming audio" (where the audio is played while it downloads) is an increasingly popular method of transfer, but the quality is about equal to a cheap AM radio (with bad reception). The technology for serving up streaming audio has become cheap enough that clubs and concerts are doing audio (and even video) netcasts. This ability has exciting potential (you'll be able to peer into club scenes from all over the world), but so far the technology lags far behind the ideal.

The next generation of Internet connections—cheap ISDN, cable modems, ADSL—could lead to a significant rerouting of music distribution channels, allowing CD-quality digital audio to be downloaded over the Net at more reasonable speeds. When this happens, it is likely that music companies and independent musicians will start selling music for downloading. For self-publishing musicians and small indie labels, the advantages of Net marketing and distribution could be tremendous. Currently, if you're a band and you want to get your music into every record store in the nation, you've got to have a record contract with a major label, or at least a contract with an indie that's distributed by a major. This seriously limits who makes it into record stores. But, if you set up your own jukebox on the Internet (or wriggle your way onto someone else's), and spend some time promoting yourself in the right places, you can attract a potentially international audience. If people like what they hear, they can order it directly from you, currently delivered by conventional mail, but eventually over the Net itself.

Of course, if you're going to sell something over the Net, you need a means of exchange. A number of virtual cash schemes are competing for dominance in cyberspace. Here's how they work: You set up a vendor's account with one of them and they handle the credit transactions with your customers and send you a check for the sales. Also, some music sites have links to big online music stores such as CDnow! Listeners can preview the music on a musician's homepage and then click on a link that takes them to an online record store where they can order the disc with a credit card. Having your music available through a virtual record store can also get you airplay in cities where your records may not be available in stores. DJs don't like to play cuts that their listeners can't have access to, but if your CD is available through an online store, they can tell their listeners to order it there. You can even make stickers that can go on the CDs you send to the media announcing that the recording is available through an online store.

All of these developments are exciting, but how will the big music monopoly of Sony, MCA, BMG, and Warner Brothers handle this challenge? There are some massively entrenched commercial interests at stake. They are not going to give up any ground if they think the Net in some way compromises their interests. MCA's former chairman Al Teller revealed a great degree of wisdom during an interview in the July '95 issue of *Wired* when he said: "I don't care how many people you have sitting around in a room trying to hypothesize where it's going to go—it's going to go where the people who create the music take it. So, out there right now are kids who are steeped in music, steeped in technology, and their synaptic connections are going to take all that stuff and synthesize it, amalgamate it, and combine it in some fashion! And then we're all finally going to look at it, hear it, see it, and say, "*Uh huh!* That's it!" For independent media producers, this can be seen as both an affirmation and a warning.

Luckily, we don't have to solve the dilemma for the mainstream music business about which future to embrace. We're here to talk about a side-stream music movement that may inspire the majors (and will undoubtedly be cannibalized by them) but, the gods willing, will never be completely controlled by them. We're talking about the no-budget fringe of the indie music biz where passion, art, and community are more important than fame and fortune.

TAPING *into the*
CASSETTE CULTURE)

**In the FUTURE,
Your Agent May Be a ROBOT
One BIG PROBLEM with
marketing and DISTRIBUTING
MUSIC** over the **Net is
mushrooming infoglut.
As commerce** of all kinds
**increases in CYBERSPACE,
and** as everybody and
their **PET PARAKEET
has a homepage
(YES,** there are tons of **pet
homepages!), your little
VIRTUAL** music store will **be
drowned in a SEA OF** other
virtual shops. **IMAGINE
the needle in a
haystack world** that will be
**CREATED when every
wired CITIZEN** has their
**own media shack
SELLING products** with
CYBERCASH.

Most people probably think that music is the only sound coming out of the audio underground, but this is not the case. "Audio networkers" (as they were sometimes called in the '80s) exchange "best of" incoming answering machine messages, phone pranks, poetry, rants, personal documentaries, found sounds and just about everything else that can make a microphone vibrate. Like zines and mail art, audiocassettes (and CDs) are circulated internationally. Also, like other noncommercial forms of media, tapes are just as often exchanged as bought and sold. Sure, there's a lot of junk and material that only its mother could love, but part of the fun is wading through all this in search of something truly unique. It's not an expensive hobby, especially if you have your own sonic noodlings to trade. Even if you're buying the tapes, they usually aren't sold for much more than the cost of blanks.

Besides tapes produced by individuals, there are also compilation tapes and audio zines. For compilation tapes, each individual sends either a completed composition or pieces of found sounds to be composed into something by the editor. Audio zines, which usually mix forms (music, rants, poetry, etc.), are most commonly done by one or a few people (like a print zine), while others are collections with many contributors. Audio zines sometimes have preannounced themes such as "Drug Experiences" or "The Most Bizarre Thing That Ever Happened to Me," or other evocative topics. For those who have no musical talent, but are still interested in working with audio, there're lots of different ways of plugging into "cassette culture."

JOHN BERGIN'S GRINDER)

John Bergin is one of those enviable humans who is so creative that he seems to enchant whatever he touches. The reserved thirty-year-old is an accomplished painter, sculptor, photographer, illustrator, cartoonist, musician, engineer, and designer. His frequently mopey demeanor contradicts his overabundant creativity and his hyperactive, workaholic schedule. From the wee morning hours late into the night, Bergin can usually be found cranking away in his old Kansas City home.

John first got involved in DIY publishing in high school, producing a writing and art journal. "I was crazy even then, editing, printing, stapling, folding, etc., etc., etc." While attending art college at Philadelphia's University of the Arts in 1987, Bergin began an art zine called *Brain Dead* and a band called Orifice. He's been obsessively producing art and music ever since, selling his creations through mail order and building a devoted following through the articles and interviews that regularly appear in comics and music zines. In 1992, Bergin created Grinder Books and Records as a publishing umbrella for his work and the work of artist and musician friends.

Given Bergin's considerable talents, it was just a matter of time before his work caught the attention of commercial interests. In 1990, Caliber Press took the bait on John's art, hiring him to do a six-volume comic book series called *Ashes*. From there, it's been bigger and better assignments, including a magnum opus 300-page full-color graphic novel called *From Inside,* published in 1994 by Kitchen Sink Press. Also in 1994, Trent Reznor of Nine Inch Nails approached John about appearing on his new label, Nothing. Unfortunately, after 2$\frac{1}{2}$ years without a release, John got out of his contract and was quickly picked up by Fifth Column Records, another popular indie label. So far, Fifth Column has released two of John's recordings and he's started to work for the record company on a number of their CD package designs.

And does this newfound stardom mean that Bergin will abandon his DIY roots? "Not a chance," says John, without hesitation. "There's something about a homemade production you can never get out of something that's been mass-produced. You can do much more interesting packaging and really put more of yourself into it. Regardless of what happens with my commercial releases, I'll continue to do my other art and music projects." Having seen the obsessive output that's poured from this man's hands and soul over the years, I don't doubt him for a second.

The SHEER volume of INFORMATION could bury all THE GOOD STUFF. Keeping up with new offerings **on the Web** HAS already BECOME **an OVERWHELMING proposition. Eventually, there will be THOUSANDS of sites competing WITHIN every** niche of interest. **When talking about music, this is compounded by THE fact that MUSIC-RELATED SITES** OUTNUMBER **every** other type of site on **THE Web. BIG COMPANIES have huge amounts of money** to spend in on- and off-line **ADVERTISING to publicize their sites. INFORMATION "AGENTS,"** software that can **TROLL the Net making decisions** about what **you're interested in,** have been **proposed AS A SOLUTION TO THIS INFOGLUT. These agents will have** LITTLE AI **(artificial intelligence) brains that will learn your likes and dislikes as you interact with them. They'll be able to make DECISIONS on the fly ABOUT NEW THINGS to introduce**

TESTING THE WIRES)
Sanjay Mishra, a classical Indian guitarist, found himself with a rare opportunity one night to meet the wife of Grateful Dead guitar legend Jerry Garcia. When Garcia himself showed up later, Sanjay seized upon an even greater opportunity. He shyly handed Garcia a copy of his self-published CD *The Crossing.* Garcia's wife

phoned a week later to say that the great tie-dyed one loved the CD and wanted to know how he could help out. Sanjay asked if Garcia would appear on his next recording. Jerry not only agreed to play on the album, but gave Mishra the use of the Dead's Club Front studio, loaned him their engineers, and gave him use of the Garcia visage for the album cover. The result is *Blue Incantation,* featuring sixteen minutes of Garcia's guitar work, some of his last recorded music before his death.

This would be an interesting enough "indie boy lucks out big-time" story, but wait, there's more. *Blue Incantation* was one of the first indie records widely marketed over the Internet. Oasis CD Duplication, Sanjay's duplicator, and Musicians on the Internet (MOI) (see Resources below) decided to target the estimated 100,000 wired Deadheads. Dead forums have always been some of the most popular areas on BBSes such as The Well in Sausalito, California, Usenet newsgroups, and online services like AOL.

Sanjay has a homepage at MOI and his CD is stocked at CDnow! An 800-number has also been set up for telephone fulfillment.

you to **OUTSIDE OF your EXISTING INTERESTS. Critics of this technology,** such as **virtual reality pioneer JARON LANIER,** say that **THE REALITY will be far MORE NEGATIVE than positive. Do you really want TO RELY ON SOFTWARE to expand your horizons? Lanier also bets that COMMERCIAL SITES will GO TO GREAT LENGTHS TO "convince" your AGENT** to show you **THEIR wares, ". . . like flowers ENTICING BEES." Whatever the developments,** it's clear that something has to be done **to help people KEEP TRACK OF INTERNET CONTENT (especially the side-stream, noncommercial stuff).**

SONIC PIRATES) Probably the two most corrosive agents in the war over musical copyright and the ownership of sound was the introduction of the portable tape machine and the digital sampler. With these two devices in wide circulation, the entire sound universe that surrounds us can be duplicated and hacked. Twentieth-century audio artists (like artists working in other media) have relied heavily on appropriation, collage, and noise. This has gotten many of them in trouble over copyright infringement. But is using the sounds that surround us any different from, say, photographers taking pictures of the urban environment around them? They don't need to get permission from the architects, builders, and owners to "sample" the physical landscape before them, so why should the audio artist? We are constantly bombarded with the unrelenting sounds of ads, television programming, cars, machines, crowds, vapid pop songs, and millions of other utterances. Copyright law has no problem with sound re-appropriation as long as the work is a parody or, as the Copyright Act states, ". . . for purposes of criticism, comment, news reporting, teaching, scholarship, or research." The problem is that many avant pop bands see their music as criticism and parody and want to be able to use the corporate soundwaves as source material. This has blurred the lines around fair use and opened up a legal Pandora's Box.

Even deeper into the legal quagmire is the use of more recognizable song samples in such genres of dance music as rap, techno, and industrial, all heavily built around sampling. After a number of high-profile cases in the '70s and '80s, starting with the group Chic suing the pants off Sugar Hill Records in 1979 for their use of samples on the ground-breaking rap tune "Rapper's Delight," many of these bands have started securing permission for anything they sample.

Music copyright holders are even more petrified about what the Net will do to their rights. Already, people are uploading copyrighted music and audio from films, making them available to anyone who cares to download, manipulate, and re-upload them. Once connection speeds makes downloading audio truly cost-effective, the Net will be flooded with audio pirates exchanging stolen booty. Even if service providers are diligent about keeping this piracy out of their public areas, people will still be able to trade sounds via email like they now trade hard-core porno images. Clearly, commercial entities are going to need to figure out a way of turning this activity to their advantage. Dozens of rock bands, from Phish and the Black Crowes to Fugazi and Jawbox, have already done such an aikido move with illegal taping at concerts. Rather than punishing the tapers, these bands are actually encouraging them, even setting up special taping areas. These bands feel as though the sense of community and openness of such a move brings their fans closer to the band and doesn't really hurt sales in the long run.

George Clinton, who along with his bands Parliament/Funkadelic is one of the most sampled artists of the funk '70s, also takes a unique approach to sampling. His 1994 release *Sample Some of Disc, Sample Some of DAT* is a series of CDs made with sampling in mind. Bands are encouraged to sample what they want as long as they send Clinton a copy and pay him "a few pennies" per copy of the band's CD sold. This way, Clinton contends, anyone can afford it and he gets to hear all of the interesting and wild things people are doing with his music.

Ram Samudrala, who makes music under the name Twisted Helices, has another unique approach to music copyright. Through a philosophy he calls Free Music, he encourages people to copy and distribute their music with only the stipulation that they give proper attribution and include the following notice:

"Permission to make verbatim copies of the music on this album, provided this notice is included with every copy that is made, is given for noncommercial, private, and nonprofit use only. If you obtained this by making a copy, and if you like the music and wish to support it, please send a donation based on whatever you thought the music was worth to the address given on this notice."

People have in fact copied his music and redistributed it, but he still feels it ends up working to his benefit. "I've gotten mail from people who got a bootleg tape of my music and then come to me to buy the CD or a T-shirt." Ram is a staunch opponent of intellectual property. "I think it is vitally important that people have the freedom to copy music, change it, and redistribute it," he says. He also doesn't believe in the high price of CDs. "I sell my CDs very cheap. I only make about a dollar apiece, but it's good to know that I'm getting my music out there." Ram's Web page (http://www.twisted-helices.com/) has been a big success in getting his music out. He gets around 200 visitors per day and averages about one to two orders per day. So far, he's sold around 600 copies of his CD.

No one knows how the great copyright/intellectual property debate will shake out, but it's clear that something needs to change to allow people to make "electronic folk art" from the sonic material that surrounds them, without it being considered plagiarism. As the band Negativland points out, in this age of media saturation, recuperation becomes a necessary form of cultural criticism. As long as our legal system and the marketplace continues to deny this, the battle will rage on and artists will continue to push the envelope.

THE AUDIO HACKER'S STARTER KIT

Getting Started **)** Just as in any DIY media, creativity and hard work can overcome many obstacles in audio hacking, including stuffy notions of talent. I have, in my tape and CD collection, music and audio art that is so bizarre it might as well be from another planet. A lot of it sounds like a 747 plowing into an interstate on-ramp or someone passing a gallstone. But among this sonic carnage can be found some of the most inspiring and passionately original material I own. These are audioscapes crafted by people plumbing their own depths, unleashing their imaginations, and experimenting for experimentation's sake. The packaging on these releases is frequently as creative and bizarre as the contents. Commercial record companies could learn a thing or two from a number of these inspired handmade efforts. When friends come over, I love to give them a guided tour of my latest acquisitions. They "ohh" and "ahh" (and giggle and retch) over the new sounds I present to them.

Mainstream music is hell-bent on re-treading formulas and dumbing down content to appeal to the widest possible audience. Yesterday's innovators become today's copycat hair bands. A steady diet of this tasteless gruel can make one mentally and spiritually malnourished. I almost consider it one of my duties in life to expose people to new music, new art, and new ideas. My mother used to say, "Put a new wrinkle on your brain every day." My obsession with all forms of fringe media is an attempt to do just that.

Recording **)**

Once you have something worthwhile to commit to tape, vinyl, or CD, you need to figure out which recording, duplicating, and distribution options make the most sense. Your choices depend on what type of music (or audio art) you're making, how many copies you plan on duplicating, how much money you have to spend, and which audience you are targeting. Let's unpack these one at a time.

[**T Y P E   O F   M U S I C :** If you desire a really high quality recording, you're probably going to end up in a professional studio (or at least a
high-end home studio). Some types of quieter music are better served by
higher fidelity production. Even if you end up in a studio, it still doesn't
have to break your piggy bank. There are lots of sophisticated home studios these days, tucked away in the basements of musicians, composers,
and moonlighting engineers. Oftentimes, these studios are underutilized
and their owners are more than happy to do your project at a reasonable
rate. They're grateful to have the business, to be working on someone else's
music, and to have another product done at their studio that they can use
for promotional purposes.

If sound quality is not of great concern to you, anything that magnetizes
sounds onto tape (or floppy disk) can be used. A lot of bands even like the
sonic qualities of degeneration and noise that low-end analog recording
introduces into the mix. If you're making electronic music, it can be done
on cheap synths and sent straight to tape. Any local mall department store
is a great source for cheap, funky electronic instruments and recording
gear. Some bands have actually made the tackiness of their dime-store
instruments a big part of their sound. Exploring the chaotic edge between
music and noise is clearly a hallmark of the postmodern artistic sensibility.
This opens up all sorts of possibilities for experimentation with instrument
hacking, using found sounds, and playing with how the recording process
affects the music.

A good way to get a handle on what level of sound quality makes sense for
your type of music (if you're unsure) is to ask other audio self-publishers

in that genre. If you have Internet access or know of a local BBS, you can look around for music-related discussion groups and ask the musicians who frequent them. Unlike mainstream commercial music, the farther you get out onto the fringes, the more helpful people become. Here there's more enthusiasm for helping others get into making music and art noise. The more participants, the greater the chances that something truly interesting will emerge from the collective rabble. Even in the more commercially focused indie rock scene, there's usually a "banding-together" mentality. Don't hesitate to take advantage of this. You're likely to meet new friends and coconspirators in the process.

[N U M B E R   O F   C O P I E S : If you're only producing a small run of tapes, you might even be able to duplicate them yourself on a good consumer-grade dual (tape-to-tape) deck. It'll take some time, but the cost will be next to nothing. A lot of low-key self-publishers only keep several copies on hand and duplicate more as people order them. Years ago, I did a one-shot audio zine this way. I bought a box of 100 cheap 45-minute cassettes from a duplicator. I had two dual decks and would make real-time copies all day as I did other work. I ended up making about fifty copies this way. My only costs were the blank tapes, the labels for the cassette shells, and the wear and tear on my decks. The sound quality was fine for that particular project (recorded on a Pro Walkman).

The next level of commitment is sending your master tape to a professional duplicator to be made into tapes, CDs, or a combination of both. Decent quality production houses have cropped up in most areas, offering

In CD production, the cost of making the "glass master" (from which all the CD copies are made) is a big chunk of the production cost. Once the press gets rolling, the difference between cranking out 300 copies and 500 copies is almost negligible. So, it's best to order as many as your budget can handle. Regardless of how many copies you order, some CD plants will go ahead and make more, storing the balance in case you reorder. So, say you ordered 500—they might press 1,000 and stash the extra 500. The scam is that, if you reorder, they'll charge you a lot more than if you had ordered 1,000 up front.

reasonably priced packages, even in small quantities. Some houses will do as few as 100 cassettes, although 300 is a more common minimum quantity. It is an increasingly common practice for duplicating plants to offer package deals that include a combination of CDs and tapes (such as 500 CDs and 300 tapes). This can be a great deal for bands looking for a substantial (but not overwhelming) inventory to sell at gigs, through the mail, at local stores, and as a way of getting reviews and airplay. Years ago, in the antiquated age of LPs, you needed to have your music on vinyl to get any media attention. Now it's CDs. Most newspapers and magazines, the mainstream ones anyway, won't give your sonic masterpiece the time of day if it's not housed on one of those little silver platters.

[**B U D G E T** : If money's no object (yeah, right), then you can let your desires for sound quality determine your budget. If you're like most of the media hackers I know, you'll need to be careful about getting satisfactory quality and production while staying within a tiny budget. If this is your first audio effort, you might want to try working with available resources (your home tape decks, friend's equipment, whatever). If you like the results, you can then pony up for a more serious home studio set-up or rent time in a professional studio. Again, don't hesitate to do a little information networking. Most cities and towns have a music paper with display ads and classifieds from musicians and others involved in the local music scene. BBSes and the Internet at large are valuable repositories for technical information, advice, and announcements of equipment sales. They're great places to meet fellow audio hackers, too. (See Resources below for some points of entry.)

Remember to consider *all* aspects of the budget when planning your project. You've got the recording costs, the cost of mixing and mastering (if you go this route), the entire cost of duplicating (which may or may not include mastering costs, test recordings, duplication, packaging, art prep, art printing, etc.), and promotion and distribution. If you're working with a studio and/or a duplicating house, make sure you're clear on all costs. Get estimates up front and ask for updates on the estimates if things change.

If your goal is basically to use a DIY production as a calling card to attract a commercial label, you're going to want to put more money and production quality into your work. In fact, you should probably spend until it hurts, especially on the postproduction end, putting together a decent media kit, doing mailings to record labels and radio stations, and tirelessly promoting yourself. If you don't manage to snag an actual recording contract, you should at least be able to attract a decent-sized distributor. There are a number of distributors cropping up that cater to dinky, even single-artist, labels.

[**TARGET AUDIENCE** : Obviously, a large factor in determining the shape of your project is the audience—who's going to be listening? A vanity tape or audio zine can get by on home recording, home duplicating, and a photocopied cassette cover, or J-card. Anything with a commercial future, regardless of how modest, should be more polished, especially in the packaging. If you're setting your sights on the mainstream, you'll probably want to go with a professional recording studio, a multicolored J-card (printed directly onto the cassette shell), and other details that fool people into thinking you're a "real" record label. And, by all means, if you're going to go this route, make up a label name. Distributors will more likely do business with you, and stores will be more interested in selling your product if you look "official." DIY media is about honesty, so you don't want to go too far in trying to play to an audience's expectations. There are far too many formula bands out there who are trying too hard to be "punk," "alternative," "metal," and it shows . . . a mile away. Just be who you are and do what you do, take some care in how you package your work, and otherwise *go for it!* There are far too many people sitting on good ideas and unexpressed passions.

Packaging)

One of the things I like the most about the DIY cassette culture is the creativity often put into packaging. As with zines, most DIY tapes are unlikely to get widespread distribution, selling instead through the mail and in specialty shops, so standardized packaging isn't necessary. You can hand-build your J-cards, produce booklets of any size to accompany the tape, put the tape(s) in Ziploc bags, in odd-sized containers—it's up to you.

John Bergin, of Grinder Books and Recordings, has developed a number of creative ways to package releases. First, he desktop publishes the J-cards on his Macintosh. You can easily set up templates in a paint or page layout program to handle the various parts of the cassette package (J-card, shell labels, lyric sheets, etc.). Since John's recording projects are steeped in dark atmospherics, he uses lots of white text on heavy black backgrounds and strange, ethereal imagery. White text on a large field of black is often a problem with laser printers and copiers, but John's figured out a cool hack. After the material has been printed, he sprays it with a fixative (available at office supply and art stores). The fixative slightly melts the toner, smoothing it out and making it darker. If you have a good cartridge on your printer/copy machine and it's well maintained, you can get near-perfect black using this method.

John's next trick is to use full-color photos for his covers. Most color copying is expensive and the quality can vary. Where he would spend over a dollar apiece for $8^1/_2$-by-11-inch color copies, John can make thirty to sixty covers with one (30-exposure) roll of color film. He sets up a shot he wants for the cover: a page from a book, a dead bug, a sculptural object he's constructed. He takes the entire roll of the same image and sends it out for cheap processing. Once he gets the prints back, he cuts them to fit the cassette box. They are slipped in front of the folded J-card. If the cover image is "ambient," (e.g., a pattern of some kind), he can cut the print in half and get two covers per print. If it's a more specific subject he's captured, he uses a template to crop and cut the print down to fit the cover dimensions. John often encloses a separate lyric sheet. These are long sheets of paper cut to the width of the cassette box and then folded several times. The whole production, done on a shoestring budget, is luscious. For one of his releases, he added another collectible item. He shot rolls of additional prints and placed five prints each inside small white boxes he had gotten from a friend. He then printed a label and signed each box. The print collection makes a kind of low-tech multimedia experience as you listen to the music.

One of Bergin's most spectacular and noteworthy packages was for the release of his album Locust. The tape was packaged inside a small cardboard box. On the outside of the box appeared the neatly printed word LOCUST. Opening the box, one was confronted by a huge locust carcass glued to the lid. The entire inside of the box was painted a gloomy matte black, and the cassette box was glued to the bottom. The J-card cover was also black, with a small square of sandpaper pasted top and center. Even before one put on the tape, it had begun to tell its frightening tale of insectoid menace, death, and destruction.

Another cassette cover design trick that John uses is to cut pieces of art gift-wrap paper to the size of the tape case and to place them in front of the laser-printed J-cards. You can get sheets of beautiful art wrap from art supply stores and mail-order art catalogs like Dick Blick and Flax (see Resources below). The paper sheets come in pulpy handmade, slick metallic, and coarse rocklike textures. It's expensive, but you'll only need 2$\frac{1}{2}$-by-4-inch pieces for each cover.

New York painter and musician Ron Anteroinen is another home-brewing musician who makes innovative, artful packages. He uses Photoshop and QuarkXPress to create the graphics on his 660AV Macintosh and then prints them to a Hewlett-Packard 560 color printer. He prints his J-cards on HP Specialty paper. The paper has a unique plasticized look and feel to it. It's somewhat expensive, but Ron thinks the results are worth it. He also prints accompanying lyric booklets using fonts he's created in Fontographer. The result is a very attractive presentation that looks accomplished and artistically compelling, but is far from slick. Anteroinen sends his tapes out to friends and people he meets who he thinks might like to hear his wildly creative and eccentric compositions. He's recently started selling his tapes as well.

If you send your sounds out to be duplicated in quantity at a big manufacturer, many of these companies offer in-house graphic arts services, everything from design to color printing. If you want something quick and dirty, you may choose to go this route. And while you might be turned off at the idea of having some assembly-line graphic artist cranking out your designs in between Hank Millstones's Country Cavalcade of Stars and the Precious Blood Gospel Choir, the results are often not half bad. You can sketch out ideas for them and they'll send you their designs and bluelines,

Most tape/CD duplicators make test recordings available, either as part of their package price or for a small extra charge. You definitely want a test recording and you want to listen to it. As obvious as this may sound, I can't tell you how many stories I've heard about musicians who got the test tape (or CD) and never got around to listening to it, or didn't listen to all of it. Listen to it several times, get others to listen to it, and don't be afraid to complain if you don't like what you hear.

or proofs, before they go to print. Disc Makers in Philadelphia reprints hundreds of CD and cassette covers and label artwork in their catalog, giving the graphically impaired valuable design ideas. Other duplicators don't do the artwork in-house but they have a network of road-tested graphic artists that they'll put you in touch with. Of course, you can always provide the camera-ready artwork yourself. If you don't feel skilled enough in graphics, maybe a friend or acquaintance can be pressed into service. It seems like half the people I meet at parties claim to be graphic artists, so you shouldn't have trouble finding one.

Duplication)

Cassette production basically boils down to either doing the duplication yourself or sending it out to a professional duplicating house. Home duplication is only practical for very small runs (unless you buy professional duplication equipment) and in situations where audio quality is not a major concern.

Sending your master tape to a professional duplicator keeps getting easier and cheaper. A number of plants across the country cater to a growing national clientele, working through mail, phone, fax, and the Internet. These companies have arisen to meet the demand for small-run full-service audio manufacturing, from cover art and cassette and CD duplication to promotion and sales consultation. They offer all sorts of package deals to fit different budgets and artistic requirements. Unfortunately, with cheap mass production and convenience comes loss of quality and generic customer service. Many of these companies are criticized in local music communities for less-than-ideal product and not being as sensitive to the needs of local artists as they claim in their promo materials. It's really up to you and your budget whether you decide to go this mass-produced route. I've heard perfectly reasonable recordings done at mass-market houses (and several horrible ones, too). These one-stop shops are especially convenient if you don't want to bother with the art preparation and you want to get the most slick-looking product for the lowest possible price. If you want a bit higher quality and don't mind paying for it, there are smaller, more musician-oriented duplicators in many local areas. Ask other local musicians about their experiences, recommendations, and warnings.

Distribution)

Once you have your masterpiece duplicated, it's time to get it into the greedy hands of the masses. Distribution seems to be a big stumbling block for many DIY music makers. It takes a lot of time and energy to shop your stuff around. Since a lot of people end up without a distribution deal, it falls upon them to negotiate with all the local record stores and to make regular trips to each store to check on inventory. Most record stores like to deal with only a few distributors. If you can convince them to carry your tapes or CDs at all, they'll probably want to do so on a consignment basis (where they pay you only when the records sell). And then they're likely to forget about you. It'll be your responsibility to "service" each store and to collect your money. If you're lucky, you live in an area that has one or more nonchain music stores that cater to a youth market, specialty interests, and the local music scene. This type of store is much easier to work with. They might even go so far as to sponsor a record release party or help promote your record in some other fashion. Most college towns have one or more of these indie-friendly stores.

If you're a working musician with lots of gigs and a mailing list, you can sell a fair amount of copies through these channels. If you have your mailing list computerized, it's pretty easy to periodically send out postcard mailings with your upcoming dates and a reminder about available recordings. If you're a real hustler, willing to put in the time to work with local stores and your fan base, your recordings can do quite well, even without professional distribution. Several Washington, D.C., rap and go-go artists actually sold more copies of their records doing it themselves than after they got signed to a major label. They apparently knew their market and how to sell to it better than the record company.

In a number of cities across the United States, there are now companies that, for a fee, will put an ad for your music in their independent music catalog. They act as a mail-order music store, selling all local indie releases. Some of these catalogs also offer a dial-up soundbite service so that someone interested in your catalog description can hear a sample of the record. If they like it, they can order it from the catalog. The problem with these catalogs is that they cover every type of music and are sent to a general audience. Mainstream music (rock, pop, folk) probably does better under these circumstances than fringe music.

Although still in its infancy, music sales and distribution over the Internet offer exciting possibilities. Oasis CD and Cassette Duplication, a well-respected duplicator in southern Maryland, offers a deal for its CD clients that illustrates how the Net can be used to serve the indie music scene. After they've manufactured your CDs, for a small additional charge they'll set up a homepage on the Web to promote your release. Web browsers can read your press materials, view pictures and videos, and hear audio excerpts of the release. If they decide to buy your recording, they can do so thanks to a distribution deal with CDnow! (www.cdnow.com), a music store on the Internet. CDnow! usually does not deal with small independents, but because you're working through Oasis and their partner company Musicians on the Internet, you have the benefit of full distribution on the

Net. If you didn't get your CDs pressed at Oasis, you can still get a home-page and CDnow! distribution working directly through Musicians on the Internet. As Net promotion and distribution of music becomes more commonplace, many more such services will undoubtedly pop up.

One thing to keep in mind when searching for a label or distributor: Don't expect a response if you send your work to them. Even if you do get a "Thank you, it's on the A&R guy's desk," this still doesn't mean anything. Most labels are swamped with unsolicited submissions and can't possibly listen to them all. It may take an out-and-out promotional assault to get any type of honest response. Your first plan of attack should be eye-catching promo materials and packaging, and, obviously, something on your tape that's worth listening to. Next, you'll want to call back frequently to check up on your submission's progress. And regardless of what they say, don't get your hopes up (until you've inked a contract). I've heard far too many stories of bands that have been told "It's definitely a 'go'," or that even had signed contracts, and still ended up with nothing to show for it. It's a cruel and nasty business (which is why some people decide to do it entirely on their own).

Promotion and Advertising)

Along with distribution, promoting oneself is reported by many DIY music makers to be the hardest thing to do. Many self-published musicians lose steam after an initial wave of sending out promo copies. Unfortunately, that's rarely good enough to get your material heard and reviewed by the media and played on the radio. Follow-up calls and mailings are essential. As someone who writes music reviews and seems to be on every label's promo list, I am inundated with press releases, prerelease cassettes, promo

CDs, and swag (stickers, key chains, T-shirts, etc.). Even though most of what I get is within music categories I'm interested in, I can't keep up, and things often get lost in the shuffle. Those individuals or labels who call and bug me or who woo me with super-cool packaging and promo items end up getting my attention sooner.

For the noncommercial end of the spectrum, a promo budget will no likely be available. That's OK, since most of the zines and radio shows you'll send your work to will not be looking for a slick commercial presentation. In the world of cassette culture and fringe music, creativity and honest work are far more valuable currencies. Make sure that you put time and energy into well-written promo materials that actually say something interesting about your work. It's amazing how many brain-dead super-hyped press releases I get that sound like they were written by an intern at a heavy metal magazine. Even small indie labels that should know better fall into this trap. Immediately setting off a reviewer's Bullshit Detector is not a good way to get his or her attention.

What you send to a reviewer or radio DJ can vary greatly depending on what type of music or audio art you make and what sort of impact you're trying to make. Just sending a tape or CD with a press release or cover letter is enough in some cases. If you're sending out music with any desire for widespread airplay and reviews in mainstream publications, you'll probably want to put together a more traditional press kit. This usually consists of a presentation folder, a bio, press clippings, a schedule of upcoming appearances, a photo, and a copy of your tape or CD (preferably CD). Even this full-blown kit doesn't need to be expensive. You can get the folders at a stationery store, along with specialty papers for the printed materials. Mail-order laser paper suppliers carry all sorts of stationery and presentation materials in small quantities. One nifty trick is to make color labels to go on the front of your presentation folders. You can have your designs color copied onto pressure-sensitive (sticky-back) paper and then cut and applied to the folders. You can also cut out extra copies to make stickers to enclose in all your mailings. You'd be surprised how much even grown-ups like stickers. For a computer program I was involved in, we printed up stickers to use for promo and to sell. We sold tons of them, shaking our heads the whole time, wondering what people were doing with them. Making your own little zine or mini-comic to go with your recording can be fun, too. Just keep in mind when putting together your materials that you are competing with thousands of others. What you have going in your favor is that most people follow the same tired formula.

Words of Wisdom)

Ron Anteroinen (Cowbrain and Saw):

: It's ok to start out small, using only the technology that you have on hand. Some of my favorite recording was done using an old Farfisa organ and some boxes, cans, pots and pans for percussion. I only had a boom box and an ancient stereo to flip-flop tapes between. Working that way, I came up with a more personal and disciplined approach to writing and recording than I might have otherwise.

: Don't make music that can be reduced to formulas ("It sounds a lot like 'so and so' with a bit of 'this and that' thrown in"). Although it's music to the ears of record execs, every time I hear music described this way I cough up a dark substance. Try to do something that's truly your own, market it like a maniac, and see what happens.

Gareth Branwyn:

: When buying audio equipment, first read about the type of gear you're interested in and talk it up with others who are knowledgeable. Never go into a store without a purchasing plan in mind (a list of the systems you know are good). Sales droids can smell your ignorance from the parking lot and will take advantage of it. Once you know exactly what system to get, you can look through the local papers and national mail-order catalogs for the best deals.

: In audio stores, you often pay up to 20 percent more for dealer assistance. By knowing what you want and ordering it from a big supplier that doesn't offer assistance, you can save some bucks.

: I've become completely reliant on the advice of the experts I find online. I now find the appropriate online forum and ask my questions before I buy any gear or attempt anything I'm not sure of. The wealth of talent and experience—and the ability to get direct answers to your questions—is staggering. When in doubt, fire up the modem!

Chase (Re-Constriction Records):

: "A parasite never kills its host." (i.e., Don't be too much of a pest when approaching people in the media, at record labels and distributors, and don't burn bridges behind you. Make good use of all your contacts and network connections.)

Ram Samudrala (Twisted Helices):

: If you're setting up a Web site for your band, and your band is fairly obscure or only locally known, you should provide other content on the site that will attract a lot of visitors to the site, and then you can channel them to your band page.

: Freely distributed music is good marketing. You should *encourage* noncommercial use and distribution of your music by other parties; encourage people to copy your music and give to friends, and encourage people to tape your live shows and spread the copies around. This word-of-mouth publicity and the distributive power it brings is extremely beneficial and simply cannot be purchased.

: Appearances are important: Choose packaging and design that will catch the attention of people who are exposed to your music, whether they be reviewers, radio station music directors, or customers wandering around a record store. At the same time, be sure it's practical and won't prevent it from being displayed in the record bins and shelves.

: Take advantage of every advertising opportunity available to you, especially the free ones, even if it is in a small zine distributed to only a dozen people or a link exchange with an obscure Web page.

Micah Solomon (Oasis CD & Cassette Duplication):

: Make sure your duplicator is speaking the same language as you.

: Make sure they can help you with promotion and distribution, as well as the simple duplication of your CDs and cassettes.

: Make sure they have quality-control standards that are at least as good as *Redbook* standards—there is nothing worse than having to recall all of your new CDs because of an intermittent problem.

: And hitch your wagon to a star—any star you can find. If a duplicator can get you on the radio via a sampler CD, make use of the opportunity, then follow up like a madman (or madwoman) to make sure the radio stations pay special attention to *your* cut. (Send follow-up postage-paid reply postcards; do anything (legal) to get the stations' attention.)

: The world is wide open to independent musicians—just keep hammering down the doors (with the help of a few well-connected friends, if possible) and you'll succeed.

Never
[C H A P T E R   T W O]
Mind the
MUSIC BIZ!

Kristin Thomson (Simple Machines):

: Don't master your record where you get it pressed. It's best to go to a mastering house where they specialize in this process.

: Be patience and persistent.

: Have realistic expectations.

: Keep on top of your dealings with distributors, get your records out, and get the money back.

: A good press run of records for a beginner is 500 copies.

Greg Werckman (Alternative Tentacles Records):

: You don't have to start your own label just because you can't get interest from major labels. The Dead Kennedys had interest from several labels but they couldn't offer the band the artistic freedom they were looking for. It's cheaper now to put out your own record than ever. The drive to start Alternative Tentacles was because the big labels insist on seeing music as a business, not as art.

: Don't go into music because you want to be successful. Don't have any delusions of fame. Do it because you love it.

: Use all the resources that are out there, including talking to other indie record companies. Call a good record company like Alternative Tentacles (415-282-9782) and ask them for some advice.

Resources)

GUIDES AND DIRECTORIES

An Introductory Mechanics Guide to Putting Out Records, Cassettes, and CDs*
KRISTIN THOMSON AND JENNY TOOMEY
SIMPLE MACHINES
P.O. BOX 10290, ARLINGTON, VA 22210-1290
EMAIL: simplemach@aol.com
WEB: www.csd.net/~musi/ic/guide/guide4.html
FIFTH EDITION, 24 PAGES, $4

> A nifty little booklet that picks up where this Starter Kit leaves off. It covers all the basics on how to get your vinyl, tapes, and CDs mastered, duplicated, packaged, and distributed. It also covers copyright and publishing issues. An address book in the back lists mastering houses, label printers, pressing plants and duplicators, distributors, and mail-order sources.

Book Your Own Fuckin' Life!

A DO-IT-YOURSELF RESOURCE GUIDE
MAXIMUMROCKNROLL AND THE BLEEDING HEART COLLECTIVE
4728 SPRUCE STREET, BOX 354, PHILADELPHIA, PA 19139
1996 EDITION, 145 PAGES, $2

> A fat directory listing resources related to regional punk scenes. It covers bands, distributors, labels, radio stations, record/book stores, promoters, venues, and zines. Listed by U.S. states, Canadian provinces, and foreign countries.

BOOKS

Cassette Mythos

ROBIN JAMES, EDITOR
AUTONOMEDIA
AVAILABLE FROM:
NONSEQUITUR, INC.
P.O. BOX 344, ALBUQUERQUE, NM 87102-0344
505-224-9483
EMAIL: robinja@halcyon.com
WEB: www.halcyon.com/robinja/mythos/aaaa.html
1990, 206 PAGES, $14

> An anthology devoted to the development of the "international cassette network home-taper underground." *Cassette Mythos* includes essays, reports, comics, documentation, manifestos, and a taste of cassette-packaging art. Many of the essays from the book are available on the Web site. There's also a cassette available called *Audio Alchemy*, which offers a nice window onto the cassette network scene of the late '80s.

Fair Use: The Story of the Letter U and the Numeral 2

NEGATIVLAND
NEGATIVMAILORDERLAND
1920 MONUMENT BLVD. MF-1, CONCORD, CA 94520
WEB: www.negativland.com
1995, 240 PAGES PLUS CD, $20

> In 1991, Negativland's infamous U2 single was sued out of existence for trademark and copyright infringement for poking fun at the Irish mega-group's anthem "I Still Haven't Found What I'm Looking For." In 1992, Negativland's magazine-plus-CD *The Letter U and the Numeral 2* was sued out of existence by the band's former record label for trying to tell the story of the first lawsuit. In 1995 Negativland released a brand new 270-page book with CD to tell the story of both lawsuits and the fight for the right to make new art out of corporately "owned" culture.

How To Make & Sell Your Own Recording*:
A Guide for the Nineties

DIANE SWARD RAPAPORT
1992, 240 PAGES, $29.95
(AVAILABLE THROUGH MIX BOOKSHELF, SEE BELOW)

A revised edition of the classic guide to DIY recording. When my wife and I decided to go into self-publishing, this was the book everyone said we should get. This latest version not only updates the old material but also adds sections related to digital music technology.

(MAGA)ZINES

Gajoob*

BRYAN BAKER
P.O. BOX 3201, SALT LAKE CITY, UT 84110
WEB: www.utw.com/~gajoob/
EMAIL: gajoob@utw.com

Sadly, *Gajoob* is one of the few remaining (and longest running) zines devoted to "cassette culture." Baker also maintains *Gajoob's DiY Report*, an Internet-based e-zine and the DiY list archive (at the URL above). *Gajoob* will soon begin putting out compilation CDs and tapes of "outstanding DIY recording artists." Write or email Bryan for submission guidelines and more details.

Improvijazzation Nation

DICK METCALF
5308 65TH AVENUE S.E., LACEY, WA 98513
WEB: www.ccnet.com/~dmic27/improv.html
EMAIL: zzajdr@mashell.com
$2.25/ISSUE, $8/4 ISSUES

I.N. has been one of the most consistent zines covering DIY music. A useful resource for anyone interested in home-brewed music and recording. If you have Web access, check out their new homepage.

MAXIMUMROCKNROLL

P.O. BOX 460760, SAN FRANCISCO, CA 94146-0760
MONTHLY, 176 PAGES, $3/ISSUE

MRR is the grandparent of punk zines at this point, celebrating its fifteenth year of monthly issues. Although it covers hard-core punk exclusively, it's also an amazing example of a zine that's hung in there for the long haul while remaining true to its roots. Every zine should be so lucky.

ND

P.O. BOX 4144, AUSTIN, TX 78765
FAX: 512-416-8007
EMAIL: mag@nd.org
WEB: nd.org
$4/ISSUE, $7/2-ISSUE SUBSCRIPTION

Daniel Plunkett's *ND* has been around since 1982. In that time, it has consistently delivered the goods on all aspects of experimental music and art. The zine is mainly composed of interviews with experimental musicians and performance artists, tape and zine reviews, and announcements of audio and mail art projects. *ND* is a major network node for the experimental audio community. *ND*'s Web site is a beauty, a perfect example of a noncommercial site that can rival the design and content of a commercial one.

Taper's Quarterly

P.O. BOX 641191, SAN FRANCISCO, CA 94164-1191
EMAIL: lava@well.com
WEB: www.well.com/user/lava
$3/ISSUE, $10/YEAR

A zine produced by LAVA, the Live Audio Video Association, "an international coalition of live music fans, concert tapers and collectors who exchange unauthorized live recordings tape-for-tape." Articles include everything from concert reports to interviews with bands to how-to instructions on live taping.

CATALOGS

Dick Blick

P.O. BOX 1267, GALESBURG, IL 61402
800-447-8192
EMAIL: info@artmaterials.com
(free catalog)

A massive catalog of art tools, supplies, and materials. They sell all sorts of materials that can be creatively fashioned into CD/tape packaging or used in countless other ways.

Flax

P.O. BOX 7216, SAN FRANCISCO, CA 94120-7216
800-343-3529
(free catalog)

While this yuppie art "lifestyle" catalog is mainly filled with overpriced beads and baubles, there are also some gems for CD/tape packaging. A $20 roll of handmade paper may be outrageously expensive for wrapping gifts, but cut into small pieces, it can make hundreds of gorgeous tape covers.

J&R Music World

59–50 QUEENS-MIDTOWN EXPRESSWAY, MASPETH, NY 11378-9896
800-221-8180

This New York mega-store has everything related to audio, from consumer-grade systems and components to low-end studio gear. They carry a nice selection of DJ and light-show equipment, too. I've bought boom boxes, mikes, a cheap 4-channel mixer, and two Pro Walkmans·from J&R. I've also bought lots of computer equipment from their sister company, J&R Computer World.

The Local Music Store Mail Order Catalog

THE LOCAL MUSIC STORE DISTRIBUTION NETWORK
2800 JUNIPER STREET, SUITE 1, FAIRFAX, VA 22031
703-641-8995
WEB: www.localmusicstore.com/
(free catalog)

A catalog offering local, independent music from several East Coast cities (mainly the Baltimore/D.C. area). Write for more information about how to get listed.

Mix Bookshelf*

6400 HOLLIS STREET, SUITE 10, EMERYVILLE, CA 94608
800-233-9604
WEB: www.mixbookshelf.com/

A great source of how-to books on the making, recording, manufacturing, and marketing of your sounds. I don't think I've ever talked to an audio hacker who didn't highly recommend this catalog. From the publishers of *Mix* and *Electronic Musician* magazines.

Sweetwater Sound

5335 BASS RD., FORT WAYNE, IN 56808
219-432-8176
WEB: www.sweetwater.com

Sweetwater Sound is a music software and hardware developer and retailer specializing in MIDI technology and recording equipment. Their free newsletter, *Sweet Notes*, provides good background information on the gizmos they sell. Back issues of it are available on their Web site.

PRESSING PLANTS

There are lots of pressing plants nationwide that offer small runs on vinyl, tapes, and CDs. Check local music publications and your phone directory to find plants in your area. Here's a tip: You can often find out who pressed the CDs in your collection by looking at the inside band of the actual disc. The company name is often stamped there. If you know of an indie label that puts out stuff that you like, try to track down their duplicator. You can always just call and ask them. Here are a few plants that I've had personal experience with:

A+R Record & Tape Manufacturing

902 N. INDUSTRIAL BLVD., DALLAS, TX 75207
800-527-DISC
(free sales information)

A good source for cheap vinyl, tape and CD pressing—no frills, fair quality. Especially good for vanity recordings, spoken art, quick-and-dirty recordings to shop to labels or to get airplay. One great thing about A+R is that they'll duplicate as few as 100 cassettes.

Disc Makers

1328 NORTH FOURTH ST., PHILADELPHIA, PA 19122
800-468-9353
EMAIL: discman@discmakers.com
WEB: www2.discmakers.com/discmakers/
(free catalog and booklets)

These folks are sort of the fast-food outlet of independent music manufacturers. A one-stop shop, offering (in addition to recordings) everything from in-house album art to promotional materials and music company logos. Disc Makers also offers some great resources for anyone doing an independent release. Their free 70-page catalog has lots of useful information on the duplicating process in general and how you can get the biggest bang for your buck. Hundreds of CD covers and CD labels are shown throughout the book to give you design ideas. They also have a number of free booklets available including: "Guide to Master Tape Preparation," "Guide to Independent Music Publicity," and the "Directory of Independent Music Distributors."

Nimbus Manufacturing

SR GUILDFORD FARM, RUCKERSVILLE, VA 22968
800-782-0778
(free CD-Audio and CD-ROM catalogs)

Nimbus is known for its quality and long standing in the industry. Their prices are higher than either A+R or Disc Makers and they charge separately for graphic services. If you want top-quality production though, and you're willing to pay for it, Nimbus is worth a look.

Oasis CD & Cassette Duplication

BOX 7256, SILVER SPRING, MD 20907-7256
301-345-6188, 800-697-5734
EMAIL: info@oasiscd.com
WEB: www.oasiscd.com

> A D.C.–area CD and tape duplicator that's well respected by the local (and national) music community. They're known for their attention to detail and the high quality of their tape production. They also offer various promotional services for their artists. Check out their "Musician's Guide to CD and Cassette Duplication," available on their Web site.

NET SITES

Audio for the Masses

WEB: www.webmonkey.com/geektalk/96/42/index3a.html

> This little primer by Adam Powell on HotWired's WebMonkey site has all the basics you'll need to know to get started in digitizing audio files for your Web pages and distribution over the Internet. Covers software, hardware, editing tips, and audio formats.

The Deterrent Tour Manual

WEB: www.islandnet.com/~moron/deterrent/tourmail.html

> This online directory provides names of and information on promoters and venues so that bands can book their own tours. A form allows you to add your own contacts and good/bad tour experiences. Covers punk, metal, industrial, rap, acoustic, and other types of music.

DiY Guide—A Guide for Songwriters/Musicians

WEB: www.ram.org/music/making/tips/DiY.html

> The DiY Guide includes sections on building a studio, recording tips, duplication and distribution, copyright and trademark issues, and marketing and promotion.

EST Magazine

WEB: hyperreal.com/zines/est/intro.html

> The Web site for the experimental/underground music zine EST. The site contains an excellent links page covering articles, reviews, radio shows, labels, zines, organizations, and Web sites related to fringe music.

The Harmony Music List

WEB: orpheus.ucsd.edu/harmony/

An excellent online music network node maintained by the U.C. San Diego Music Library. Covers artists, instruments, equipment, events, labels, music stores, magazines, radio stations—you name it, they have it.

The Hollow Ear

WEB: www.hear.com/hollow/index.html

The Hollow Ear is a gorgeous Web zine dedicated to "The gap between the aural cavities, to music and art that defies easy categorizations or quick quips . . . a sideways glance at commercial culture." They have interviews with avant-garde artists and musicians, fiction, poetry, reviews, and links to homepages maintained by artists and musicians associated with *Hollow Ear*.

Independant Artists' Services

WEB: www.idiom.com/~upend/ias/

Billed as "yet another DIY site for independent musicians," IAS provides band and club databases, a bulletin board, indie music news, and an international area. Includes audio clips of bands.

IndieCenter*

WEB: www.csd.net/~muji/indiecentre.html

An amazing resource for independent musicians and teeny labels. It contains articles; the entire text of *An Introductory Mechanics Guide to Putting Out Records, Cassettes, and CDs* (see Guides and Directories above); how-to sections on home recording, mastering, manufacturing, printing, promotion, and booking; and words of wisdom from fellow audio artists.

The Indie Label List

WEB: www.cs.ucl.ac.uk/external/twicks/ill

A listing of some 600 independent music labels. New additions to the list can be entered online.

Indie Music Resources*

WEB: kathoderay.org/music/

This site has tons of links to labels, music zines, bands, radio stations (including pirates!), regional music scenes, mailing lists, and more.

The Internet Underground Music Archive

W E B : www.iuma.com

> The grandpappy of Internet music sites. They have over 800 indie artists on their site, organized by music category. You can scan the archives, read bios, look at promo pictures, and download audio samples. A chat feature lets you leave your feedback. Getting your band page on the archive used to be free. Currently, they charge $240 per year.

MACOS

M U S I C I A N S A G A I N S T C O P Y R I G H T I N G O F S A M P L E S
E M A I L : macos@io.org
W E B : www.io.org/~macos/

> MACOS is a nonprofit organization and international network of musicians who oppose the copyrighting of samples. Participating musicians allow the general public to sample from their material freely without incurring any legal ramifications.

The Mixmasters' List

> Mixmasters is a worldwide group of people who exchange audiotapes and advice. For more information on the list, send the command "info" in the body of an email message (not in the subject line) to: *mixmasters-request@infopro.com*. To join the list, send the command "subscribe" in the body of an email message to the same address above.

The Monster MIDI Links Page*

W E B : www.albany.net/~xygxag/MIDI/Monster_MIDI.html

> Just like the name implies, this site links you up to everything MIDI: equipment manufacturers, MIDI files online, MIDI-related Web sites, MIDI tips, etc.

Musicians on the Internet (MOI)

3 7 8 3 2 0 T H S T R E E T # 1 9 , S A N F R A N C I S C O , C A 9 4 1 1 0
4 1 5 - 2 8 2 - 7 4 2 0
E M A I L : rpisen@escape.com
W E B : oasiscd.com/www/MOIhome.html

> For a modest fee, MOI will build a homepage for your CD music project, complete with text, images, video, and sounds. They will also set up a link to CDnow! so that you can sell your CDs over the Net.

Online Music Stores

WEB: rsrecords.com/jump/mu_store.htm

A link page of over forty online music stores.

SonicNet

WEB: www.sonicnet.com

A New York-based computer network dedicated to alternative music, independent labels, and building closer musician-fan relations. SonicNet has chat areas, netcasts of concerts, reviews, interviews, and show schedules.

Sound Management Music

BBS: 847-949-6434

An important networking node for those involved in electronic music, synths, and MIDI. It has an archive with information and sound files, including a nationwide listing of MIDI BBSes.

Sound Wire

WEB: soundwire.com
EMAIL: info@soundwire.com

Sound Wire is a Net-based record store specializing in indie/underground music and hard-to-find titles. It has audio clips and videos available. It also sells zines and videos.

World Wide Internet Music Resources*

WEB: www.music.indiana.edu/music_resources/

A site maintained by the music library at Indiana University. It has tons of links to musician's Web sites, sites devoted to specific genres, music history and research, composers and compositions, journals, and magazines.

Music-related Usenet newsgroups:

alt.music.4-track
alt.music.independent*
alt.music.tape-culture
rec.audio.pro

Multimedia
for
the MASSES

Computers in
THE FUTURE may
weigh no more
than **1.5 TONS**.

—*Popular Mechanics,* **1949**

What is **THE USE**
of a book, thought Alice,
without **PICTURES** or
CONVERSATION.

—Lewis Carroll,
Alice's Adventures in
Wonderland

When Apple Computer released its HyperCard program in 1987, the computer world scratched its pointy little head, not quite sure what to make of it. The computer press struggled to explain it ("It's a graphical database system," "It's an alternative to the Macintosh desktop," "It's a software construction kit"). Consumers were intrigued but largely clueless as to how to use it. We heard it was easy to use, even easy to program, and that it could magically link together text, images, and sounds into something called "hypermedia." In today's world of multimedia CD-ROMs and the World Wide Web, what HyperCard heralded seems obvious, but at the time it just didn't click. Like a lot of the technology that Apple has given us, it was ahead of its time.

CLICK!) I got my first inkling of what hypermedia was all about when a floppy disk from a friend, Peter Sugarman, arrived in the mail one day in January 1989. It had a coarse, digitized picture of Peter, in a particularly pensive pose, on the label. At the time, even a dig-itized photo on a disk label was extravagant. Booting up the HyperCard document (called a "stack"), I discovered more pictures of Peter, some of his family, and a map of Virginia that made goofy sounds and had a little animated guy skulking about. I found myself peering at some weird hybrid media, a cross between an interactive letter, a family album, and a whimsical stroll through someone's mind. While it was obvious that Peter was basically doodling, testing out the capabilities of the new medium, I was instantly struck by its potential.

Around this same time, I was running a monthly salon (or was it a saloon?), called Cafe Gaga, in Washington, D.C. The purpose of these gatherings was to send a group of people from different professions and viewpoints on a journey deep into a specific idea. Some events were experiential, others cere-bral. The credo of the group was "art, information, noise." Each event was supposed to have some component of art and information exchange, and, of course, everything produces noise. When I saw Peter's HyperCard stack, I immediately thought of how this technology could be used to create little "salons" on floppy disks. After several weeks of blathering to others about this idea, someone sent me a stack called *Passing Notes*. It was exactly what I was talking about, a broadly cast conversation threading its way through art, science, religion, and philosophy, all grappling with a single idea (in this case, the question "Are we more than the science that explains us?"). The stack even had a link to a BBS so that you could add to the conversation and see how others responded to the stack. Again, this all sounds like ancient history when counted in computer years (where a year equals a life-time), but back in 1989, this was pretty profound stuff.

Peter and I began having regular phone conversations about hypermedia and how it might change the nature of storytelling, media delivery, and

information organization. I'd always been struck by cyberneticist Gregory
Bateson's idea of always balancing "rigor and imagination" in one's pursuit of knowledge. It seemed to Peter and I that hypermedia provided a perfect environment to pursue ideas deeply, while building in fun, whimsy,
and a sense of the unexpected—a kind of orchestrated chaos. We began
kicking around various ideas for a collaborative HyperCard project.

THE *BEYOND CYBERPUNK*

^
comic BEYOND CYBERPUNK, by G. Branwyn and
Mark Frauenfelder

STORY) *Beyond Cyberpunk (BCP)* had very casual origins. Peter and
I wanted to get our hands dirty with hypermedia and were looking for
a suitable subject. I had discovered a rather exhaustive list of cyberpunk
sci-fi novels on the Well BBS and thought about using that as the backbone
for a stack. The idea was simply to create a "data bucket" into which we
could toss all of the information on cyberpunk that we found while surfing
the Net. But, like a lot of hypermedia projects, once we started building
our little pocket universe—filled with a teeming brew of multimedia life—
Beyond Cyberpunk quickly took on a life of its own. We decided to go all
out, to make it as exhaustive as possible, and to release it for sale. At the
time (1990), the Internet was not yet in the media spotlight and so-called
cyberculture was in its heyday. We could sense that all things "cyber" were
about to pop into the mainstream and we wanted to chart the course cyberculture had taken, from its sci-fi and early hacker origins through the
Internet and into everyday life.

The project quickly mushroomed. We sweet-talked Mark Frauenfelder of
bOING bOING and a brilliant Silicon Valley designer named Jim Leftwich
into signing on and their involvement kicked us into high gear.

As we talked about our plans on-line, we attracted more contributors. One of the things that surprised us most was the caliber of people we were able to get on board. Somehow, approaching a well-known writer seemed much easier on the long end of an email message. We sent mail to many of the founders of the cyberpunk sci-fi genre and were shocked to get encouragement and contributions from Bruce Sterling, Rudy Rucker, Richard Kadrey, Robert Anton Wilson, Joan Gordon, Mark Laidlaw, Paul DiFillipo, and many others.

Flash-forward: The second annual CyberArts Festival in Pasadena, California, November 1991. Peter, Mark, myself, and several other contributors meet and shake hands *literally* in front of the program as it merrily chugs and gurgles its cyber-industrial soundtrack. Some of us are meeting for the first time. We've spent hundreds of hours working together in a virtual computer lab, and now we're here to press the flesh and look at the fruits of our labors. *Beyond Cyberpunk* has been chosen as a featured exhibit in the CyberArts Gallery. We're munching cheese and sipping wine while proudly showing off our digital baby to the world. We're immediately struck by the sight of our low-budget, indie project running alongside expensively produced commercial programs. *BCP* looks humble and unassuming on its little black-and-white Mac SE, but as soon as people start playing with it, they're drawn to its dense content and periodic "chaos events."

In the months that followed, the critical acclaim for *Beyond Cyberpunk* was overwhelming. It received positive reviews in *MacWeek, MacWorld, TidBITS, Mondo 2000*, even the *New York Times* and *Newsweek*. *MacWeek* claimed that *BCP* "put the Mac back on its revolutionary track." University of Iowa professor and sci-fi scholar Brooks Landon published a lengthy essay on *Beyond Cyberpunk* in *Science-Fiction Studies* (Vol. 20, No. 3, Nov. 93), arguing that *Beyond Cyberpunk* was one of the more important documents "in the first generation of canonical hypertexts."

I'm not telling you this story to brag about my multimedia accomplishments
(well, ok . . . maybe a little). The point is that, despite all of the positive press
and the wild enthusiasm of early purchasers, *BCP* never went anywhere.
Ultimately, we poured into it thousands of hours of work and thousands of
our own dollars. The critics loved it, but *BCP* bombed at the box office. *BCP*
itself probably wasn't the problem . . . it was the ugly specter of distribution that plagues many DIY projects. We can only imagine how things
would have been different if we'd hooked up with a software company, or
even a small aggressive distributor. But, as with many of these projects, the
real riches gained are not measured in dollars or units sold. We made
tremendous connections and friendships that continue today. It was one of
the happiest times of my life. We enjoyed valuable exposure of our ideas in
major media venues and got work opportunities out of it. If we had it to do
all over again . . . well . . . we'd probably do it all over again.

THE STUNTED GROWTH *of* DESKTOP MULTIMEDIA)

HyperCard heralded the
beginning of the digital media onslaught. The next big development was CD-
ROM. It took about four years of the computer industry declaring "This is the
year that CD-ROM will break" before it finally did, in 1994. But even with all
the fanfare and thousands of titles flooding the market, CD-ROM didn't deliver
on much of its promise. Even today, many CD-ROMs are plagued by poor performance, excessive "bells and whistles," and kitchen sink content (called
"shovelware"), preexisting, weak material put onto disc with little regard
for its relevance. The average price of CD-ROM is also way too high, given
the quality of the content and the fact that you can now get lots of similar
content on the Web.

Just as CD-ROM and "multimedia computing" was being accepted by consumers, the World Wide Web was growing like a bread mold over the Internet. With a growth rate that was downright scary, the Web went from relative obscurity (outside of geek circles) to a mainstream phenomenon inside of a year. The World Wide Web, with its ability to deliver multimedia content globally and to change that content constantly, has given the CD-ROM market an identity crisis. Who needs a movie database on CD-ROM (which will quickly become outdated), when you can access several of them, updated frequently, on the Web?

Of course, modem speed is still a big limiting factor in Web-based multimedia. In an effort to stay alive, the CD-ROM industry is moving into "hybrid multimedia." With hybrid, multimedia online is combined with disc-based media. Using such a scheme, a complex interactive virtual world can be created. The rendered environments can be stored on the disc while the characters and real-time events are delivered and integrated via the Net. Or all the memory-intensive graphics, animatimations, typefaces, and other fixed components of an online magazine or Web site can be stored on disc. The Web browser on the user's computer composes the final hypermedia documents by fetching elements from the disc and the Web server as needed.

Until connection speeds become supersonic, hybrid multimedia solutions make a lot of sense. At the moment, hybrid technology is new and not readily available for small-scale multimedia authors, but this is changing as I type these words. The proliferation of CD-ROM service bureaus, inexpensive disc duplication, and dramatic price reductions for CD-recordable drives have made CD-ROMs a reasonable option for low-budget amateur publishers.

BAR-MIN-SKI:
CONSUMER PRODUCT) If you're interested in art—

enough to want to experience it firsthand—you usually go to a show, a museum, or a performance space or see it in books, magazines, and documentaries. There's plenty of art-related media out there, but it's limited to a small universe of artists who've reached a certain level of success and can afford to distribute their work. For all the other struggling artists looking to reach a wider audience, CD-ROM is a useful medium. With its ability to interweave text, video, sounds, animations, and images, CD-ROM also offers a new way of exploring not only the art but the process and the ideas behind it. It's like touring an art gallery, going to a lecture by the artist, listening in on art critics droning on about the work, and snooping around the artist's studio . . . all from your desktop.

> BAR-MIN-SKI CD-PACKAGE >

Avant pop artist Bill Barminski shows off his multifaceted talents in *BAR-MIN-SKI: Consumer Product*. The disc not only serves as a catalog of Barminski's enamel on canvas paintings and his controversial underground comics, but it's also a documentary about Barminski himself. There's even a wacky role-playing game about life in an ad agency.

In Barminski's dark and twisted world, everything is a Madison Avenue ad slogan; people literally talk out of two mouths at once. His work exists in an alternate universe where the history of American consumerism comingles and tempts us with a mutant blend of nonsensical products (Utopia Tires, Atomic Sky Detergent, Cathode Ray Spray). On the CD-ROM, clicking on a box of detergent or a bottle of squeezable margarine will only take you deeper into Barminski's maze of insane consumer culture and mix-and-match ad slogans.

BAR-MIN-SKI: Consumer Product includes a game called SubVert in which you play a hapless Dilbertesque ad designer who's bullied into creating two instant ad campaigns by a mutated boss-monster named Mr. Saki. If you make the right (totally foolish) choices in assembling your ad campaign, you're rewarded with seeing your ads on buses, the sides of buildings, etc. If you screw up by choosing the wrong (equally foolish) elements for your campaign, you'll see your ads on discarded shopping carts and on the walls of condemned buildings. And whatever you do, don't let Mr. Saki catch you watching the boob tube in the employee lounge, or your ass is fired!

Besides *BAR-MIN-SKI: Consumer Product* being a perfect example of CD-ROM as a new medium for art distribution, it's also a great example of street-tech multimedia. Barminski created the program with filmmaker Webster Lewin and programmer Jerry Hesketh. They worked after hours, on weekends, and even while they were at work. It was made on a shoe-string budget, with Barminski and Lewin trading artwork and favors, and often using hijacked equipment. The result looks and feels like a zine but is polished enough that it can rival some of the big-budget multimedia titles out there.

DIGITAL STORYTELLERS)

WE MAKE MEMORIES, A
by Abbe Don

San Francisco artist and multimedia author Abbe Don is first and foremost a storyteller. Her installations have included *We Make Memories*, a videodisc project (made with the Director authoring program) that contained a timeline of sixty-five family photographs as well as forty-five oral history video clips of her great-grandmother, grandmother, mother, and Abbe herself. The project

Check the Jamming the Media Web site at home.earthlink.net/~garethb2/jamming/ for late-breaking news and updates on the technologies and resources mentioned in this book.

examined how a family history is constructed and how different generations express themselves. The experience of *We Make Memories* inspired in others a desire to share their own life stories. This prompted Abbe to create *Share with Me a Story*, which allowed users to scan in their own photographs and tell their own stories, creating an evolving community album. Users could also access the stories of the other contributors.

Abbe's personal art work continues to develop in two directions. With pieces such as *We Make Memories*, and her live solo performances, she is first and foremost the "author." In other pieces like *Share with Me a Story*, she acts more as a catalyst, creating a framework to spur other people's creativity and storytelling impulses. Works such as TPTV—a video response system about environmental issues—have been installed in public settings such as nightclubs and professional conferences where users can wander by, view the animations, the responses from other viewers, or add their own comments. For more information about these and other projects, check out www.abbedon.com. Her latest interactive storytelling project, a spin-off of *Share with Me a Story*, is called *Bubbe's Back Porch*. It can be reached via the Web at www.bubbe.com.

WE MAKE MEMORIES, ∧
by Abbe Don

Is it disk or disc? For this book, disc is used to refer to CD-ROMs and videodiscs. disk refers to floppy diskettes. When the two types are considered together, I've used disk. Don't blame me for the confusion, it's the CD-ROM and videodisc industry that insists on disc.

IT'S THE CONTENT, STUPID!)

When people think about, and begin to develop, CD-ROM multimedia, they tend to get all worked up over the media that are available: text, graphics, movies, sounds, and animations. They make the big mistake of letting the media dictate the content. When I was asked several years ago to contribute to a book on multimedia, and to choose the best titles on the market, my choices ended up almost entirely on the low end of the development spectrum. Topping my list was Pedro Meyer's *I Photograph to Remember* (Voyager Company). This disc contains only black-and-white photos and an audio narrative by Meyer (with accompanying piano music).

I Photograph is an intensely moving portrait of Meyer's parents in the last year of their lives. It is an attempt by Meyer to come to grips with his parents' death through pictures and audio journals. It certainly would have been easy for him to add QuickTime movies of his parents, interviews with them and other family members, a follow-along transcription of the text, biographies, and "back stories" about his parents, and other extras common to disk-based multimedia. But he had the wisdom to realize that the power of his images and the emotional impact of his spoken words were more than enough.

Morton Shubotnick, author of the CD performance piece *All My Hummingbirds Have Alibis*, coined the term *chamber art* to describe the "intimate one-on-one relationship that an artist can have with a consumer of computer-based art." Pedro Meyer's portrait of his dying parents is a powerful example of chamber art and the unique abilities of computer-based multimedia. If you were watching *I Photograph* on television, with a group of people, or thumbing through a coffee-table book, the experience would be entirely different. In the solitary confines of your computer, listening to Meyer's words on headphones, you're free to experience your true emotions.

I Photograph to Remember is a reminder that, given potent content, your production can have a powerful impact on the reader/viewer regardless of how skimpy your budget. Meyer obviously had a decent budget and the support of Voyager behind him, but even if *I Photograph* had been done on a shoestring, the impact would have been similar.

IS DIY DISK-BASED MULTIMEDIA DEAD?)

> TAPE-BEATLES SINGLE: "Grave Implications"

The sad truth is that disk-based multimedia has all but capsized in the wake of the Internet. It's easier to learn Web publishing than "authoring programs" such as Director, HyperCard, and SuperCard, and there are hardly any distribution hassles over the Net. Some multimedia zinesters, like Ted Kusio, editor of the e-zine *Monkey Spew,* keep the faith by offering both Net- and disk-based versions of their publications:

"I still try and keep all my multimedia projects at about 1.4 megabytes so they can fit onto a floppy disk. Although I have a Web site, I feel that the Web is kind of limiting since it's still slow and mainly text and graphics. "

The Internet is also only a means of distribution to those who have a connection. Estimates put the number of people with computers at 40 percent of the U.S. population and less than half of that group have modems (and an even smaller percentage are actually online). If you want to reach those who have computers but aren't yet on the Web, a disk-based zine makes sense. Certainly when we're all connected via ISDN, cable modems, or some other high-speed connectivity scheme in our future, and can gobble up Web media in almost real time, CD-ROMs will fall by the wayside. Since this isn't likely to happen in the immediate future, CD-ROM is still a viable publishing medium.

DIGITAL PIRATES)

To get some idea of how prevalent software piracy is, let's do a little impromptu research. Everyone reading this who's ever copied (stolen as far as the software industry's concerned) and used software without paying for it raise their hands. If we're all being honest, almost all of us now have our thieving mitts skyward. The majority of computer users in the United States (and it gets even worse overseas) don't think there's anything wrong with copying and distributing software for personal use. The level of interest in obeying the software copyright laws run the gamut. Some feel it's about as naughty as tearing the warning label off a pillow, others liken it to making copies of audio recordings for personal use. A common moderate position is "try before you buy," copying a program to evaluate whether it's going to be useful or not. If it turns out to be a program that might be used frequently, a legal copy is bought. This makes good sense if it's a program you'll be working with frequently, in which case you'll want the manuals and tech support.

Many of today's computer users may not be aware of the fact that in the early hacker days software was intended to be free. The idea of selling it ran counter to the "information wants to be free" ethos of hackerdom. Hardware would be bought and sold, but software would be freely distributed and built with an open architecture so that fellow users/hackers could tinker with it. What a far cry that is from today's multi-billion-per-year software industry, where paying up to several thousand dollars for a high-end program is not uncommon. It is this schizophrenic atmosphere—where information wants to be free and software companies want big profits—that we inhabit.

The development of shareware was an attempt at developing a software distribution system that takes into account the realities of how people actually use software. By paying only for those programs that you actually use (versus the ones you buy or pirate, goof around with once or twice, and then never launch again), you're saving a lot of money and you're supporting the software developers who are providing you with the tools you need. The problem with shareware is that it's left to one's personal initiative to mail in the registration fee. It's a shame more people don't pay for their shareware programs, but they don't. Enough do that it keeps the shareware community alive (barely), but not enough that mainstream software vendors see it as a viable alternative to charging what the market will bear.

Many people involved in amateur multimedia are not as uptight about having their work copied and distributed as the commercial software business. The idea of getting wide exposure through people passing one's software through the Net saves the expense and hassle of duplicating disks and mailing parcels yourself. For floppy- and CD-ROM-based projects that are too large for practical distribution over the Net, a sampler version of the program is often posted on the Net with the blessings of the creator to distribute. These samplers then contain ordering information for the full product. Those wishing their program not to be pirated, often enclose a plea ("Please, I need the money to pay my heating bill!") to help discourage many would-be pirates. Most netizens remain more sympathetic to the little guy than the software executives of the corporate world.

THE MULTIMEDIA HACKER'S STARTER KIT

Getting Started) To get started in DIY multimedia, the first thing you'll need is a computer, or in geek parlance, a box. If you want to go with cheap tech, you can get a used system either by snooping through the classifieds or by visiting a computer reseller. You don't want to venture too far back into computer history or you might end up producing multimedia that nobody can run. The current crop of RISC processor-based machines—such as the PowerMacs and Pentiums—have compatibility problems with some older programs wired with earlier CISC-era technology (e.g., Director 2.0 files will not run on a PowerMac).

An entry-level used machine could be any Mac family member running System 7 and stuffed with plenty of RAM and hard disk, or on the PC side, a color 486 with plenty of RAM and disk space. Since computer shelf-life is insanely short, you should be able to find some sort of machine no matter what kind of budget you're on. Of course, how much you spend will affect what type of multimedia you can make.

To produce full-blown multimedia with the capability to input and edit audio and video, you're going to need a sound and video card. Macs have come with sound cards built into them for years and most PCs now include them standard as well. AV Macs come with video input standard. All other Macs and PCs require a video card. Multimedia takes up a lot of storage space (especially sounds and images) and requires decent processing power (16 megs of RAM is bare bones, 32 megs is better). You need as much hard disk space as you can stand to pay for, too. A removable backup, such as the Iomega Zip drive with 100-megabyte disks, is also recommended. A scanner, which will allow you to digitize non-computer-based images, is also invaluable.

The hardware and software considerations for disk-based multimedia are similar for Web publishing and desktop video. See chapter 7 for additional information about Web publishing.

Design and Authoring)

When buying a computer, it's always a good idea to know which software programs you're going to use and base your hardware decision around that (and don't forget to figure your software costs into your budget). For disk-based multimedia, you'll need the suite of software outlined in the chart below. You should make sure—if you're buying a computer expressly to do multimedia—that you get a system that can handle all of these software types (and the specific packages you'll be using). Talk to friends or knowledgeable people online before making your final decision. Plan your purchases. Don't be sucked in by ads and sales pitches and succumb to impulse buying. You'll regret it, I can assure you, based on hard-won personal experience. Your hardware and software choices will also have some effect on the design of your multimedia creations (e.g., if you have no video input capability, you'll have to work with already-existing video clips or no video at all).

Once you have your hardware set up and have mastered the rudiments of the necessary software packages (see you in several years), it's time to plan your project. There are a number of directions in which you can go. Many people fall into the trap of thinking that they have to do multimedia because it's the hip new medium. Balderdash! Once you know what your content is, you need to ask yourself whether disk-based multimedia (as opposed to say print or Web publishing) is the best vehicle. And don't forget to think about your audience. Is this the best way to communicate with them? If it is, then you need to figure out what specific form the project should take. Some common forms are:

: **electronic book, or e-book** (mainly text, with some sound and graphics)

: **digizine** (any combo of text, images, and sounds in a magazine format)

MEDIUM	TYPICAL SOFTWARE	PLATFORM	SPECIAL HARDWARE
Text	B B Edit Lite*	Mac	None
	Microsoft Word	Mac/PC	None
	SuperPad*	PC	None
	MacWrite Pro	Mac	None
Graphics	Graphics Converter*	Mac	None
	PaintShop Pro	Mac	None
	Photoshop	Mac/PC	None
Sound	SoundEdit 16	Mac	Sound card**
	Sound Effects*	Mac	Sound card**
	D-SoundPro*	Mac	Sound card**
	CoolEdit*	PC	Sound card
	Wham*	PC	Sound card
Movies	QuickTime	Mac/PC	Sound and video card**
	QuickEdit*	Mac	Sound and video card**
	Video for Windows	PC	Sound and video card
	Adobe Premiere	Mac/PC	Sound and video card**
Animation	Director	Mac/PC	Sound card**
Authoring	Director	Mac/PC	None
	HyperCard	Mac	None
	SuperCard	Mac	None
	Visual Basic	PC	None

*Shareware or freeware.
**Most current Macs come with audio input built in. Older Macs may require a sound
digitizing device. AV Macs come with audio and video capture standard.

In the planning stages, you should decide whether you're going to want
your project to eventually end up on both "platforms" (Mac and PC). If
you want a cross-platform project, it'll save you a lot of hassle in
the long run if you know the software you'll be using for both platforms and what exactly you'll need to do to convert from one platform
to the other.

: **self-running "slide show"** (images with soundtrack)

: **interactive art** (an art piece or performance on disk)

: **interactive catalog** (a database of text, images, sounds cataloging a set of ideas, a product line, etc.)

: **game**

: **kiosk** (installation-based project)

Once you've decided that multimedia is your soapbox (if not, see the other chapters of this book), and once you've decided on the specific form your project will take, it's time to start collecting the content (or getting it ready for importing into your authoring program). We won't go into the authoring process here; the manuals that came with your software will give you those instructions. For some of the more difficult authoring tools such as Director, you might want to take a class to speed up your learning time. Most cities have schools that offer all sorts of software training classes. Look in the business section of the newspaper or the Yellow Pages.

The most important thing to stress—which is often not stressed enough in multimedia training and literature—is the importance of storyboarding. You really want to take your time scripting your presentation. You are telling your audience a story, generating an experience for them. The more you think about your story and how to tell it best, the more powerful your multimedia experience will be. Your storyboards don't need to be works of art (forget all those cool movie storyboards you've seen in documentaries on filmmaking), they simply need to "block out" the action. You can use a blackboard, post-it notes on a wall, a sketch pad, a computer outlining program, anything you're comfortable with. By thinking of this process as storyboarding, as opposed to say outlining, you emphasize the storytelling aspect over the other trappings of multimedia.

Besides the story, the interface you use is critically important. The interface defines how people will interact with the content. It's the buttons they click, the pull-down menus and pop-up boxes, and the other tools that are used for getting around your little idea universe. Spend plenty of time planning the interface. What should it look like (what part of the story does it help to tell)? How will navigation work and how will the interface facilitate that? The interface should draw the users into the content and help them find their way through it. It's amazing how many bad interfaces there are in today's multimedia products. Often, great content is ruined by a crummy interface and/or a bad navigation scheme. Try creating several different interface designs and compare how they function and feel to use. Drag other people into your hack shack and ask their opinions. If it's 2 A.M. and you don't have anybody handy, pop onto the Net and deputize someone there as your beta tester. If you spend a lot of time on creating/acquiring good content, scripting it to maximize its impact, and wiring it all into a well thought out interface, your project should work out great (and it will instantly outshine about 75 percent of what's currently out there).

Production)

When the authoring process is done, it's time to move your multimedia masterpiece onto the appropriate storage medium so that you can send it around for "beta testing" (getting other people to try and break it). Of course, you should have already considered what type of medium is best for the project during the planning process. On the next page is a chart showing the most common storage media affordable to DIY media makers.

Artist/musician Brian Eno has a technique for critiquing his own work. He looks at it (or listens to it) while pretending that someone whose aesthetics he's familiar with, or someone whom he knows would be hypercritical, is also judging it. Looking through their eyes, he imagines their reactions.

STORAGE MEDIA

MEDIUM	CAPACITY	POPULARITY LEVEL	NOTES
Double-Density Diskette	800 K	High	It is still common on many older computers.
High-Density Diskette	1.4 MB	High	Most common format.
CD-ROM	~600 MB	High	For cost-to-capacity and popularity, this is your best bet for large multimedia.
CD-R (CD Recordable)	~600 MB	Moderate	One-off CD-ROM, CD-Audio, or EDC. Good for testing.
Enhanced CD	~600 MB	Low	CD-Audio/CD-ROM hybrid medium. Increasingly common in music biz.
Photo CD	~600 MB	Low	Used for picture archiving, but can also be used as a multimedia platform for pictures, sounds, and music.

After the beta test phase of the final program, it's time to get your disks duplicated. There are a number of disk duplicators nationwide that handle most of the media available. For floppy disk projects, these duplicators will handle everything from small (25-50 copies) to huge runs. Even at the lower end, most of these places will label, assemble, package, and shrink-wrap your software. Of course, if you want to save money, you can do all that yourself. For floppies, you can even do all the duplicating yourself, if the number of copies you're making is small. One great feature of digital media is that no quality is lost with successive duplication. If you suspect the rate of distribution of your final product is going to be slow, you can just duplicate the disks as you receive orders. But consider this: Prices at duplicating houses are cheap enough that you can save yourself a lot of time without spending too many of your hard-earned doubloons.

For CD production, there are also duplicating houses that can handle all sizes of jobs. Compact Disc technology has become affordable enough for both the storage and distribution of all types of digital data. You can send your project to a duplication house for multiple copies, get a one-off done at a CD-R (compact disc-recordable) service bureau, or buy a CD-R deck and roll your own. Many of the duplicators that handle CD-Audio also do CD-ROM. See the Audio Hacker's Starter Kit for a list of several of these companies.

Photo CDs can be made by taking your film (or slides or negatives) to a Kodak photo shop where they will put up to 100 images on a Photo CD disc. Many photo and computer service bureaus offer this service. Using Kodak's Build-It software, you can add spoken word and music to your presentation. Photo CD is also used as a way of archiving large numbers of photos for complex multimedia projects.

Packaging)

Packaging of your multimedia program can be anything from a disk label on the final duplicated disks to fancy full-color boxes. For low-budget floppy-based projects, one easy solution is to put the disk in a plastic bag with a printed card behind it (sized to the bag). You can even go lower budget than that and put your disks in one of the plastic sleeves that protect floppies when you buy them blank. For one of my projects, I used these sleeves with a color photocopied sticker to seal the disk inside. It looked great and cost almost nothing (you can get a lot of small stickers color photocopied onto a single sheet of sticky-back paper). If you want to go a little more highbrow, you can get clear and colored plastic boxes that will hold different numbers of disks. Full-color cardboard boxes are, of course, out of the question for anything low budget. One solution I've seen is to get generic computer software boxes and paste a printed or photocopied front onto it. This is often tacky looking, but several small-scale software publishers have done it with great success.

Cool CD-ROM packaging doesn't have to be expensive either. There is a new type of clear plastic envelope (one brand name is Viewpak) for CDs. There's a place for the CD, a booklet, and "tray card" art. These Viewpaks are not only a cheap packaging option, but they make storing CDs and CD-ROMs a lot more sensible for the user. Hundreds of CDs can fit in a very small space. The print part can be done in anything from black-and-white photo copy to full-color printing. If you're looking for more traditional packaging in jewel boxes, you can also hand-build covers and booklets and buy the boxes from a disk vendor. Used CD stores often sell empty jewel boxes. If you send your CD-ROM to a duplication house, it usually will handle the package printing and assembly for little or no additional cost.

If you can't afford to be slick, or have high-budget packaging, then do your best to be unique. Creativity doesn't cost extra. One of the coolest floppy-disk packages I've ever received consisted of a disk with a handmade color-copied label folded inside of an envelope made out of a road map. It was fastened by an astronaut sticker and placed inside a simple cardboard fold-over made out of an old product box for a model airplane. It was a beautiful hand-built artifact made out of trash. Another was a disk envelope cut from corrugated cardboard spray-painted matte black with a glued-on label

that had the name of the program printed in gold foil (which can be easily
done using laser-compatible foil ribbon bought at mail order suppliers such
as Paper Direct).

Distribution)

The process of hunting down a distributor for disk-based multimedia is
basically the same as for music (see the Distribution section of the Audio
Hacker's Starter Kit). If you want to sell your wares through traditional
outlets (stores, mail-order catalogs, etc.), you'll find this to be quite difficult
unless you can get a distributor. Direct sales is another traditional route
that can work out well for small operations as long as your sales are modest and you have no-cost or low-cost venues (such as zines) in which to
advertise. If you become dependent on paid advertising and direct mailings, you'll need to be moving a lot of product to generate the kind of revenue that you can feed back into advertising.

If you're more interested in getting your media out there than in getting
rich, you might want to make your project shareware or freeware. For
shareware, you distribute your wares for free but ask users to pay a fee if
they like what you've done. You can give them an incentive to send in their
shareware registration money by offering them a newsletter, free updates,
additional content, or something else they won't get otherwise. Shareware
is usually priced much less than commercial software. Freeware is given
away at no charge, usually with the understanding that users can distribute it freely as long as no one else makes money on it and as long as the
author's identifying information remains attached to the program.
Shareware and freeware are very common on the Net.

There are also shareware compilation discs published by major computer
book and software publishers that provide a much broader distribution for

"best of" shareware. Getting involved in any type of compilation project can boost your distribution tremendously. There are a number of CD-ROM magazines and various compilation discs of freeware, shareware, art compilations, etc. Since CD-ROMs have lots of room on them, these compilations are often starved for good content. You can submit a sampler/demo of your program or the entire thing.

There are lots of program storage sites on the net (called FTP sites or software libraries). By getting just a few of these sites to store a sampler of your multimedia zine, you're making it available to a potential global audience. And it's likely that once it's out there, it will make its own friends and travel around the planet on its own steam. We initially released a *Beyond Cyberpunk* sampler to two sites. We watched by the week (using the Archie search program) as *BCP* ping-ponged from site to site across the globe. Within weeks we were getting email orders from South Africa, Japan, and Australia, not to mention numerous other sites in the United States.

You can also create a site on the World Wide Web to distribute a sampler/demo, or even the full-blown program. Modems continue to get faster and more schemes for e-cash, and secure credit card transactions are being introduced that will allow you do sell software directly over the Net.

Pricing)

The rule of thumb in pricing is to charge twice as much as your production costs. Another says to charge within the current range of commercial offerings of a similar nature. A third approach says to charge what the market will bear. The rationale here is that you're unlikely to sell very many units of your program, so you might as well get what you can per unit. If it's a specialty piece that appeals to a niche market, a certain number of hard-core fans will pay any reasonable price.

If you anticipate that a lot of your sales are going to be through stores and distributors, you need to have a high enough list price so that when they take their discount (often 40 percent for stores and between 50-60 percent for distributors), you still have enough left over for you.

Promotion and Advertising)

Most of the general promotion and advertising ideas have already been covered in previous chapters' Starter Kits. DIY media is marketed through similar channels using similar low-cost methods. Zines are always a great source for free promotion (through reviews) and cheap advertising. And the Net is the other no-cost/low-cost avenue for promoting and selling your work. Usenet discussion groups don't take kindly to blatant advertising, but you can still announce your wares if you do so in the appropriate groups and with the appropriate tone. Make your posting informational in nature and then ask people to email you for more information on price, ordering, etc. Creating a Web page is all the rage . . . and a great way to promote your wares (see the Net publishing chapter for details on how to create Web documents).

One unique avenue of software promotion and advertising is computer users groups. These clubs usually have newsletters in which you can announce your work and meetings where you can demo your program. Look on local BBSes, in computer store magazine racks, and other places where computer geeks hang out for information on users groups in your

Don't forget to take advantage of your local papers, cable access shows, the evening news, and other local media. Many of these outlets are often starved for interesting local people, events, and products to cover. Every time you release a new program or do something interesting and newsworthy, send press releases to the local media. Make sure your press releases are creative so they'll attract attention (most media types are swamped with boring releases).

area. And, of course, you can mail a review copy of your software to users groups throughout the country. As you get reviewed in these various newsletters, clip and paste up the reviews and add them to the promo materials that you send to subsequent publications. Make sure you have a good press release in your promo pack that adequately describes your project. You'd be surprised how many publications lift the material right out of these releases. So make sure you have nice things to say about yourself and your software.

The importance of editorial coverage for low-budget projects cannot be stressed enough. Paid advertising is far too expensive for anything other than well-funded commercial ventures. But if your project is newsworthy or is cool enough to tickle a reviewer's fancy, the sky's the limit in terms of who might choose to cover you. We were stunned to get a $3/4$-page review of *Beyond Cyberpunk* in the *New York Times* and coverage in almost every computer magazine, newsweekly, and several dailies. We wouldn't have been able to afford even a business-card-size ad in any of these publications.

Also, don't forget to target stores that cater to your subject. If your disk is on amateur robot enthusiasts, try getting into electronic shops and hobby stores. If it's on book collecting, independent and used bookstores might be a good target.

Words of Wisdom $)$

Robert Carr (Lamprey Systems):
: Never rely on your computer operating system's "undocumented features" when programming. Today's undocumented feature is tomorrow's unsupported feature . . . with disastrous results.

: Leave your user's computer in the same state you found it. Don't let your program change their pixel depth or sound volume without setting it back when they quit.

: The right sound at the right moment can really make your program. Don't go overboard with the sounds however, as sound effects require a large amount of space. Here's another thing to keep in mind: Since the mid-1980s, almost every sound in the universe has been copyrighted. The good news is that if a nobody uses a couple of copyrighted sounds for their obscure program, it's unlikely to raise an eyebrow. On the other hand, if you lift ninety seconds of tunes out of a Nine Inch Nails CD and your game is the next *Doom*, don't be surprised when Trent Reznor's lawyer comes knocking on your door.

: You can't compete head to head with commercial programmers. These guys program for a living while you maybe only have a few hours a week, so (of course) they are going to be better than you. Your advantage is that you don't have editors, bosses, or coworkers to slow you down or make you compromise your work. At one Redmond software megacorp, a programmer has to take three meetings and draft a mission statement just to go to the bathroom. You are like a small furry mammal about 65 million years ago. You can leap out of your hole, bite the lumbering software corporation in the ass, and be back in the safety of your burrow before the message even makes it halfway to the dinosaur's puny brain.

: You can skimp on computer equipment but not on programming software. Lots of folks spend huge sums on a computer and then refuse to spend anything on software. Poor programming software is a much greater handicap than poor equipment. It is important that you research your choice of software. When you have completed your research, make your choice on quality—not price. Take into account that in addition to your software, you'll probably need reference books. These usually run about $40 each.

: If money is a problem, consider buying your programming software secondhand. Many people buy programming software only to find that they are not interested in programming. They often try to recoup their loss by reselling the software at a discount. If possible, get software that is unregistered (still has the warranty card). Software that has already been registered should be deeply discounted and should come with a letter of transfer (stating that you are now the owner). The classified section on AOL is an excellent place to check for secondhand software.

: Write stand-alone applications. If your creation requires another program to run, such as HyperCard or ToolBook, you are limiting the number of people who can run it. In addition, you are now at the mercy of producers of your player software. If they go out of business or release a buggy version of their software player, you've got problems.

: Keep your program lean. It should fit in a compressed format (such as Zip or StuffIt) on the most common transportable media at the time. Right now that would be a 1.44-meg floppy disk. SneakerNet is still an important avenue of distribution. Furthermore, online users are more likely to download your program if it is a reasonable size.

: Pirate your own software. You can write the greatest program ever, but that does not mean anything unless people are playing it. Distribute your creation as widely as possible. If your goal is to make money, charge for extra levels or for giving the user information necessary to win (if it's a game). Remember, the first fix is always free.

: Start small and don't get discouraged. Don't expect to write a megahit right out of the gate. Instead write small throwaway programs that allow you to build up your skills while being creative.

Abbe Don (Abbe Don Interactive):

: Use personal stories and idiosyncratic structures to organize information and users' experience. People naturally weave stories together in a multilinear or polylinear manner, but in school they learn to organize things linearly in a very top-down fashion. Once you have the linear flow, free things up.

: Use characters to represent multiple points of view. The most effective use of characters in the interface is to use them to represent information from multiple points of view, especially in domains such as history, news, or storytelling. In addition, characters can be used to help users find information from a particular point of view rather than requiring them to struggle with a more traditional query interface.

: Work with people who can engage in simultaneous top-down and bottom-up design. In other words, balance a user-centered perspective based on user scenarios and the ideal world with a functionality and system perspective based on the limitations of hardware, software, and bandwidth.

: Provide experiences in which the user co-creates and transforms the content, not just branches through shovelware consuming randomly accessible data.

: Use improvisation and performance in the early brainstorming phases or at any point when the design, production, or programming teams are stuck. Take improv and performance courses to keep you on your feet and not get stuck with the same old techniques and same old approach to design problems.

: Keep your sense of humor, passion, and patience, especially when collaborating. (Copyright © 1996 by Abbe Don)

Peter Sugarman (The Computer Lab):

: Full motion video may not be necessary. Still pictures, along with a good sound track, can tell a powerful story.

: Remember that you're having a conversation with your viewer. If you can anticipate and respond to the reaction your media is likely to inspire, the conversation becomes that much more intimate.

: Never break faith with your viewer. Once they expect a certain action, such as pressing a button to produce a certain result, don't disappoint . . . unless you're doing so to make a point.

: Images fill the screen, but sound fills the room. Use sound to define the world you've created.

Sean Carton (Cool Tool of the Day):

: Never underestimate the power of the Ziploc freezer bag. Ziplocs are cheap, tough, completely resealable, and even waterproof! Just stuff all your materials inside, zip it up, and put a staple or two in it to make sure that little hooligans don't empty your booty into their pockets. You can also punch a hole in the top of the bag so that it can be hung on a hook in the store.

: One alternative to software boxes is to get clear plastic boxes to pack your stuff in—either jewel boxes if it's a CD-ROM or plastic disk boxes if you're packaging floppies. Put your disks and a cover/insert inside, seal it up with a sticker, and you're set! Your cover art will be visible through the front of the box.

: Another simple packaging idea is to design your cover in such a way that you can fold it over to secure all the contents inside. Print your cover onto a light card stock, score along the spine, and fold over. To hold the whole thing together, put stickers on the three remaining edges. You can go as simple as plain, pre-purchased colored stickers, or get fancy and laser-print or photocopy your own. Avery sells sheets of adhesive-backed materials that can be run through a copier or laser printer. This method works well for disk labels, too. You can even buy pre-cut disk labels, create your artwork on the computer, and then print in color (or black and white) right onto the disk labels. If you don't have a color label printer, take your color art on disk to a service bureau.

: Scanners? Expensive, right? Not really. If you're on a budget, you can purchase a handheld gray-scale scanner for a reasonable amount. Plug that baby in, grab some artwork, and start scanning. Even without a much more expensive color scanner, you can do a lot, scanning in gray scale and colorizing it in a graphics program such as Photoshop.

Resources)

SOFTWARE

Here's where you can get the multimedia programs mentioned in this chapter:

BAR-MIN-SKI: Consumer Product (Mac/PC)
DE-LUX'O
P.O. BOX 661635, LOS ANGELES, CA 90066
800-338-BOOK
EMAIL: deluxo1@aol.com
WEB: evolutionary.com/deluxo/

$40 regular edition, $100 signed limited edition. Sampler available for downloading.

Beyond Cyberpunk
THE COMPUTER LAB
WEB: www.streettech.com/bcp/

BCP is no longer available on disk, but you can download or view portions of it from our Web site.

eSpew (Mac/Windows)
TED KUSIO, EDITOR
SLOWX PRESS
WEB: www.logical.net/users/slowx

Available for downloading. Along with *Bizara*, Ted's other e-zine.

eWire (Mac)

KIERAN CHAPMAN
37 BALTIC ST. #3, S. ATTLEBORO, MA 02703
EMAIL: wirezine@aol.com
WEB: www.ici.net/cust_pages/wire/home.html

I Photograph to Remember (Mac/PC)

PEDRO MEYER
VOYAGER COMPANY
WEB: www.voyagerco.com

Lamprey Systems

ROBERT CARR
EMAIL: smurfboy@aol.com
WEB: users.aol.com/lampreysys/index.html

Robert Carr makes seriously inappropriate games and other programs that poke fun at the sacred cows of our society. *MacJesus* dispenses heavenly wisdom at the click of a mouse. *Geraldo-matic* takes TV sleazy talk shows to a new low. *Hexon Exon* replaces naughty Net pornography with the names of senators and other truly offensive people. *Operation Rescue* . . . well . . . you don't even wanna know.

Reverb (Mac/Windows)

DAN SICKO, EDITOR
EMAIL: reverb@hyperreal.com
WEB: hyperreal.com/zines/reverb/

MULTIMEDIA AUTHORING SOFTWARE

Adobe Acrobat

Creates universal electronic documents that can be viewed across computer platforms (Mac, Windows, Unix) and online. Existing documents created in PageMaker, QuarkXPress, and Word can be exported into Acrobat, retaining their formatting, graphics, and fonts. Using Adobe Distiller software, you can "print" your layouts to a PDF file that can be read by the Adobe Acrobat Reader. Acrobat documents can include hyperlinks within the text and URL links to the World Wide Web. From Adobe, 800-833-6687, www.adobe.com.

Apple Interactive Music Toolkit (Mac)

WEB: 17.254.3.54:80/imt/imt.html

The rage these days is enhanced CDs (or "ECDs"). This is an audio CD/CD-ROM hybrid that includes both musical and data tracks. The Apple Interactive Music Toolkit allows you to create Blue Book–compliant ECDs that run on both Mac and Windows. It's available for free from the Web address above.

Build-It (Mac/PC)

Photo CD presentation software that lets you create Photo CD "Portfolio Discs," Photo CDs with added audio. From Eastman Kodak, 800-866-5533, www.kodak.com.

Common Ground (Mac/PC)

Similar to Acrobat. Allows you to create electronic documents that can be read on a variety of platforms (Mac, Windows, Unix) while retaining all the formatting of the original documents. No Hands Software, 800-598-3821.

Director (Mac/PC)

Director is the undisputed leader in authoring programs. It has many more capabilities than HyperCard but is much harder to learn. Director expertly handles animation, color, and is adept at cross-platform translation. Shockwave, a free Director player that works over the World Wide Web, means that MacroMedia (www.macromedia.com) is likely to cast a big shadow over the multimedia world for some time to come.

DocMaker (Mac)

An inexpensive shareware program that allows you to make simple disk-based presentations for the Mac. You distribute your zine on disk with a self-running viewer so that your readers don't need an outside program to view it. You can find DocMaker in many software libraries on the Internet.

HTML/Web Browsers (Mac/PC)

HTML is a series of mark-up tags that you put into the text documents you want formatted for reading in a World Wide Web browser such as Netscape or Internet Explorer. HTML and Web browsers, although designed for Web-based media presentation, work on individual computers, too. You can create a multimedia zine in HTML and put it on disk for those who don't have full Internet access. "Webs on disk" are not common, but they work just fine. See the Net Publisher's Starter Kit for details on how to get HTML-related software and Web browsers.

HyperCard (Mac)

HyperCard is the closest we've come to a software vox populi: a cheap (it used to be free), easy-to-program hypermedia toolkit. Although fading in popularity, HyperCard still forms the backbone of many commercial multimedia product (such as many Voyager titles and the breakout hit *Myst*). Great for low-tech multimedia. A HyperCard reader comes with all Macs, but to create HyperCard stacks you'll need the full-blown program (around $100). From Apple Computer (www.apple.com).

Museum (Mac)

A very simple shareware program that allows you to cut and paste text, images, and sounds into a self-running "slide show" or electronic book. From Rustle Laidman at members.aol.com/raymeow.

PageBoy (Mac)

A simple and cheap shareware program that lets you create stand-alone publications that anyone with a Mac can view. From Rustle Laidman at members.aol.com/raymeow.

SuperCard (Mac)

Very similar to HyperCard, SuperCard has more advanced color capabilities and animation tools. It uses a scripting language, SuperTalk, that's similar to (HyperCard's) HyperTalk. From Allegiant Technologies (www.allegiant.com/supercard/).

Writer's Dream (PC)

The DOS/PC-equivalent to DocMaker. Not nearly as versatile, but just as easy to use. Available from software libraries on the Net.

BOOKS

The CD-Recordable Bible

ASH PAHWA, PH.D.
EIGHT BIT BOOKS
462 DANBURY ROAD, WILTON, CT 06897
1994, 185 PAGES, $24.95

A useful primer for those who want to get started in CD-R. It covers basic terms, standards, procedures, software, how to select a CD-R deck, and how to duplicate the discs.

Demystifying Multimedia:
A Guide for Multimedia Developers from Apple Computer, Inc.*

KEN FROMM AND NATHAN SHEDROFF, EDITORS
RANDOM HOUSE/NEWMEDIA, 1995, 304 PAGES, $30

An extremely useful, densely packed book covering multimedia production, marketing, and sales. It is definitely geared towards commercial enterprises (with lots on management, team assembly, high-end production, etc.), but there's plenty here for the noncommercial media maker, too. The book is jam-packed with overview information, how-to instructions, profiles of successful multimedia producers, and resources. The book's a hypertext document itself with lots of marginalia, pointers to other sections, and color-coded icons that indicate the various stages of multimedia development. (It covers both Mac and PC platforms.)

MAGAZINES

EMedia Professional (formerly called CD-Rom Professional)

P.O. BOX 401, MT. MORRIS, IL 61054-0401
800-806-7795
WEB: www.onlineinc.com/emediapro
$55 PERSONAL / $98 CORPORATE PER YEAR

A trade journal for those who are serious about getting into the CD-ROM business. It has a number of useful articles and interesting industry news, along with some how-to instructions.

NewMedia*

HYPERMEDIA COMMUNICATIONS, INC.
901 MARINER'S ISLAND BLVD., SUITE 365, SAN MATEO, CA 94404
415-573-5170, FAX: 415-573-5131
WEB: www.hyperstand.com

A controlled-circulation trade journal for the multimedia business. It covers all aspects of multimedia and related technology, as well as industry gossip, breaking news, and cyberculture coverage. If you're a multimedia insider (hint: you'll qualify for a free subscription), you need this magazine. A qualification form is available on their Web site.

CATALOGS

Voyager Catalog

578 BROADWAY, SUITE 1106, NEW YORK, NY 10012
800-446-2001
EMAIL: catalogs@voyager.com
WEB: www.voyagerco.com

The Voyager Company's magalog contains their entire line of CD-ROMs, Expanded Books (e-books), and paraphernalia. There's also lots of background information and marginalia, including interviews with the programs' designers and their subjects. The catalog is beautifully designed and infinitely browsable. Voyager continues to lead the industry in releasing and distributing the best CD-ROMs around. And they're not ashamed to pick up the little guys (*BAR-MIN-SKI* and *BLAM!*, for instance).

Eastgate Systems

134 MAIN STREET, WATERTOWN, MA 02172
800-562-1638
EMAIL: info@eastgate.com
WEB: www.eastgate.com/
E-LIST: eastgate-list@eastgate.com
(send a note saying you want to subscribe)

A distributor of disk-based hypertext/hypermedia, Eastgate carries many of the innovative first hypertexts such as Stuart Moulthrop's *Victory Garden*, George P. Landow's *The Dickens Web*, and Jaime Levy's e-book *Ambulance*. They're very friendly folks and sympathetic to modestly produced hypermedia (as long as the content is good). If you have a project you're looking to distribute, Eastgate is worth contacting. They also sell a hypertext authoring program called Story Space.

DUPLICATORS

Disc Manufacturing, Inc.

800-433-DISC

Disc Manufacturing, Inc., offers full CD replication services. It also has a number of excellent technical pubs for free, including *Compact Disc Terminology, A Glossary of CD and CD-ROM Terms*, and *An Overview to Multimedia CD-ROM Production*. All the booklets are weighed down by industry geekspeak, but you might be able to get some value out of them. You can't beat the price!

NET SITES

CD-ROM FAQ*

FTP: ftp.cdrom.com/pub/cdrom/faq

CD-ROM Information Center*

WEB: www.cd-info.com

> A major information source for anything having to do with CD technology. This site includes articles on the history of CD-ROM, an extensive bibliography, links to all of the major online CD-ROM magazines, industry news and information, and sections on all the different CD formats and available technologies.

CD-ROM Info Web Site

WEB: www.uscchi.com/cdrom/index.html

> An information resource on CD-ROM drives, hybrid systems, CD-R devices, CD-related software.

Creating Audio CDs on your PC

WEB: www.westnet.com/~gsmith/cdrecord.htm

> Greg Smith's excellent guide to audio CD recording.

D.FILM

WEB: www.dfilm.com/

> "D.FILM is a traveling festival that showcases the innovative ways people are using technology to make low-budget and independent films. This includes people editing films on their home computers... people creating vivid new worlds through desktop 3-D animation... or shooting digital video cameras. And people taking film in bold new directions with custom software and weird cameras like Pixelvision and Connectix."

The HyperCard Home Page

WEB: www.glasscat.com/hypercard.cgi

> An online resource for HyperCard programmers, teachers, and enthusiasts.

Index to Multimedia Information Sources*

WEB: viswiz.gmd.de/MultimediaInfo/

The CD-Audio manufacturers listed in the Audio Hacker's Starter Kit section also do CD-ROM duplicating.

A major link node for all aspects of multimedia production. There are sections on audio, video, 2-D and 3-D graphics, authoring, storage media, and much more.

J.R.'s WebFlux Page

WEB: members.aol.com/jrspacer/ixmag.html

A Web site that grew out of *FLUX,* a HyperCard zine. The site has articles from the HyperCard stacks and links to HyperCard authoring tools.

MMDEVX

E-list covering cross-platform (Mac/PC) multimedia issues. To subscribe, send the message: SUBSCRIBE MMDEVX FirstName LastName to Mail-Server @knex.mind.org.

Multimedia Wire

WEB: www.mmwire.com

A weekly Web magazine focusing on the multimedia business. It covers videogames, interactive entertainment, CD-ROM, online services, and interactive TV.

ResFest '97

109 MINNA STREET, SUITE 390, SAN FRANCISCO, CA 94105
EMAIL: Jonathan@resfest.com
WEB: www.resfest.com/

"The goal of the ResFest Digital Film Festival is to expose and inspire innovative films and videos created with desktop digital tools. The focus of the Festival is how computers and other digital tools affect the way people are making independent films and videos today. Films screened in past years have been made using all types of production tools including 35mm, 16mm, Super 8, Betacam, Hi8, MiniDV, Pixelvision, various types of animation manipulated on the computer, and the full range of non-linear editing and effects software."

Resource Guide on Distributed Media

WEB: www.teleshuttle.com/resource

A technical guide to CD/online hybrid media. It includes general information and links to white papers, tools and services, standards documents, and other resources for those considering this form of hybrid media.

Usenet Newsgroups:

alt.authorware
alt.cd-rom
comp.multimedia*
comp.os.ms-windows.programmer.multimedia
comp.publish.cdrom.hardware
comp.publish.cdrom.multimedia
comp.publish.cdrom.software
comp.sys.mac.hypercard
misc.education.multimedia

Developing a CRITICAL
consciousness
about the
COMMUNICATIONS
industry is a
necessary first step
towards DEMOCRATIC
control of information
RESOURCES.
—*The Paper Tiger Manifesto*

Don't just WATCH TV
(or kvetch about it),
Make it!
— cable-access motto

THE BIRTH *of* COMMUNITY TV) I'm sitting on a big bed with three other people and a wiry little dog named Gracie. We're all in our pajamas, lounging like Turkish royalty on colorful pillows and cushions. The one woman in the group, an attractive Brit named Lucy, is clad in a tiny champagne-colored slip. The men are all overdressed in an uninspiring mishmash of robes, T-shirts, pajama pants, and well-worn socks. Gracie, curled up at our feet, has begun licking Lucy's leg. As the slightly awkward conversation trips along, Gracie continues the sensuous leg lapping. After what seems like an eternity of licking, I'm getting a little more . . . ah . . . enthusiastic than seems appropriate. As soon as I point out the mutt's antics, Lucy brushes the dog aside and we all laugh. The last of the ice has melted.

In case you're wondering, this is not the opening maneuvers of an orgy. I'm a guest on *Slumber Party*, an Arlington, Virginia, cable-access chat show. The premise of the show, now in its fifth year, is simple: Local poets, writers, artists, musicians, actors, and other D.C.-area bohos mix it up amidst the oversized pillows and the late-night-in-the-group-house ambience. The show is the brainchild of Hap Heubusch, a musician and fan of the arts who got tired of seeing local artists and musicians not getting the respect and exposure they deserve. He decided to do something about it, creating *Slumber Party*, and talked friend and fellow musician Miles Anderson into being one of its hosts. Current co-host Lucy Symons, a local actress, came on board in 1992.

"I wanted to create something completely different from what you usually see on TV," says Heubusch. "I was sick and tired of watching the arts get shafted by Jesse Helms and his lot. I saw the show as a way of making a political statement." *Slumber Party* has grown from Hap's one-man after-hours hobby into a small TV production collective. "It's become a big wonderful family," enthuses Lucy. "We've had the same crew now for two years. We even hang out together, going to see music, performances, or whatever." Having a larger pool of people involved has relieved Hap of the burden of producing all the shows. Now there's a team of alternating producers. "Hap's kicked himself upstairs into an executive producer position," says Anderson. "It's really great for him to get a break. He's been doing this show for so long, they ought to erect a monument to him at ACT (Arlington Community Television)."

The sleepy-time trappings of *Slumber Party* create a playful, even erotically charged atmosphere. Guests are sometimes surprised when they realize that the show really does take place in a bed, with guests in their under-wear, jammies, and lingerie. "I have more lingerie than any other women in the Western world!" blurts Symons. The hosts and producers have found that putting everybody in their pajamas levels the playing field to an extent and gets people to loosen up. "It's a good way of selecting out people for the show," says Miles. "If you're too uptight to get in your pajamas and climb into bed with strangers, you probably take yourself too seriously to be on our show anyway." Lucy tells the story of a nationally known mystery writer, Laurence Block, showing up for the show in a suit and tie. "Apparently he didn't think we were serious about the pajamas bit." After convincing him that climbing into bed in full business regalia was out of the question, they managed to get him into one of Miles's spare outfits. After a few minutes of Block sitting wooden and uncomfortable on the edge of the bed, he began to loosen. "By the end of the show, we couldn't get him out of bed!" giggles Lucy.

Even when the conversations on *Slumber Party* end up on a road to nowhere (which they frequently do), the unpredictable dynamics of the weekly bed-in are fascinating to watch. And true to Heubusch's vision, the show has become a frequent watering hole for the D.C.-area artists and musicians. Future plans for the show include trying to get it "bicycled" (circulated through the mail) to more cable-access channels and getting it funded. Right now, Hap and the other producers pay for the production out of their own pockets, with two episodes (taped back-to-back) costing about $160.

SLUMBER PARTY ∧

WAYNE'S WORLD...*not!*)

If you ask a random sampling of people on the street "What is cable access?" they're likely to feed you bits of cable parodies from *Saturday Night Live*. People will usually mention how awful and unwatchable most amateur TV shows are. Basically, the majority of Americans have no idea what public access TV (or PATV) is and they don't really care. You won't find PATV shows listed in *TV Guide* and you're lucky if you can find them in your local paper's TV section. To get a PATV show on your radar, you'll have to wade through an on-screen bulletin board of ads for shows such as *Book Nook*, *The Young Republican Hour*, *Bridle Call of Christ*, countless community board meetings, and other equally stimulating fare. Once you've targeted a worthwhile show, you'll have to remember what night it's on and what its rerun schedule is (e.g., every first Tuesday is new, the other Tuesdays are repeats). OK, so this isn't rocket science, but compared to the ease with which one can stumble onto programming on commercial TV, it's difficult to stay abreast of cable-access programming. Most cable-access stations also have limited cablecasting hours (e.g., 3:30 P.M.-11:30 P.M.), giving only a small window of opportunity to viewers and show producers.

Real-life cable-access TV may be struggling with obscurity, mediocrity, and hand-to-mouth financing, but Hollywood's version is flourishing. *Wayne's World* has become a lucrative franchise, *Daily Affirmations with Stuart Smalley* was a major motion picture, and *Coffee Talk*'s Linda Richmond (Mike Meyers in drag) has appeared onstage with "her" idol Barbra "Like Buttah" Streisand. Blue-collar film critics Bucky and Vinnie (who had a show on Manhattan Cable) became TV spokesmodels for Subway sandwich shops.

(sidebar, vertical:) PAPER TIGER TELEVISION

A rent TV ad from our local cable company is outrageous in its omission of cable access when listing its benefits to the community. The ad talks about the wonderful cable content the company offers, its excellent service record, and the fact that it even pipes educational programming into our schools. Nothing is mentioned of the fact that it also provides the local community with TV equipment, training, studios, and the potential for any resident to start his or her own TV show!

In the formula Gen-X film *Reality Bites*, Winona Ryder plays a camcorder-wielding junior filmmaker whose work bleeds so much truth that her tapes get bought by the film's equivalent of MTV. With all this mainstream media attention, it's somewhat surprising that cable access is not more popular and more creatively utilized. After decades of operation, cable access still looks like a medium waiting to happen.

TV from the TWILIGHT ZONE Manhattan's cable access **CHANNELS** are **LEGENDARY FOR** their **BIZARRE,** envelope-pushing shows (and **SHOW NAMES).** I wish we had this **KIND of programming ANARCHY** in Arlington, Virginia. **Our IDEA** of naughty, **RADICAL ACCESS** in Arlington is a **subdued** pajama party, *LaRouche Connection,* and a **Greenpeace show.**

PATV'S INFREQUENTLY ASKED QUESTIONS) So what *is* PATV? Public access was created in the 1960s and '70s as a means of providing a media outlet to local communities. Regulatory support for public access wavered until the 1984 Cable Act when the FCC mandated that cable companies be responsible for providing cablecasting access to citizens in the cable company's service area. In order for cable companies to get their franchise license, they had to agree to make TV facilities readily available to the community. A percentage of revenue from the cable company was to be fed into a budget that would support equipment and training for cable-access channels. This money was then used to create access channels for public use, education, and government information (or PEG, as it's commonly abbreviated).

Public access has, among other things, been very useful to ethnic communities who often have little or no other opportunity to program in their native languages. Some of these shows are general-interest news and entertainment, while others are geared towards newly arrived immigrants, offering information about the local community and basic survival skills like how to use an ATM machine, how to get around on public transportation, and how to take advantage of other local services.

Political and religious groups of every breed have found an exploitable niche on cable access. The Moonies, the LaRouchies, the KKK, the Neo-Nazis, Greenpeace, witch covens, Satanists, and various bizarre New Age churches all have cable shows. And just as there are personal zines ("perzines") in the print world, there are numerous cable shows built around the creator's eccentric views and behaviors. For instance, Manhattan Cable's *Kitty's Kronicles* offers an ongoing record of one woman's exhibitionism. In each episode, Kitty scouts out a site, sets up her cameraman "Honey," and then disrobes, capturing the reactions of stunned and embarrassed passersby. Count Devio, a self-proclaimed vampire, also haunts Manhattan Cable, dispensing his advice on dating and blood sucking. In Arlington, *Naughty Bits* features two guys sitting around trading lame jokes and painfully strained repartee.

No matter which cable-access channel you punch up in the United States, you're likely to see some sweaty host sitting in front of a cheap set and a potted plant, stumbling through his idea of a TV program. It almost doesn't matter what the subject matter is; this agonizing scene is universal and screams out: "change the channel, quick!"

So why is cable lousy and populated with hardly any interesting, creative content? Two big reasons: time and money. A cable-access producer/creator can spend dozens of hours preparing and shooting a single show . . . and then *pay* for the privilege of doing so. Most cable shows have no grants or outside funding, so the production costs, albeit modest, come out of the producer's pocket. This can quickly become a drag on a show. Another stumbling block is general public ignorance and indifference towards cable

Acid Lolly-pops —
Experimental entertainment

Addicted to Jesus —
Religious

Boot Eating Scooter Trash —
Comedy

Count Devio's Midnight Snack
—Vampire dating tips

Dyke TV —
Gay/Lesbian pride

Freak It Wit Da Fellaz —
Music and sports

Guttervision —
"High-defiance television"

It's Lucifer! —
Horror, war, destruction, heavy metal

Live from the Morgue w/host MZ D'Luxe —
Homemade horror

Mad Dog's House of Young Lust
—Variety show

Monkey Butt Sex —
Music, video show, movies, comedy, and camp

The Adventures of Antenna Man—
One man show and entertainment

Time Takes a Cigarette —
Experimental video show

Young, Gifted, and Broke —
Comedy

Check out the **MANHATTAN CABLE ACCESS Guide** on the Web at: **www.mnntv.com/**

access. Most wired humans are unaware of it, both as potential content creators and as an audience. For a cable-access producer, it's very discouraging to realize that after putting all your hard work and hard-earned moollah into a show, nobody's likely to watch it.

Another obstacle to cable access is the fact that most potential viewers have been brainwashed by mainstream television's slick, smooth-talking production values. Almost every cable-access show falls into the trap of trying to mimic commercial TV. Restless thumb-happy channel surfers are unlikely to stop on an access show long enough to give it a chance.

Mimicking mainstream television is probably the most common production mistake that cable-access producers make. Today's cameras are portable enough to go anywhere and to film under most conditions. One doesn't need to be chained to the studio or to existing broadcast formats. The cable-access shows that work best are often the ones that do not obsess over production values and viewership. As one access producer said with a big chuckle: "I never get nervous in front of the camera. I just say to myself: 'Don't sweat it, nobody's watching anyway!'"

Public access cable and camcorder technology offer us the opportunity to learn about people, places, and issues unencumbered by the normal constraints of commercial TV. There are no sponsors to please, no ratings to compete for, no requirement for slickness or sound bites. The only requirement is to tell stories that make a difference, that communicate something.

ROX: THE STONED AGE *of* TELEVISION)

The show opens with two nerdy twenty-somethings enthusiastically stuffing their heads into the lens of a palmcorder that one of them is holding. They're sarcastic and punchy, loud, and most likely stoned. They're making it up as they go along; every week they dangle their Hi-8 into the swift-moving current of their lives and show us—for good or ill—the footage. In the process, they make one of the coolest shows on TV, cable access or otherwise.

Weekly cablecast on Bloomington, Indiana's Channel 3 from 1992 to 1995, *ROX* (short for the original title, *J and B on the ROX*) played like a no-budget, more honest version of MTV's *Real World* crossed with Michael Moore's *TV Nation*. *ROX* was a mainstay of the local (dare I say it?) slacker scene. Each show featured "J" (Joe Nickell), "B" (Bart Everson), and a cast of other regulars, passersby, and hangers-on.

The first episodes were recorded in the small dingy basement of J's house located in the "campus ghetto" just south of Indiana University. In front of a camera mounted on a tripod and a bare lightbulb, the boys talked about whatever popped into their heads. Originally the show was dedicated to "The Responsible Use of Alcohol" (they would later drop the "responsible" part). During each episode, J, a bartender of dubious distinction, mixed up surreal rotgut concoctions that made you want to heave just reading the list of ingredients (which appeared on-screen in the style of cooking shows). "Those early shows were mainly about sitting down in front of the camera, getting drunk, and seeing where things would end up," says J. About five to eight shows were taped in this house. J & B soon moved in together into a larger house apartment. Not having a suitable studio space (like the musty basement of J's old pad), they ditched the tripod and began to wander around with the camera, first inside the house and then onto

Here are some *ROX* episodes of note.

#60: *Sustaining the Buzz*
"After Episode 59 aired ("J & B Get Baked"), we were virtually overrun by rabid TV reporters and pencil-scratching journalists. So we made a TV show about it."

#62: *XY in NY*
"Christy Paxson spent the summer of 1994 as an MTV intern/slave in New York City. Her video diary offers a unique glimpse into the pit of corporate hell."

#68: *Raw Footage*
"People often ask if we videotape everything we do. Those people obviously haven't seen this episode. Our editing deck broke, so all we could come up with was this: completely unedited footage drawn from a couple of old, previously unseen tapes."

#70: *Head Jobs*
"Our ode to jobs. Of course, we don't have 'real' jobs, so it's more about others: Jim at Sega, Terry at The Eye, Linda at home with the kids, Chris burning forests, Worm at the Beanery."

#74: *Slaves to the Bean*
"Virtually the entire
ROX Video Troupe is addicted
to coffee . . . and we're all
just giddy about it . . .
featuring the long-lost
anti-caffeine film,
Java Madness, as well as a
guided tour of Bloomington's
coffee houses."

#77: *How to make
your own TV show*

"In response to a letter sent
from some inmates at the
Monroe County Jail, the *ROX*
Video Troupe bares all,
offering their deep insights
into the world of television
production. Featuring tips on
how to get your own equipment
without paying a cent, and
how to make sure your
program gets on the air even
if your parents don't
want it to."

#78: *Luv on the ROX*

"The *ROX* Video Troupe is
pairing off at an alarming rate.
What's happening? For this
Valentine's Day, join us as we
examine the dark side
of love."

#80: *The Potable Gourmet*
"Well, it's about time:
an entire episode full of mixed
drink recipes. Learn how to
create concoctions you didn't
even know exist. See J mix
'em until he drops."

the streets of Bloomington. J recalls: "It was here that we really started to focus in on our lives." It was also at this point that *ROX* began to break away from the laboring pack of cable-access shows to distinguish itself as something special, beyond the typical amateur fare. After putting together some twenty-five shows at this second address, J & B moved into a nearby group house in the summer of 1993. It was here that Christy Paxson, Jenny Beasley, Kelly Worm, and T-Black moved in and became a more integral part of the show.

While the *ROX* crew experienced communal living, relationships, shitty jobs, drugs, cockroaches, harsh winters, and the everyday humdrum, the viewing audience was taken along for the ride. Unlike MTV's *Real World*, where sex and drugs are only mentioned (and cockroaches are conspicuously absent), *ROX* kept the camera rolling as much as possible. The show generated controversy, and a large cult following, when they began smoking pot on-camera in Episode 59: "J & B Get Baked." This got the attention of *MTV News*, *The Howard Stern Show*, and the executive director for the Governor's Commission on a Drug-Free Indiana. His letter, accusing J & B of "the overt promotion of anarchy," became the theme of Episode 64. That's what *ROX* was always about, rolling with the punches, turning obstacles into opportunities, creating "reality-based television."

So how does *ROX* get away with firing up doobies on the idiot box? Traditionally, cable companies have shied away from getting into the business of censorship on their access channels. Most access programming agreements, which cable producers must sign before a cablecast, stipulate that the show must conform to the law and to local community standards.

"We just happen to be very lucky to live in a community where the standards are rather liberal," says J. But what about the weed? That's illegal everywhere. The *ROX* FAQ file on the Internet gives this explanation:

"If you ask the authority figures (i.e., cops, prosecutors, etc.) about this, they'll grumble something about how you can't prove it really is cannabis that we're smoking. But a lawyer in town told us there's some sort of legal precedent about "stale information"—you can't get a search warrant based on old info, and since we don't do the show "live," there'd be no way for them to prove exactly when we were there in front of the courthouse, or in our living room, or on our porch, or driving to Chicago, etc., smoking pot. So we're safe (famous last words?). In fact, the lawyer guy was so confident that we wouldn't get busted, he said he'd represent us for free if we did get hassled. And lawyers don't waive fees lightly. Please knock on wood after reading this."

Whatever the reasons, this leniency, and the overall freedom and advantages of cable, allowed *ROX* to create an extremely honest, warts and all, portrait of a community of struggling, young Hoosiers.

With all the press enthusiasm (*Wired* dubbed *ROX* hipper than MTV) and a program that was getting more sophisticated and sure of itself by the episode, one would think the future of *ROX* would have been rosy. The trouble was funding. Because *ROX* is cable access, they couldn't advertise sponsors or ask for donations on the air. J again: "We looked into leased access, but that didn't look cost effective for regional programming. It's more for low-budget infomercials." After they tried in vain to find some sort of sponsorship that could keep them alive, the group finally decided to call it quits. They still maintain the *ROX* Quarry site on the World Wide Web and sell their videotapes through the mail. On the Web, they immodestly bill

#82: *The RCA State*
"Despite having cut the benefits of their low-level workers, Thompson Consumer Electronics doesn't seem short on cash. They've spent $10 million to change the name of the Hoosier Dome to the RCA Dome. J&B go to a Colts game and ask the fans some penetrating questions."

#85: *Global Village Idiots*
"The Internet is everywhere. You can get there . . . for free! Join us for our first journey around the world, as we introduce *ROX* to the Internet, and the Internet to *ROX*.

ROX Update:
The cable access program that refused to die. As this book went to press, ROX was resurrected by Free Speech TV (www.freespeech.org) and bicycled to cable access channels around the country. The Free Speech Web site also includes video excerpts of the show that can be viewed with VDOLive or RealVideo software.

themselves as the first TV show to be available on the Internet. They have several of their shows online (divided into chunky multimegabyte segments) and lots of additional material, all as clever and whacked out as their show.

T-Blackrox Crew (from left to right) Joe Nickel, Christy Paxson. Black photo by Paul. T-Blackrox photo by Paul Wershba.

VIDEO VIGILANTISM)

A deep male narrator's voice, filled with concern and edged by fear, speaks of dastardly crimes and natural disasters. The TV screen races through an unsettling montage of images: people being unceremoniously gunned down in convenience store stickups, a hurricane ripping a house to splinters, a college-party-turned-street-riot, police hammering defenseless protesters. The commercial ends with a pitch asking you to be a video watchdog for your local news program. Send in your videotapes of senseless crimes and cruel acts of God and get a pat on the back by your nightly newscaster.

Commercials similar to this played on TV stations across the country in the late '80s, each hailing the camcorder as the people's news-gathering weapon and deputizing their viewers as video gunslingers. Some people have taken this idea to heart, always traveling with their camcorder by their side, waiting for something newsworthy to happen within their viewfinder. The truly dedicated even scan police, emergency, and news team radio traffic, hoping to beat the pros to the scene. Welcome to the exciting world of eyewitness video.

Ever since the introduction of the portable camcorder in the 1980s, the media and the public have been enthralled by the idea of camera-equipped citizens operating as video vigilantes. The Scud missile attack on the U.S. military barracks in Saudi Arabia (caught on video by civilians in a neighboring hotel) and the Rodney King beating were two events that escalated the fervor over eyewitness video. Besides local news bureaus' celebration of amateur news gathering, TV shows like *I Witness Video* and *America's Funniest Home Videos* encourage viewers to send in tapes of crimes, accidents, and family pratfalls. Even the most gruesome images are presented, somehow made acceptable through the amateur's lens. Even the idea of "funny" gets stretched and twisted. *America's Funniest Home Videos* has shown a bride with her hair on fire, a toddler tickling his father while he bench-presses weights (causing the barbell to slam onto daddy's chest), a woman with her hair tangled inside a dishwasher, and a skier slamming full force into a tree. This is a TV executive's idea of sidesplitting fun.

The video vigilante crime and disaster shows are even more disturbing. This seems to be Hollywood's idea of what average citizens can and want to do with their camcorders. Interestingly enough, there's no show on mainstream TV that encourages citizens to use their cameras in the way that *ROX* and a handful of other quality cable-access shows do.

"OPEN CHANELS, OPEN MINDS") "Opinionated

individuals speak in their own voices at their own pace, free of the limitation of sound bites, makeup, or the framing of an interviewer's question. Underscoring their critiques are colorful hand-lettered placards bearing informative graphics which pass before the camera. This handmade look, a PTTV trademark, consciously encompasses both set enhancements (colorful backdrops and on-screen characterizations) and sound cues, camera shots of the crew and their technical transgressions. These 'mistakes' disrupt the insular nature of television production, proving to viewers that individuals of varying talent and economic circumstances (maybe even themselves!) can make worthwhile TV."

The speaker is Adriene Jenik of the infamous TV collective Paper Tiger Television (PTTV). Since 1981, PTTV has been cablecasting its multifaceted vision of people's TV on Manhattan cable and other access stations across the United States. The show was started when video producer DeeDee Halek had the bright idea of sitting author/media critic Herb Schiller down, letting him have his way with an issue of the *New York Times*, and recording the results. The show was such a success that Halek and the crew of independent producers she'd recruited decided to get other media critics to give their from-the-hip opinions on other popular and influential publications. Paper Tiger Television was born.

Over the years, PTTV has grown and expanded its coverage from critiquing print media to critiquing all forms of media and consumer culture. Another group, Deep Dish TV, has spun off from PTTV to distribute alternative programming to stations throughout the United States. An additional PTTV collective has been started in San Francisco. Over the years, Paper Tiger/Deep Dish have become the biggest success stories in cable access/alternative TV. Besides their own programming, these collectives are very helpful in getting the work of other groups distributed and in helping to teach people how to get involved in DIY media. In 1995, the group produced two shows, "Staking a Claim in Cyberspace" and "NetRoots," to examine the so-called digital revolution with questions about equal access and its relevance to diverse American communities.

FUN WITH LOW-FIDELITY
and ENDANGERED CINEMA) It could be argued that
film is not suited to the DIY mind-set of this book. It is usually not cheap
to shoot film, requiring expensive gear, a crew, outside processing, spe-
cialized equipment for projection, and a suitable projection space. But there
are some unique aspects of film that make it worth considering.

The so-called small-gauge or home-gauge film technologies (Super 8,
Regular 8, Pixelvision) embody DIY potential because they, like video, offer
aim-and-shoot ease, but with far more appealing photographic quality than
video. And in today's video age, the obstacles facing small gauge producers
—locating hard-to-find equipment and processing, finding ways to exhibit,
creating distribution channels—provide a challenge not unlike saving an
endangered species, or in this case, an endangered media technology.

The workability and spontaneity offered by the small gauges has brought
amateur artists with new visions onto the scene. Not surprisingly, small-
gauge filmmakers celebrate the grainy, low-tech production values that
"film professionals" disdain. It's the challenges of low/no-budget filmmaking that knit the small-gauge community together. They need each other
for technical and moral support, equipment sharing, and production tips.
Also, these makers share an idealism that says it's worthwhile to make and
share personal images different from the dominant visual aesthetics of
Hollywood and mainstream TV.

To the growing hordes of high-tech media hackers, film may seem
anachronistic and limiting because of its reliance on nondigital
technology for recording and presenting images. Without the translation
to digital or video, film cannot be broadcast, appear on home video, or find
its way onto the Internet. But there's a very positive social aspect to

consider: unlike television, home video, or computer-based imaging, film—due to the special conditions under which it must be presented— requires people to get off their couches to gather at screenings, festivals, exhibitions, and public art spaces. This social dimension helps sustain local and regional film scenes, and directly or indirectly supports the development of member organizations, film festivals, arts centers, and alternative publications.

Even people who don't have direct exposure to experimental and no-budget filmmaking are no doubt familiar with many of the techniques pioneered by these artists: layered film, defaced film, found or appropriated footage, handmade effects, nonnarrative structures, disjointed editing, optical print- ing, and so forth. MTV owes (but will never pay) a huge debt to experimen- tal filmmakers who've developed a visual vocabulary that music video producers (and the ad industry) have capitalized on in a big way.

Increasingly, independents are choosing to combine the best of available media in new ways: to combine the photographic superiority of film with the advantages of video, computer graphics, and digital editing. This mutant blend of technologies has been dubbed *low-fi* filmmaking. Lissa Gibbs of Film Arts Foundation in San Francisco says: "Low-fi is both an aesthetic and a method of production. As an aesthetic, it implies a certain distressed, funky, organic, or simple look. It's a home version of high tech and may include co-opted or appropriated sounds or images. As a method of production, *low-fi* generally means that the work was made with cheap technologies and with a bare-bones crew (often the filmmaker does every- thing him/herself). It also refers to the low-end technologies used in pro- duction, such as home computers and software, pro-sumer DAT and four-track recording decks, Fisher-Price Pixelvision cameras, Super 8, 16mm Bolex cameras, Hi-8 video, and Casio keyboards."

One of the best examples of the resurgence in Super 8 is the Flicker film group in Athens, Georgia. Started in 1992, Flicker holds well-attended screenings every other month at Athens's popular 40-Watt Club. Many producers have taken film courses there with local filmmaker Jim Herbert, who has produced music videos for REM. Flicker has had lots of outside interest from independents who want to submit their work, but organizer Angie Grass and company stay true to Flicker's original vision of only showing work by those in, or with a strong connection to, Athens and only films that have originated on Super 8. Inspired by the success of Athens's Flicker, other groups have started up in Tampa, Florida, and Chapel Hill, North Carolina.

It's very significant that groups like these still exist and that new ones continue to emerge. In the late '80s, artists who worked in and celebrated this medium long after home users flocked to video saw a virtual stampede of Super 8 production. It's a tricky endeavor to make 8mm in the '90s, yet any demand these makers can create will keep the medium alive. Clearly, Super 8 makers get a monster buzz from producing under the commercial radar, raiding closets of extended family members and haunting flea markets and yard sales in search of footage and forgotten equipment. They're actively thinking of ways to strengthen their network and to make Super 8mm more accessible and equipment more serviceable in the future.

INDEPENDENT VIDEO COALITION)

FROM "MEDIA BUST" by E. Saks >

Every eighteen months in Los Angeles an amazing thing happens. All across the L.A. sprawl, in the oddest places, media art screenings pop up. One night it might be at a community center or high school, the next, at a grungy bar downtown. Suddenly, local public access stations, which beam into nearly half the homes in town, begin screening hours and hours of experimental film and video. This inclusive, multicultural festival, as diverse as Los Angeles itself, is put together by a band of curators and community representatives who call themselves L.A. Freewaves.

Although emphatically consensus-driven, L.A. Freewaves is very much the brain- and love child of Anne Bray, a film curator and teacher. The festival is put together by curators from all corners of the L.A. demographic, and its success depends on their knowledge and familiarity with each venue and audience. A representative of the Latino community center might have a program already in mind; other groups might want Freewaves to put something together for them. Organizers participate according to their needs and abilities, with a month-long program of politically focused work, or one night of shorts from the local high school's animation lab. The resulting Freewaves printed program is a dizzying menu of media art delicacies served up in diverse locations, offering Angelenos an opportunity to interact with one another in a manner slightly different from flipping one another off on the freeway.

Freewaves was formed rather casually in 1989 on a shoestring budget of $15,000. "We were the only people coming to each other's screenings," says

Bray, who is as proud of the group's networking as she is of the festival itself. "It's been an educational process for all of us." The mission statement is an affirmation of the community-forming power of art, and especially media art, which is viewed in groups. Other Freewaves goals include "empowering communities with control over their own images and access to the images created by other cultures," sharing resources, fostering multicultural collaboration, challenging audiences, paying artists, creating more knowledgeable viewers, and encouraging public awareness of the media art community in general.

Currently operating with a budget of about $40,000, Freewaves has recently achieved non-profit status and received grants from the country's leading foundations. Bray is exploring new media with her usual gusto and Freewaves is sponsoring a three-part conference series on digital film and video, multimedia, and networks. These "DigiDaze" vary slightly from other Freewaves projects in that they're aimed at media makers. There are hands-on seminars, theoretical panels, displays of the latest work, and speakers who discuss the transitions and pitfalls of new formats. Other projects include free distribution of tapes of Freewaves programming to local high schools and public libraries, a night of screenings at a drive-in theater, and a Web page of local media resources.

 **PIXELVISIONARY)** While independent film is currently in vogue as a launching pad for directors on their way to the studio system, fringe filmmaker Eric Saks remains staunchly low budget and self-financed. When grant money dried up in the early 1990s, Saks turned from feature work to shorter, cheaper formats, using puppets instead of

actors, and embracing the grainy world of the Fisher-Price Pixelvision toy camera. In a series of Public Service Announcements (PSAs) over the past few years, Saks has managed to comment on the National Security Agency's Clipper Chip, the tiki revival, phone phreaking, and more, all within the constraints of the thirty-second format. But he is best known for his work with Pixelvision.

Introduced in the early 1980s, the Fisher-Price PXL2000 camera was originally designed for children, recording chunky, black-and-white motion images onto ordinary audiotape. With its low price and retro-trash aesthetics, it was a natural for artists to take up the medium. Saks was among the first, and in 1989, he released *Don from Lakewood,* created with Saks's frequent collaborator, Patrick Tierney. *Don* is the story of a prank, an endless phone call from hell, acted out by puppets. Tierney plays the title character, who repeatedly calls an unsuspecting furniture salesman with a series of off-the-wall demands. In this adversarial conversation, a strange sort of relationship unfolds as each character speaks according to his diametrically opposed moral viewpoint. *Don* contains many of the hallmark themes of a Saks production: a disturbing failure to communicate, two parties held hostage by the duplicitous potential of conversation, and the subversive possibilities of everyday technology.

Saks went on to become a leader in the Pixelvision "movement," organizing its first national shows and introducing haute pixel artist Sadie Bening to the rest of the world. Throughout his career, Saks has worked to develop and expand independent media. For one year, he served as president of L.A.'s Film Forum, an organization that brings underground and experimental films into the coffee shops normally filled with studio production assistants and executive wannabes. Oddly enough, Saks seems prouder of his work in the state prison system, where he's worked with inmates in a variety of formats. One assumes that this place of confinement and codification will be seeping into his future work. (One also wonders what the hell the prison authorities were thinking.) You can rest assured that whatever Eric gets out of this experience, he'll twist the expected themes and assumptions to his own provocative ends.

CRAIG BALDWIN:
FILMMAKER, DUMPSTER-DIVER) Working in a porn theater in San Francisco in the early '70s, Craig Baldwin found himself literally up to his eyeballs in film. Celluloid strips cluttered the walls, the floor, and the other surfaces around him. As the theater projectionist, Baldwin spent hours watching film after film, gradually discovering that he preferred viewing films when he was close to the screen, obsessively studying the array of textures, the washes of color, and the cacophony of flickering grain. Picking up footage from the booth's floor, Baldwin began to put his own films together. His first project, *Flick Skin,* marked the beginning of his obsession with what he calls "electronic folk culture." "I felt totally empowered," he says. "I had a theater, I had all these projectors, and I had all this footage. I could re-fashion it, re-purpose it, and invite my friends over to watch."

> ^
> CRAIG BALDWIN,
> Photo by L. Eanes

Rejecting the gloss of Hollywood, along with its considerable psychological lures—catharsis, identification, and cheap vicarious thrills—Baldwin chose instead to cobble together projects from the detritus of the film industry. He used the "trash" that was readily available in the dumpsters around the city, on odd reels, trailers, and quirky industrial films, all of which Baldwin still avidly collects. "My whole approach is really about collage, or bricolage, and it's basically a natural, intuitive response to my environment, which is a media-saturated one," he explains. "With humor, playfulness, and a little bit of perversity, I create these hand-made subversive gestures. I call it 'Cinema Povera.'"

After his porn theater stint, Baldwin spent several years creating multiple-projector shows for clubs. He then attended film school, where he made several films, including *Wild Gunman* (1978), another collage and found-footage film. Over the years, Baldwin's work has grown increasingly political. *Tribulation 99* (1991) is a hyperkinetic gloss on conspiracy theories, visions of the apocalypse, and a host of governmental blunders, rendered through found footage. *!O No Coronado!* (1992) takes on colonialism, again through found footage. Baldwin's most recent film, his first feature, is *Sonic Outlaws*, a wild ride through the world of found sound/audio collage artists such as Negativland, The Tape-Beatles, and John Oswald, querying along the way issues of copyright, fair use, and the ownership of the public airwaves.

Since 1983, Baldwin has programmed weekly screenings of alternative media under the banner "Other Cinema" at the Artists Television Access (ATA) space in San Francisco. "It's a one-person operation, more like a garage than a regular theater," explains Baldwin. Using the collector sensibility that makes his found-footage projects so remarkable, Baldwin hunts down unusual films, conjuring brilliant and eclectic programs and creating a place for work that may not be programmed in other venues. "I like the stuff that falls between the cracks, the more political issue-oriented and contemporary stuff," says Baldwin. And, living up to the "povera" of its nickname, the place itself is resolutely, uh, comfortable.

"I'm usually peeking down at the bulb, chanting to the projector not to quit, and holding the sound cable together in my hand," says Baldwin, who takes a kind of perverse pride in creating this type of Band-Aid and bailing wire cinema.

THE EXHIBITION(ISTS)) The following filmmakers share a lot in terms of resourcefulness, problem solving, and suspicion of traditional filmmaking and exhibition. There's a definite trend afoot to undermine the prestige-based screenings of museum programs and competitive film festivals.

Experimental Filmmaker Jon Rubin)

Throughout the late '70s and early '80s, Jon Rubin explored ways of letting people experience film without the usual professional or commercial "filters" such as television and film programmers, marketing whizzes, museum curators, and the humming hype-machinery of Hollywood. Rubin and his accomplices (generally his students) created situations in which people could encounter experimental/alternative film through happenstance. Rubin pioneered ambulatory screenings, live film processionals with thirty to forty participants, sometimes in costume, hoisting a rear projection system—projector, screen, speakers and all—through the streets of Boston. At Hampshire College, Rubin taught an experimental film course as part of a summer institute. At the end of the course, he and the students showed student films on a raft in the campus pond using a makeshift rear-screen projection. The evening turned into something of a bacchanal. Rubin decided the event had "fit a key into a particular psychic lock," and that he would develop the idea even further. He began traveling by river—at least in part because it's one of those great American romances—with a group of students and two pontoon boats. They traveled down the Allegheny River, the Ohio River, and had a two-week outing on the Erie barge canal. Heading westward, they began trying to find places where people would hang out on the river's edge. They would set up completely out of site and then send the first pontoon out with a film image of a disembodied pair of lips saying, "Where am I?, Where am I?" Soon, the other pontoon would follow, offering some kind of response, and the show would begin. On moonless nights, claims Rubin, these projections rivaled the strangeness of a UFO experience. Rubin would hide on shore, where he would radio technical instructions to his crew and occasionally eavesdrop on crowd reactions, which he found fascinating. Once onlookers felt sure the apparitions weren't selling anything or touting a political candidate, they'd be attentive. Rubin's favorite occurrence: Two eagle-eyed state troopers raced onto the scene, hands on holsters. At a loss to identify the crime being committed, they soon sat down on the river's edge and began enjoying the show.

[J A M E S   S T E W A R T : The revenge of Toronto independent filmmaker James Stewart won't soon be forgotten by organizers of the 1993 Toronto Film Festival. Stewart's film *Teen* was rejected for their Perspective Canada series. Deciding he wanted his fellow Torontonians to at least have the chance to judge for themselves, he secured a special xenon-bulb projector, a set of powerful speakers, and set up across the street from Eaton Centre, one of Canada's largest shopping malls. He beamed his film onto the center's vast windowless white exterior, stopping traffic on Yonge Street and attracting local television and print media coverage as well as the police. Naturally, Stewart had timed his screenings to catch the festival attendees across the street going into (and coming out of) one of the festival's gala events. Stewart enjoyed more visibility this way than if he'd played by the rules. *Teen* later won the audience award at a festival in Belfast.

Highway Cinema)

Once a year, Hunter Mann of Bellingham, Washington, climbs onto his souped-up mountain bike, hitches on a hefty trailer, and hits the low roads of North America. The 200-pound custom bike and trailer carries a 16mm film projector, a folding screen, a sound system, and Mann's life support for the next few months. For three years running, he's brought his Traveling Film Festival to cinema-deprived locations: islands, tiny desert towns (population 75), and Native American reservations. Mann embarked on his first Highway Cinema tour in 1993, huffin' his way from Washington State to Minnesota. In '94, this cinematic missionary hauled his church from Seattle, Washington, to Southern California, to the "twilight zone desert towns" of Nevada. In 1995, Mann toured the San Juan and Gulf Islands of Washington and western Canada. For one showing, Mann had to row out to an island with a 400-foot electrical cord in tow.

"Jamming the Media? You bet!," boasts Mann. "I've shown movies in the darnedest places: laundromats, bowling alleys, campsites, churches, bars, a rock quarry, barbershops, Indian reservations, rooftops, trailer parks, RVs." He doesn't do it for money, he doesn't even charge for the showings. He just gets off on sharing the communal experience of film and the memorable responses he gets from viewers. He tells one particular story about two men at a small-town showing who seemed to really be enjoying each other's company, staying seated after the rest of the audience had left. "You seem to be having a good time," said Mann, as he packed up his gear. Turns out, this was the first time they'd spoken in over four years. The two ranchers had locked horns over a land dispute and had not talked to each other since. The next morning, as Mann was blowing out of town, he saw the men again, in the local diner, chatting over breakfast. "Lots of people are under the impression that small-town people are all close and friendly to each other," offers Mann. "This hasn't been my experience. Highway Cinema provides an excuse for them to get together. Many of the places don't have a theater, or if they do, it's perpetually showing *Waterworld 3* or *Rambo 14*. My films are different." The roster includes old comedy and cartoons (Laurel and Hardy, Betty Boop, Chaplin), independent shorts, and a feature-length low budget film by Harrod Blank called *Wild Wheels*. Mann, who does TV and movie production work when he's not on the road, plans to start work soon on his own no-budget feature that he'll eventually add to the Highway Cinema program. He also dreams of taking the show overseas, to places like Puerto Rico, Latin America, Spain, Italy, Greece, France, and Africa. So far, he's hauled his theater on wheels over 7,000 miles and has given 286 screenings. "Sometimes I think about upgrading from a bike to a Harley, but whenever I mention this to people, they seem disappointed . . . like I'd be killing the charm of the thing. I have to agree." Mann has to end the phone interview now. He's calling from the road, and that road, and the little entertainment-starved town at the end of it, is calling. Highway Cinema rides again.

The Low Res Digital Film and Video Festival)

In 1994, Bart Cheever and Jonathan Wells threw a Christmas party in their San Francisco basement to show their short no-budget digital film *Slacker Cop 3* and some other friend's digital shorts. They realized how many people were doing interesting work on home computers and after hours at multimedia and film companies (both worked at Digital Pictures). They decided, since they had drawn a crowd to their little informal screening, that they should organize a festival. The result is the Low Res Digital Film and Video Festival, a touring festival with films by such well-knowns as Spike Jonze, Sofia Coppola, Emergency Broadcast Network, and Dame Darcy, and such undiscovered talent as *ROX*, Cameron Noble, and Uruma Delvi. "The goal of the Low Res Digital Film and Video Festival is to expose and inspire innovative films and videos created with desktop digital tools. These digital tools have enabled filmmakers and videographers to write, shoot, edit, create visuals effects, and mix sound on a single desktop computer . . . " The 1996 festival included work done in computer animation, Hi-8, 16mm, and 35mm. It traveled through San Francisco, Los Angeles, Rotterdam (Holland), and New York. After the '96 Low Res festival, Bart and Jonathan parted company. Bart is now heading up D.Film Digital Film Festival, and Jonathan is organizing Res Fest '97. Both festivals are now accepting submissions for future festivals.

PAPER TIGER TELEVISION

BROADCAST PIRATES)

Everybody loves a TV pirate . . . or at least the romantic image of one. If you bring up TV pirates, and the apocryphal stories that surround them, in a discussion, you'll get lots of interest from people, but little hard information. Documentation of known acts of TV piracy are few and far between.

On April 27, 1986, TV viewers watching *The Falcon and the Snowman* on HBO did a collective doubletake when the screen was replaced by a color-bar test pattern with a message typed onto it: "Good evening HBO from

Captain Midnight. $12.95 a month? No way! (Showtime—Movie Channel Beware.)." Several seconds into this image jamming, the screen started flashing back and forth in a tug of war between the HBO signal and the pirate message, which went on ranting about cable's new scrambling practices. This bizarre battle for the cablewaves lasted for $4\,^1/_2$ minutes.

"Captain Midnight" turned out to be John R. MacDougall, a satellite dish salesman from Ocala, Florida. His pirate broadcast was no great media hack. MacDougall was an employee at Central Florida Teleport, one of the few satellite transmission facilities with enough juice to overpower an HBO satellite feed. This facility was quickly singled out and the media spotlight soon trained on MacDougall.

TV pirate stories are the stuff of urban legend: widely reported, but with shady origins. There's the one about the guy who made a small transmitter, bundled it with a VCR, a timer, and an antenna, and put it all in his car. He parked the car next to a cable satellite uplink and when the timer went off (and he was elsewhere), his pirate signal was beamed skyward. As the story goes, when the timer stopped, he nonchalantly got back in his car and drove away. The tale does not include the details of his message or motive. Another pirate story that I've heard told by people from different regions of the country involves a guy in a Max Headroom mask brandishing an arsenal of sex toys and spouting nonsense.

A British fellow sent me email recounting a well-known incident of U.K. pirates using BBC 2 after hours to transmit porno movies. They "borrowed" a medium-power relay from the BBC/ITV transmitter relay station at Brighton Race Course on the south coast of Britain. At the time (at least as he tells it), the BBC was powerless to stop the signal jamming as they had yet to find the need for an "off" switch. Needless to say, they found one.

Given the few documented incidents of TV piracy, it's interesting to discover how easy it actually is to get an audio or audio/video signal onto the TV airwaves. One can create a microTV station using a VCR, an antenna amplifier, a VHF antenna, and a matching transformer. The resulting signal will reach about a mile. Other more powerful units for both VHF and UHF broadcasting can be built with off-the-shelf parts and plans available in electronics magazines and on the Internet.

The main reason for lack of activity in pirate TV is the severity of the law. While the FCC is serious enough with tracking down and fining unlicensed radio broadcasters, they have no tolerance for those disrupting TV signals. And neither does the TV industry or the general public. When Captain Midnight pulled his little media rant, industry spokespeople and citizens were outraged. They spoke of being violated, ripped off, terrorized. Even those sympathetic to pirate pranks wouldn't tolerate them too often. Who wants to be interrupted in the middle of an *X-Files* episode with some semi-intelligible rabble about cable rates? Don't tread on my TV! (at least not during one of the few decent shows on the box).

THE EDGY BROADCASTER'S STARTER KIT)

This Starter Kit has been divided into two sections, one covering Public Access Television, the other Video and Filmmaking.

Public Access TV (PATV))

GETTING STARTED

The steps to public access are usually short and easily negotiated. There are differences depending on who your cable company is and what arrangement they've made for providing access, but most PATV facilities have similar procedures. The first thing you'll want to find out is if you, in fact, have cable access or some other form of community-accessible TV. If you have a cable company in your area, you probably have an access channel. If you live in a rural area that doesn't have cable, you still may have a low-power broadcast community station you could get involved in. Your phone book and public library would be good places to start.

ONCE YOU'VE FOUND THE CABLE-ACCESS CHANNEL:

1) Call and ask for the person who coordinates access. Ask them for a schedule or more background information. Some channels have orientations and tour nights. To be able to do anything else, you'll probably have to become a supporting member of the channel (usually requiring a nominal annual fee).

2) The next thing you'll need to do is get training and the certification needed to actually work on cable shows. There's usually a basic training, more advanced training (for things like location shooting), and periodic seminars in various specialties (interviewing, sound, etc.).

3) Once you have certification—if you have a show you want to program— you can put your name on a waiting list. You'll need to work with the program coordinator to nail down the schedule. The waiting list doesn't necessarily mean that you'll have a long wait. The channel likes to at least have enough lead time to publicize your show in their newsletter, the on-screen electronic bulletin board, and/or the local TV listings. A month is a common waiting period.

4) Before your show can be cablecast, you'll also need to sign a Channel Use Agreement. This indemnifies the channel and makes you responsible for

the content of your program and the transportation of your videotapes to and from the station. These agreements usually tie your show's content to local and state indecency laws and specify that your show has no overt commercial content.

Production)

Make sure you set realistic goals for your first effort. As the folks at Paper Tiger Television suggest, don't knock yourself out producing fancy sets and on-screen computer-generated graphics and titling. Make sure the content is strong and let everything else work off of that. PTTV uses painted backdrops and simple handheld placards.

You don't have to commit to a series of programs, either. Once you've been certified, you can put a show together whenever you're inspired to do so (as long as the equipment is available). After your show is complete, you work it out with the program coordinator how frequently it can run. If you get a good response, you might be inspired to produce more episodes, eventually going for a regular schedule.

Most channels use ³/₄-inch U-matic tape and require that your show be delivered in the same format. The channel's studios will usually have facilities to transfer to ³/₄-inch if you've shot part or all of your show in some other format.

Since it's unlikely that you can single-handedly produce a cable show, you'll need to assemble a crew. Most CATV studios have sign-up sheets where certified members can volunteer to crew different programs. While these volunteers represent a crew pool you can draw from, it's best if you can put together a crew of people you want to work with. That way, you know everyone is on the same wavelength in terms of the show's approach and content. It's much more fun working with a creative team when everyone's working towards a common vision. But if you find yourself short a crewmember or two, you can get a list from the station of available volunteers.

Distribution)

Getting your show distributed on your local access channel is done through the program coordinator. But you don't have to stop there. Through a process called *bicycling*, you can get your show cablecast on access stations throughout the country. This process takes a fair amount of work and isn't something you should jump into right away. You'll need to find people in other cities and towns who want to sponsor your show on their access station. They'll probably need to be a member/supporter of the station and willing to fill out a form (Channel Use Agreement) making them responsible for the content of your show. If you can find people willing to do this, you probably have a pretty great show. Once you get a number of these out-of-town venues lined up, you'll need to coordinate getting show tapes to them to meet their station's schedule. This can get confusing, so it's best to start with one additional cable station at a time and add stations as time and energy permit.

Another way of distributing your show is via mail-order tapes. This is probably not an option for most access producers, but it has worked for some shows. Mail-order distribution will generate a demand that cannot be met through bicycling or any other means. You can dub the videos yourself (if you have tape-to-tape capability) or find a local tape duplicator to dub them in bulk. Obviously, if you go this route, you'll have to put energy into promoting your program outside your access area (See Promotion and Advertising below).

....

If you do a cable-access show, make sure to give a postal and/or email address so that interested viewers can get in touch with you. If you've just done one installment and are wondering if you should do more, ask people for their input. You might also get volunteers this way who can help you with production or financial support.

It's also becoming possible to distribute programming over the Internet. The *ROX* cable show from Bloomington, Indiana, and *CamNet* have sites on the World Wide Web with episode segments available for downloading. The *ROX* site includes an episode summary and ordering information. Current modem speeds and affordable hardware make distributing even parts of shows over the Net unrealistic, but that will change soon enough. In a few short years, you'll be able to easily download a half-hour show cheaper than if you bought it on tape through the mail (although the quality will remain sub-standard for some time to come). The current rage on the Internet is streaming video, which delivers video as it's downloading. This technology is crude but improving.

Promotion and Advertising)

Promoting a cable show can feel like an uphill battle. Talk to the program coordinator to take advantage of whatever promotion and advertising the station provides. Some areas now print the cable-access schedule in the Sunday paper's TV listings. You should also try to get your show listed in other local newspapers, magazines, and zines. If you're feeling ambitious, you can print up flyers and post them around bookstores, cafes, college bulletin boards, and other public places.

You'll also want to have an exemplary episode or a "best-of" compilation on VHS tapes that you can give out to the press. Most of the access shows I contacted for this book were more than eager to send me a "reel" of shows and promotional materials.

Speaking of promo materials, you'll also want to put some together your-self. It doesn't need to be elaborate, just a factsheet about your show and any reviews you've received.

Of course, if you want to get involved in public access, you don't have to start your own show. There may be existing shows, or shows in the planning stages, that could use your help. Check sign-up sheets and bulletin boards at the station or talk to someone who's involved in access.

Video and Film)

In covering film for this book, I've only looked at super-low-budget efforts. I've limited discussion to a particular spectrum of filmmaking—the small gauges: Super 8mm, Regular 8mm, Pixelvision, and very low-end 16mm.

<u>GETTING STARTED</u>

There's no way to be comprehensive about small-gauge film and video aesthetics and technology in such a short section. I've tried to give an overview, and more importantly, to suggest key resources and areas for further exploration.

[**C O N S I D E R I N G   V I D E O** : Video is relatively cheap to make, produce, duplicate, and distribute, and almost everyone has access to a playback machine. If you don't own a camera, you undoubtedly know someone who does. By borrowing a good camera, a video deck or two, and a good external microphone, you're in business. Once you get your feet wet, you can invest in your own equipment. Mail-order electronics houses and the classifieds are good places to look for cheap new and used gear. If you want to go the desktop video route, you'll need a high-end audio-video computer with special software.

[**C O N S I D E R I N G   8 M M   F I L M** : The "home movie gauges," Super 8mm and Regular 8mm, the point and shoot (or wind, point, and shoot) cameras that many baby boomers will remember from their childhood, seem like a thing of the past. Gear for these gauges is no longer widely available and processing labs that handle 8mm are now hard to find. But this hasn't stopped the fringe art community from embracing 8mm. The simple

For simplicity sake, I'm using the term 8mm to refer to both Super 8mm and Regular 8mm filmmaking. When I need to specifically refer to one type over the other, I add "Super" or "Regular."

operation, the particular aesthetic qualities, and the attraction to appropriating a dead medium have drawn many artists to 8mm (especially Super 8). These resuscitators of a near-dead technology sometimes go to great lengths for their art, including buying 16mm film, slicing it down the middle, and punching sprocket holes to make 8mm stock. For those who do choose to get involved in 8mm, you will find a great community of artists, hobbyists, and technicians dedicated to keeping this medium alive.

For makers eager to create personal or diaristic works, 8mm has the considerable benefit of being the gauge onto which your parents and grandparents captured family footage, making it easy to incorporate vintage 8mm material into your film.

[C O N S I D E R I N G   1 6 M M   F I L M : The technical requirements of 16mm can be intimidating for the novice. Depending on your choice of location, you'll need light meters, special lighting for indoor shoots, as well as an understanding of filters, film speeds, and complicated editing processes. Once mastered, 16mm offers technical sophistication and better exhibition potential opportunities. Some 16mm makers like San Francisco independent Greta Snider—whose experimental short *Futility* cost almost nothing to make and now sits in the Museum of Modern Art— exemplify a certain breed of filmmaker who uses cast-off equipment (cameras and projectors are getting ditched all over the place by schools and other institutions), found footage, non-sync sound, and hand processing. If you find yourself attracted to working in 16mm, go for it. As long as you don't make some huge initial investment, you can always move on to a medium less challenging and less expensive. Before you jump in, be sure to read up on no-budget filmmaking (in magazines such as *Filmmaker* and *The Independent)* and try to talk to some filmmakers. Most low-budget practitioners are open about sharing the trials and tribulations of working with no money, no crew, and begged, borrowed, or stolen gear.

TOOLS AND EQUIPMENT

[**V I D E O** : What type of video equipment you'll need depends a lot on how you'll use it and how much money you care to spend. As I've said above, borrowing equipment first might be your best bet. You can even try borrowing a number of different systems until you find the one that works best for you. Today's 8mm video camcorders are reasonably priced and super lightweight. Their portability makes them easy to carry. People even seem more open and less intimidated by videographers wielding smaller cameras. One drawback to these cameras is that they require an adapter cassette to play on a VHS-type deck and they need to be transferred to VHS for distribution. Hi-8 is the best quality consumer-grade video camera. This improved picture quality can be important if you're going to be doing multiple generation edits and dubs. Hi-8 is the high-end of consumer grade and continues to improve in quality and added features (and price) all the way up to professional grade. If you really get into it and want to produce tightly edited material with titling and other effects, you'll need to buy (or gain access to) multiple editing decks and other editing and effects equipment. Other amateurs who've invested in lots of video gear are usually underutilizing it and are good candidates for loaning (or renting) their equipment.

If you want to explore digital video, you'll need special hardware and software. Besides a good camera (at least a Hi-8), you'll need a video card, a fast computer, and lots of hard disk space. You will also need software for video capture, editing, and effects. Some popular packages are Adobe Premier and VideoShop (capture and editing), AfterEffects and Elastic Reality (for compositing, graphics, and special effects), and SoundEdit 16 and Sonic Foundry (audio editing and processing).

[**8 M M   F I L M** : The international community of 8mm makers must employ a hunter and gatherer approach to locating out-of-production items like cameras, editing equipment, vintage film stock, etc. Technical self-sufficiency in 8mm can be achieved by investing only a small amount in hardware, as opposed to self-sufficiency in 16mm or video which requires a lot more money. Film-related publications and Internet sites (see Resources below) are great places to find equipment for sale and labs that do 8mm processing. Don't forget to ask friends and family as well. You'd be surprised how many people have old 8mm equipment tossed into the backs of closets and attics.

[**1 6 M M   F I L M** : Should you decide to create in 16mm, you may be able to find training, access to equipment, technical and moral support from a media arts center (see Organizations below). Of course, the fates of these organizations in the United States are tied to that of the National Endowment of the Arts, so staking your creative efforts on their future may be tricky. If you decide to become technically self-sufficient in 16mm (i.e., buying your own camera and editing equipment), you'll need to spend lots of money, even for old, used gear. Again, your best bet is to initially borrow gear for your first project to see if 16mm is the gauge for you. If you decide you're serious and want to take the plunge, you can use the zines, guides, and organizations listed below to help you hunt down reasonably priced equipment. One good thing about 16mm is that, unlike 8mm, film stock, cameras, and editing equipment are still in production, readily available, and easily serviceable.

PRODUCTION

Learning the ins and outs of video and film production is not hard, but you should consider some learning time. Many local communities offer courses on home video production. Taking the inexpensive classes at your cable-access station is a good and inexpensive way to learn basic studio and field production. Much of what you learn there can be applied to all types of video and film production. There are also a large number of useful books available on video and filmmaking, as well as courses available on video-tape. Check your local library and video store for these. *Videomaker Magazine* (see Resources below) has an excellent introductory course on video making available at their Web site. Filmmaking classes may be harder to find. Local/regional media arts centers are good places to start looking.

DISTRIBUTION

[**V I D E O** : See the Distribution section in Cable Access above for ideas on distributing video.

[**8 M M   A N D   1 6 M M   F I L M** : Film distribution is a rough-and-tumble, dog-eat-dog business. There are, however, a few avenues open to the low/no-budget alternative filmmaker:

1) Many media arts centers take on a quasi-distribution role for their members. They might do anything from member screenings to maintaining a membership database or film/video databank that can be consulted by interested visitors. Staff members may also aggressively promote their member artists' works to outside programmers. Contact NAMAC (see Resources below) to find the media arts center closest to you.

One of the most basic production tips for film and video makers is called "The Rule of Thirds." Think of the image in your viewfinder as a tic-tac-toe board divided into thirds horizontally and vertically (nine sections). To add dynamism to your shots, your subjects should ideally fall somewhere along the lines or at the points where the lines meet. If your subject is off to one side or smack in the middle all the time, you'll have a more static image. Of course this is a rule of thumb, and you know what they say about rules.

2) Two of the most accessible options for new unknown film- and video makers are Canyon Cinema in San Francisco and Film-Maker's Cooperative in New York (see Resources below). Both distribute 16mm, Super 8mm, and video. Canyon Cinema was established as a cooperative of filmmakers in 1967 and has been operated as such ever since. They ask $40 yearly for membership, which includes a listing of members' film(s) in their catalog. They have 400 members, and represent 3,500 film titles (mostly 16mm) and 500 video titles.

3) There are few options for getting your 8mm work screened beyond your local supporters. Exhibition is limited and tends to be organized on a grass-roots level. Your finished film can, however, be transferred to 16mm or video (with grainier results) and possibly, if you've got something really special, have a life of its own on the festival circuit or with alternative exhibitors (refer to *AIVF* and *AEIOU* guides listed in Resources).

Currently, there are virtually no 8mm distribution channels. The gauge enables personal expression and complete artistic control. It attracts both professional and nonprofessional artists alike.

....

Before you go putting your entire life onto videotape, be forewarned: all forms of magnetic tape (audio, video, and data) have been found to be vulnerable to what's called the "sticky-shed" syndrome. After about ten years, the layer beneath the oxide begins to deteriorate. If the tape is played, it may function the first time, but the stress will begin separating the substrate layers, rendering the tape "dead." Rumor has it that much of the network archives of video from the 1960s and 1970s is already unusable, or in bad shape. People who've dubbed their old 8mm home movies onto video now find that it's deteriorating faster than the original film (having been subjected to too many wedding and birthday videos, this may not be such a bad thing after all). There is one home-brew remedy that's reportedly able to prolong terminally ill tapes. Placing them in an oven set to 120 degrees Fahrenheit for six hours will temporarily "cure" the sticky-shed problem for up to a month. During that time, the tape can be played several times without disintegration (enabling it to be copied or transferred). After that, the tape will quickly degrade and re-baking will not work. Bon appétit! [Thanks to Jim Leftwich for this tip.]

Ironically, while 8mm may be harder than ever to produce, it will soon be enjoying increased visibility thanks to a major exhibition that opened at New York's Museum of Modern Art in the fall of 1996 and runs through 1998. Jytte Jensen of the Museum of Modern Art and Steve Anchor of the San Francisco Cinematheque have devoted two years of research to the project tentatively titled *The Small Gauges: An American History*. Jensen describes the process as "a kind of archeology we have undertaken to discover what artists have put on Super 8mm and other small gauges from the '50s onward." Jensen says that the project has begun to take on a preservational dimension.

Words of Wisdom $)$

Rob Campanell (*Cyberia* TV show):

: If you're going to be doing your own show, don't watch network or major cable television. The more TV you watch, the greater the temptation is to produce programs that are similar to the status quo. You stand a better chance of producing creative and original programming when you avoid perceptions of standard programming.

: Collaborate with other DIY TV producers. Make friends with others who are producing similar shows. They can be helpful in locating resources. Friendly competition from other producers helps you improve the quality of your program, too.

: Check out CU-SeeME technology. This Internet-based broadcasting technology gives you the potential to send video images to a worldwide audience. Seize this technology now so that DIY producers can be the ones who shape and develop it.

: Don't rely on technology to improve the quality of your program. Determine the quality by the program's content, not a three-chip video camera or some other new techno-toy.

: Produce what you love. DIY television is very personal. Be proud of what you do. Your programs are video documentation of today's subculture trends. They will be important to social scientists in the future. Adopt good tape preservation practices and adequately document your efforts.

"J" (*ROX*) Video-making Tips

: Like most cable-access programs, *ROX* was a distinctly low-budget, homegrown affair. We held no pretense that it was anything but amateurish. However, despite our many technical, financial, emotional, and intellectual shortcomings, we did try to make the best of what we had. It's an endless learning process, and we're by no means experts. However, we have picked up a few useful ideas along the way, some of which might translate well to your particular approach to making video:

: Buy all your equipment on credit at major department stores. Find out their return policies. Use the equipment for as long as you can. Then take it back and tell your happy returns/exchanges clerk that "it just doesn't suit my needs," and demand a full refund.

: Always loop the camera strap around your neck. When you're looking through that little viewfinder, you're prone to trip over anything. Trust us; we've had too many near misses and one terrible tragedy involving J's motorcycle, a stop sign, and some very hard pavement.

: Take the lens cap off! Turn the camera on. Aim at your subject. These may seem like simple concepts, but you'd be surprised what happens when drug-laden fools like us pick up a camcorder.

: Don't forget freshly charged batteries. And extra tape.

: Don't tell the arresting officer that you're working for us, even if you are.

: Get close to your subject. Since video is usually shown on a much smaller screen than film— and because of basic differences between the two media—head-to-toe shots rarely look as good as up-close face shots. As an added bonus when not using a wireless or external microphone, this technique will also help keep the audio . . . um . . . audible.

: Focus on the action. If someone's talking about the blister on his/her left big toe, point the camera at the left big toe. If someone describes something they did yesterday, ask them afterward if they'd mind acting out the scene for use as a dramatic reenactment.

: Medium shots should generally frame your subject with his/her head near the top of the screen, rather than at the center or bottom. This rule does not apply in cases where your subject is standing on his/her head, or when he/she does not have a head.

: Vary your shooting angles. Be creative. But whatever you do, don't try climbing a tree with a rented camera!

: Don't shake the camera. Trust us. Most low-budget programs already look like one of those frenetic AT&T commercials. The picture shakes enough without any help from you. So try to move slowly or stand still. That way, it'll still have that homemade look without going overboard.

: Videotape outdoors whenever possible. Indoor video lights are expensive and a pain in the ass; and they don't allow for much spontaneity.

: Avoid extremely bright backgrounds, such as windows or nuclear explosions, and extremely dark backgrounds, such as outer space or black curtains. The former will reduce detail on your subject; the latter will make them look washed out.

How to Become a Successful UNDERGROUND Video Artist (or Just Act Like One) by Mikki Halpin, former contributing editor of *Filmmaker* magazine:

1. Be related to someone FAMOUS.

2. Dress really HIP and BE SEEN in all the RIGHT places.

3. PEPPER your speech with INDIE terms like *FOURWALLING*.

4. ESCHEW beepers and cell phones; instead, WRITE everyone's phone number ON LITTLE pieces of PAPER. KEEP ALL of these pieces in your pocket. When someone mentions that YOU OWE them a call, mumble about how DISORGANIZED you are, and CHANGE THE SUBJECT to your WORK.

5. Use EDGY, out-of-date media like PIXELVISION and Polaroids. APPROPRIATE their limitations as your "VISION."

6. Adopt a disjunctive NARRATIVE STYLE to make up for your ATTENTION DEFICIT DISORDER.

: Avoid using the zoom; get closer to your subject instead—unless you're taping lions or sharks at the zoo. Most new camera operators are zoom-happy; the resultant videos look like they were made during an earthquake.

: Use a wireless or directional microphone whenever possible. Even a cheap job will probably give you more focused sound than the mikes on your camera. Besides, it'll give your subject something to fidget with.

: Work with what you've got. Be creative with your resources. Did you ever see *Roger & Me*? One of the best flicks of all time, centering around a guy's failure to get an interview with the subject of his film. The trick is to transform weaknesses into strengths. Don't be tunnel-visioned and don't be anal.

: Reality, reality, reality. There's something about the nature of video as a medium that makes staged action almost always look stupid and fake. Use film if you're trying to create illusion; use video if you're trying to capture reality.

: Blow lots of tape. It's absurdly cheap, and if you're really stingy, you can even tape over the old crap. Whenever you're looking through the viewfinder, you might as well be recording (unless you don't plan to edit your videos later).

: Let your subject speak his/her/its mind. Feel free to talk from behind the camera, but if you're gonna say anything more than a sentence or two, hand the camera to someone else and talk to the lens.

: As you edit your videos, constantly ask yourself, "who is my audience, and will they care about this?" Don't be a pack-rat: Narrative succinctness is usually more important than exhaustive accuracy (tell that to your libel/slander lawyer!). Inside jokes and subtle cultural/media references tend to alienate all but your most loyal viewers.

: Focus on who you are and what you know. Honesty is key. Don't speak for others. Aim above the mundane but below prophesy . . . at least the first few times around. Be less than boastful but more than timid. Speak your mind.

: Brevity is the soul of wit. 'Nuff said?

A final inspirational message from your bartender, Joe Nickell:
: It's always better to make a video than not. You'll never make the perfect video. You'll never even make one you're completely happy with. If you do, then you're wrong. Or else I'm wrong. But the point I'm getting at here is that there are plenty of people out there who think forever about making a video, but they never get around to it, because they're afraid it'll suck, or they keep thinking of new ideas, or they think they just need to read one more of these inspirational books in order to know everything about making videos. Ideas are worthless if you don't share them. Creativity never happens through complete understanding of a process or medium. And the only way to learn is to just do it. Bump into walls, trip over yourself, but do it. And have fun. Because if you don't, you've wasted your time.

Tony Barreca (CEO, Magic Circle Media, Inc.):

: Here's a suggestion for anyone looking to break into film and video: Get your hands on a camera and go out and make films!

: If you want to learn to direct, I'd suggest that you start an acting company, shoot scenes from scripts that are generally recognized to be great, or at least very well written (so you can tell the difference between problems caused by the writing and problems caused by the directing —i.e., if the script is great, all the problems are caused by the directing), and try shooting them in a couple of different ways to see which ways work best. I did something like this several years ago on a shoestring—the whole thing cost me less than $1,000. And I learned an incredible amount about directing.

: To put together the acting company, I just put up flyers announcing a "Scene Study Workshop" at every acting school in the Bay Area. Almost 200 people showed up at my first meeting. I tried to scare most of them away, and ended up auditioning about 60 people, of whom I selected about half for the workshop.

Julia Pelosi (film programmer):
Advice to first-time filmmakers on getting your work shown:

: No matter what gauge or format your original work is on, you'll need to make VHS video copies of it to send out. You can access a lot of information about how to send your preview tapes to alternative venues and festivals with the *AEIOU Guide* for alternative venues and the *AIVF Guide to International Film and Video Festivals* (see Resources below). They are terrific references that will give you an idea of who accepts unsolicited work and what kinds of programming they offer. Most festivals charge entry fees and require that you fill out a special entry form and send it along with your submission. These charges can add up quickly, so before you write all those checks, remember: You may be able to attend a festival for the same price. On the other hand, the alternative venues in *AEIOU* don't usually charge and many program year-round so there are no deadlines to keep up with. If you are really interested in a particular exhibitor, you may want to call them and get on the mailing list for their program calendar. It will give you a good sense of what their specific interests are.

: Once you have a good-quality VHS preview tape to send out, don't forget to include the following essentials:

: An eye-catching one-page description of the film. Make sure the graphics and tone of the one-sheet parallel the sensibility of the film. Include any reviews you might have.

: Black-and-white stills of one or more images from your film (not of the director or crew). Color photos are good for impact but they generally don't reproduce well.

: A self-addressed stamped envelope if they ask for it. If you can get dubs done cheaply enough (by buying bulk VHS tape stock and doing tape-to-tape dubs yourself), you may not need to bother with the SASE since the required postage and shipping packet needed for it could cost more than your per-tape dubbing costs. If you do want the tape back, always write your name, phone, and address *on* the tape itself (not just the tape dustcover) as these things will likely get separated. If you got your dubs made by a professional duplicator, they often stick their own label and address on the finished product—make sure you cover this up. You'd be surprised how often a tape will get sent back to them instead.

7. **Get a significant other with good GRANT-WRITING SKILLS.**

8. **Do a BEASTIE BOYS video.**

9. **Remind people constantly that you DIDN'T GO to film school, THEN STUDY up secretly on Bazin, Mulvey, and Metz, so you seem like an IDIOT savant.**

10. **Claim that you NEVER, ever WATCH TELEVISION.**

It's impossible to overstress that you should generate the
most intriguing and striking photos possible because:

1) They will entice the receiver to view your film sooner rather than later (or not at all).

2) Programmers are always on the lookout for striking images to put in their program calendars and for publicity purposes.

3) If it gets used in the calendar or in a write-up, you'll have a great tool for promoting your film further.

4) If you get it published enough times, or in some publication that lots of programmers read, that photo can become a signature image for your film.

Resources)

BOOKS

AEIOU Guide*

FILM ARTS FOUNDATION (FAF)
346 NINTH STREET, 2ND FLOOR, SAN FRANCISCO, CA 94103
FAX: 415-552-0882
$6 AND A SELF-ADDRESSED MAILING LABEL

> Douglas Conrad of Film Arts Foundation (FAF)—with help from Mimi Brody, Mark Taylor & the Zellerbach Family Foundation—has created a truly wonderful thing known as the *Alternative Exhibition Information of the Universe Guide*, or *AEIOU*. *AEIOU* is an extensive guide to exhibitors of alternative film and video that tells you what gauges and formats they preview and exhibit. *AEIOU* gives basic instructions on how and where to send preview tapes of your film or video. The bulk of the listings are in the United States, but it's being continually expanded to include more international venues. Unlike most festivals, the presenters listed in *AEIOU* do not require entry fees (usually just a SASE for returning your preview tape). They also don't have entry deadlines or insist that the work be very recent as is usually the case with festivals. FAF staff is open to suggestions and continues to update the guide. *AEIOU* can be ordered from FAF at cost, and they encourage purchasers to photocopy the guide and make it available to others.

Desktop Video Studio

ANDREW SODERBERG AND TOM HUDSON
RANDOM HOUSE/APPLE NEW MEDIA LIBRARY
1995, 432 PAGES WITH CD-ROM, $40

A digital video toolkit with a basic print guide and a CD-ROM containing demos of the major desktop video software (Premiere, Apple Media Tool, Director, Sonic Foundary, SoundEdit 16). The book has a digital video primer and sections on hardware, software, techniques, and product reviews. Besides the demos, the CD contains animations, video, lots of video-related utility programs and the full-blown versions of the commercial software. If after using a demo, you want the application, you can call an 800-number, spend lots of money, and get a password key to unlock it.

Feature Filmmaking at Used Car Prices: How to Write, Produce, Direct, Film, Edit, and Promote a Feature-Length Film for Less Than $10,000

RICK SCHMIDT
PENGUIN BOOKS, 1995
WEB: 204.250.144.70:80/lightvideo/

A step-by-step guide to super-low-budget filmmaking. The book covers everything from choosing and developing a story concept for low/no-budget to new digital technology for editing, sound mixing, etc. The Web site includes a useful filmmaking FAQ.

Flicker Guide*

C/O DAILY GROCERIES CO-OP
197 PRINCE AVE.
ATHENS, GA 30601
52-PAGE BOOKLET, $2

The *Flicker Guide* is an invaluable sourcebook for 8mm filmmaking, with basic "getting started" information and a listing of mail-order sources for cameras and film, labs, and other valuable resources. It includes a history of Athen's Flicker group.

ROAR* The Paper Tiger Television Guide to Media Activism

DANIEL MARCUS, EDITOR
PAPER TIGER TELEVISION COLLECTIVE
339 LAFAYETTE STREET, NEW YORK, NY 10012
212-420-9045
1991, 64 PAGES, $12

A guide to doing media activism on public-access television by members of the PTTV collective and other public-access veterans. It contains mostly essays on the history, philosophy, and working approach behind Paper Tiger, along with a few how-to articles. It also includes resource listings and even schematics for building a pirate radio transmitter. An electronic version is available at www.papertiger.org/roar/.

Shot by Shot: A Practical Guide to Filmmaking

JOHN CANTINE, SUSAN HOWARD, BRADY LEWIS
PITTSBURGH FILMMAKERS
477 MELWOOD AVENUE, PITTSBURGH, PA 15213
412-681-5449
1995, 155 PAGES, $12.50

A great resource for Super 8 and 16mm techniques with lots of useful information presented in a simple, direct approach.

Super 8 in the Video Age*
Using Amateur Movie Film Today

BOB BRODSKY AND TONI TREADWAY
INTERNATIONAL CENTER FOR 8MM FILM
(See IC8 under Organizations below)
1994, 124 PAGES, $18 *(check payable to Brodsky and Treadway)*

A nuts-and-bolts guide to finding and using cameras, editing equipment, film stock, etc. It covers everything from the fundamentals to transferring to videotape to advanced techniques and troubleshooting. The simple GBC-bound book is itself a fine example of DIY publishing. If you're looking to embark on a journey into Super 8 production, you could not ask for a more inspirational and knowledgeable guide.

Video Compression for Multimedia

JAN OZER
ACADEMIC PRESS/DOCEO PUBLISHING, INC.
ONE MECA WAY, NORCROSS, GA, 30093
770-564-5545
EMAIL: info@doceo.com
400 PAGES PLUS CD-ROM, $49.95 (WINDOWS ONLY)

Video Compression for Multimedia teaches you techniques to capture, edit, and compress digital video using Video for Windows. The accompanying CD-ROM illustrates the products, technologies, and techniques outlined in the text.

(MAGA)ZINES

AV Video and Multimedia Producer

KNOWLEDGE INDUSTRY PUBLICATIONS, INC.
701 WESTCHESTER AVENUE, WHITE PLAINS, NY 10604
800-800-5474, FAX: 914-328-9093
WEB: www.kipinet.com/av_mmp/

A controlled-circulation magazine that's free to qualified video, multimedia, film, and television professionals in the United States and Canada. The Web site has articles and reviews from the print magazine and a qualification form.

B & T Little Film Notebook

TONI TREADWAY, EDITOR/PUBLISHER
INTERNATIONAL CENTER FOR 8MM FILM
(See IC8 under Organizations below)

A periodic newsletter loaded with technical Q & A, editorials, trade/swap information, news on Super 8-friendly labs, etc. As of now, there is no set subscription fee for this newsletter (there may be soon). If you send off for some back issues, please enclose a decent donation. IC8 has been widely publicized (due to the fine quality of their material) and they've been swamped with requests. If you write them, be nice, and make it worth their while.

Celluloidall*

TIMOLEON WILKINS

Timoleon Wilkins started *Celluloidall* in 1993 and produced five issues. His zine dealt exclusively with Super 8, Regular 8, and 16mm (no Pixelvision or video). Film and its unique qualities was celebrated here. Issue topics included how to process your own film (saving money and being in control are Super 8 fixations it seems), how to deal with labs (finding friendly labs that won't censor unorthodox imagery and content), and how to use different film stocks and equipment. Issue #5 included a lab/services guide for Super 8/16mm. Sadly, Wilkins has ceased publishing *Celluloidall*, but it's worth asking around on the Internet to borrow (or copy) someone else's old issues.

Community Media Review

$25/YEAR NONMEMBERS (FREE TO MEMBERS)
(see ACM under Organizations below)

Bi-monthly journal of the Alliance for Community Media. It publishes articles on policy, community activism through cable access, Alliance news, and other information of interest to cable access programmers and organizers.

Filmmaker: The Magazine of Independent Film

5858 WILSHIRE BOULEVARD, LOS ANGELES, CA 90036-0926
800-FILMMAG
WEB: WWW.FILMMAG.COM
$14/4 ISSUES

An excellent quarterly focusing on independent feature films. It includes interviews with directors, producers, actors; practical information on budgets, equipment, distribution; and technical updates. It is mainly for the "high-end" independent *(Crumb, Before Sunrise, Barcelona),* but it does carry frequent low/no-budget pieces.

The Independent Film and Video Monthly

304 HUDSON ST., 6TH FLOOR, NEW YORK, NY 10013
212-807-1400
$45/10 ISSUES ($25 STUDENTS, $100 NONPROFIT)

The Independent is published ten times a year by the AIVF as part of their membership package (See AIVF under Organizations). It features interviews and profiles with independent filmmakers, experimentalists, animators, educators, and students; media news; funding information; festival listings; and classifieds.

Videomaker Magazine*

P.O. BOX 4591, CHICO, CA 95927
1-800-A-VID-CAM *(free sample issue)*
WEB: www.videomaker.com/
$22.50/12 ISSUES

A magazine (and Web site) catering to video amateurs, hobbyists, pro-sumers, and professionals who want to stay abreast of the latest trends in video making. From simple editing techniques to breakthroughs in digital video, most every aspect of the world of the camcorder is explored. The *Videomaker* Web site is highly recommended. It is a free online course in video preproduction, production, and postproduction.

CATALOGS

J&R Music World

(see Media Hacker's Starter Kit section)

Great source of competitively priced video cameras, editing gear, tape, and other tools and equipment.

VIDEOS

Channel Zero

507 KING ST. EAST, SUITE 16, TORONTO, CANADA M5A 1M3
416-868-1851
EMAIL: zero@channel-zero.com
WEB: www.channel-zero.com
$25/ISSUE, $90/4 ISSUES

Channel Zero is an innovative quarterly TV newsmagazine distributed on videotape. The shows, professionally produced and beautifully packaged, are sold through the mail, at video and music stores, and via *Channel Zero*'s Web site. *Channel Zero* is an attempt at building "a media culture that is global and participatory." The Web site links participants together and gives them a chance to respond to the video programming. The first three-hour/2-cassette issue is called "Planet Street" and includes an interview with media critic Neil Postman, a trip through the crack houses of Belize, profiles of the Neo-Nazi movement in Slovenia, and male streetwalking in Paris, an ode to pot, a goofy conspiracy rant, and lots more. *Channel Zero* is an impressive example of what a small cadre of young filmmakers can accomplish armed with a small investment money, Hi-8 cameras, and a Web site.

Don from Lakewood

ERIC SAKS, DIRECTOR
VIDEOACTIVE
2522 HYPERION AVENUE, LOS ANGELES, CA 90027
213-669-8544
EMAIL: hat@earthlink.com
WEB: www.sirius.com/~sstark/welcome.html

> *Don from Lakewood* and Saks' other films are available from Franklin Media at the Web address above.

Rox

P.O. BOX 3241
BLOOMINGTON, IN 47402
1-800-414-MIND
WEB: www.rox.com/quarry/

> Tapes of select *ROX* episodes are also available by mail or can be ordered over the phone. Descriptions of the shows and video clips are available at the *ROX* Quarry Web site. Additional *ROX* material is also available at Free Speech TV (www.freespeech.org).

ORGANIZATIONS

Alliance for Community Media (ACM)

666 ELEVENTH ST., N.W., SUITE 806, WASHINGTON, DC 20001-4542
202-393-2650

> A nonprofit organization for those involved in cable-access television. "The alliance represents the interests of more than 950 public, educational, and governmental (PEG) access cable centers..." ACM is dedicated to making television technology available to people of all walks of life and the creation of "electronic town halls." They offer technical assistance, trade shows, access advocacy, and various publications and videos. Their books include *Access Producer's Handbook* ($40), *Community Media Yellow Pages* ($20), *Cable Access Advocacy Handbook* ($15).

Association of Independent Video and Filmmakers (AIVF)*

304 HUDSON ST., 6TH FLOOR, NEW YORK, NY 10013
212-807-1400

A national service advocacy organization that provides a multitude of services for independent makers. They publish *The Independent Film and Video Monthly* (see Magazines above) and the *AIVF Guide to International Film and Video Festivals.* The guide is global in scope and lists acceptable gauges, entry deadlines, entry fees, basic descriptions of each festival, and occasionally publishes good-sized articles from AIVF correspondents who've attended the festivals. AIVF's guide has helpful multiple indices by subject, geography, deadlines for entry, film category, and so forth.

Canyon Cinema*

2325 THIRD ST., SUITE 338, SAN FRANCISCO, CA 94107
415-626-2255

Canyon Cinema operates a cooperative distribution center for independent film and video makers. A $40 fee makes you a co-op member and gets your work listed in their massive catalog. The catalog (with supplements) costs $20 to those interested in renting or buying members' work.

D.FILM Digital Film Festival

564 MISSION ST., SUITE 429, SAN FRANCISCO, CA 94105
415-541-5683
EMAIL: bart@dfilm.com
WEB: www.dfilm.com/

"D.FILM is a traveling festival that showcases the innovative ways people are using technology to make low budget and independent films. This includes people editing films on their home computers . . . people creating vivid new worlds through desktop 3-D animation . . . or shooting digital video with the same quality as broadcast TV for a fraction of the price with consumer digital video cameras. And people taking film in bold new directions with custom software and weird cameras like Pixelvision and Connectix."

Deep Dish Television

339 LAYFAYETTE ST., NEW YORK, NY 10012
212-473-8933

Deep Dish is the first national public-access satellite network. They distribute grass-roots TV programming to cable-access stations, media arts centers, and home satellite dish owners. They "link independent producers, programmers, activists, and community members" in an attempt to cover issues that are often ignored by mainstream TV. One series, "Visions of Ourselves," presented a selection of programming from around the country and around the world (from Palestine and South Africa to Latin America and the United States). One of their latest, "Staking Claim in Cyberspace," takes a critical look at cyberspace and the impact it may have on average citizens. It is possible to get DDTV shown on your local access station. Many stations have satellite downlinking. If your access provider does not have a dish (and you can't convince a local dish-owner to nab it), you still might be able to have it "bicycled" from another location. Contact Deep Dish for details.

Film-Maker's Cooperative

175 LEXINGTON AVE., NEW YORK, NY 10016
212-889-3820, FAX: 212-477-2714

Started in 1961 by twenty-two New York artists, Film-Maker's Cooperative is an alternative exhibition and distribution co-op for underground and experimental cinema. It's the oldest artists-run distribution co-op with 700 members currently and over 4,000 films. The co-op deals in all formats of film and video. It costs $35/year to join. Once a member, you get to write listings for your offerings to be placed in the biannual catalog. You set the rental price and split the money 60/40 with the co-op (you get the 60 percent).

International Center for 8mm Film (IC8)*

BOB BRODSKY AND TONI TREADWAY
P. O. BOX 335, ROWLEY, MA 01969-0735

The International Center for 8mm Film, or IC8, produces the newsletter *B & T Little Film Notebook* and publishes the invaluable *Super 8 in the Video Age*. A must for anyone wanting to produce in Super 8 film. IC8 gets a lot of requests for information and newsletters. If you request anything, send a donation, too. This is a two-person organization that tirelessly crusades for the home movie gauges.

L.A. Freewaves

2151 LAKE SHORE AVE., LOS ANGELES, CA 90039
213-664-1510
EMAIL: freewaves@aol.com
WEB: www.pixels.filmtv.ucla.edu/community/LA_Freewaves

Media arts network that holds annual celebration of independent video, film, and TV. They also hold workshops and provide video programming for schools and libraries.

National Alliance of Media Arts and Culture (NAMAC)

655 THIRTEENTH ST., SUITE 201, OAKLAND, CA 94612-1220
510-451-2717
EMAIL: namac@aol.com

National organization of media arts centers. It is an excellent national advocacy group and source of information on media arts centers around the country. NAMAC prints a calendar and publishes a directory of member arts centers. Membership is $30/year for an individual and $50-250/year for an institution.

ResFest '97

109 MINNA ST., SUITE 390, SAN FRANCISCO, CA 94105
EMAIL: jonathan@resfest.com
WEB: www.resfest.com/

> The goal of the ResFest Digital Film Festival is to expose and inspire innovative films and videos created with desktop digital tools. The focus of the Festival is how computers and other digital tools affect the way people are making independent films and videos today. Films screened in past have been made using all types of production tools including 35mm, 16mm, Super 8, Betacam, Hi8, MiniDV, Pixelvision, various types of animation manipulated on the computer, and the full range of non-linear editing and effects software.

NET SITES

Artists Television Access (ATA)

WEB: www.sirius.com/~ata/Welcome.html

> Artists Television Access is an alternative film and video exhibition space in San Francisco. They have a weekly cable-access show on Channel 52 and a Web site with art-related information and a calendar.

Austin Community Television

WEB: www.eden.com/~actv/

> A good example of a Web page for a local community access channel. It covers how to get involved in Austin cable, late-breaking news, schedules, and available training and seminars.

Digital Movie News

WEB: www.el-dorado.ca.us/~dmnews/

> A Web-based journal focusing on digital video (especially the emerging digitial video disk, or DVD, technology). The site also includes *How to Make Motion Pictures Using Your Personal Computer*, a how-to guide that covers all the basics from script creation to desktop video editing and distribution. The how-to guide is focused on DVD, but much of it can be applied to all forms of digital moviemaking.

DV—Digital Video Magazine

WEB: dvlive.com

> An online magazine dedicated to the digital video professional. It has product reviews, tutorials, news, case studies, and announcements of upcoming conferences and events.

The Director's Template

WEB: www.inforamp.net/~bpaton/

B. Paton makes a device called the Director's Template, a filmmaker's tool that allows you to plan shots on paper, select required lenses (16mm and 35mm), measure distances, and lots of other useful stuff. The Director's Template site not only contains information on how to order and use this tool but other general how-to info, a great link list to the "Filmmaker's Top 30+ Internet Links," and a list of filmmakers' homepages.

Flicker

WEB: www.sirius.com/~sstark/

Flicker is a resource for "media artists, cinephiles, perceptualists, scanheads, art junkies, sabateurs, inverts, agoraphobics, researchers, programmers, educators, media literacists, and disaffected elements of the mainstream media technocracy." The site has artists' pages (new and old films and videos organized by individual makers, with some film clips); a calendar listing places that show experimental and art cinema, information about festivals, grants, workshops, seminars, and resources for media artists. This site is not related to the Athens Flicker group.

(Another) Flicker

WEB: www.cradle.com/flicker/

Flicker is a bimonthly film festival in Chapel Hill, North Carolina. North Carolina Flicker was started in September 1994 with help and inspiration from Angie Grass and Lance Bangs of Flicker in Athens. They welcome filmmakers' Super 8 and 16mm short films and film transferred to VHS. The only requirement is that it originates on film (or an alternative source like Pixelvision).

Flux TV

WEB: www.flux.net/

A great example of what can be done with a Web site dedicated to an access show. *Flux* is cablecast in New York, on Manhattan Cable, Channel 17, and San Francisco on Viacom, Channel 53. The show, shot on Hi-8 video and edited entirely on the desktop, covers techno music, digital culture, fashion, and the club and cafe scenes. The Web site provides schedules, news related to what's covered in the show, and links to other sites of interest.

Hot Links to Digital Video Vendors

WEB: www.doceo.com/links.html

A nice link list to digital video vendors selling video capture boards, editing software, stream audio and video, video clip art, and digital audio publications.

The Independent Film and Video Makers Internet Resource Guide

WEB: www.echonyc.com/~mvidal/Indi-Film+Video.html

A hypertext reference to resources on the Internet for the independent film and video community. The site also contains information on joining organizations that are dedicated to keeping public media alive (which is currently threatened by cuts in art-related funding, fundamentalist moral crusades, and the Telecommunications Act).

Index to Multimedia Information Sources

WEB: viswiz.gmd.de/MultimediaInfo

See description in the Resource section of chapter 3.

Low Res Digital Film and Video Festival

WEB: www.lowres.com/

The Web site also contains information on the 1996 festival, a DIY area with reviews of film and video equipment and computer hardware and software, plus tips and tricks from low-res filmmakers. There's also information on submitting to the next festival.

ROX Quarry

WEB: www.rox.com/quarry/

The *ROX* Web site contains background on the TV show, an episode guide, QuickTime movie clips, and original online content. Videotapes of the TV show can also be ordered online.

SimMike's Complete Guide to Non-Linear Editing on your PC*

WEB: members.aol.com/simmike/beguide.htm

This excellent guide tells you the basics you'll need to know about digital editing on a home computer. The instructions are geared toward Windows computers, but most of the information and words of wisdom are applicable to both Mac and PC platforms.

Small Movies*

WEB: www.city-net.com/~fodder/index.html

Small Movies is hands-down the most useful Web site for small-gauge filmmakers. This beautifully designed site contains an invaluable directory of film processing labs in the United States, Canada, and Australia, listing format, stock, and process and print costs. There are also how-to sections with info on the art of splicing, home processing, building your own processing tank, and mixing chemicals, with excerpts from *B & T Little Film Notebook, Celluloidall,* and S.F. filmmakers Greta Snider and Bill Daniels. One really cool feature of the site is an illustrated trip through a film-processing lab (with tips on how to improve your film's chances of surviving the lab in good shape). The navigation through the site is more exploratory than straightforward, but the time wandering around is well spent. If you're involved in small-gauge film and you have Web access, you'll want to check out this site.

The Ultimate Access List*

WEB: 153.18.60.51/ual/

A large international list of cable-access stations, programs, organizations, and vendors of video and camera equipment. This site is link-central for the cable-access community in cyberspace.

Video/Film Glossary

WEB: www.videomaker.com/edit/other/glosliz.htm

A useful video and film glossary maintained by *Videomaker Magazine*.

Usenet Newsgroups:

alt.cable-tv.re-regulate

A discussion group centered around regulatory issues affecting cable television and community-related access.

alt.tv.public-access

A low-traffic newsgroup devoted to public access. There are announcements of upcoming shows and events, plus discussions of cutting-edge and future tech such as cable radio and cable modems, video on demand, as well as regulatory issues.

rec.arts.movies.production

Discussion of all gauges of filmmaking. This is where lots of Super 8 filmmakers hang out.

rec.video.production

Discussion of everything from video equipment and techniques to digital video.

rec.video.desktop

The newsgroup for discussion of all aspects of digital video.

Surfing
the
AIRWAVES

Hide the GEAR, here come the magic station WAGONS!

—from alt.pirate.radio **newsgroup**

Twilight has settled over the sprawl—you've got work to do. You're on the air in an hour and you haven't even set out for your "studio" yet. Your lookout is late—isn't even within walkie-talkie range—but you can't hang back any longer. You heft on the massive backpack and head for the hills where you've already stashed fresh batteries and a folded antenna. Once on-site, you quickly wire up the rig and begin loading and tuning the transmitter. The lookout buzzes into your earpiece announcing his position just moments before you begin radiating your voice into the ether. All over town, loyal fans, obsessive radio geeks, and a Chevy Suburban full of FCC goons begin honing in on your signal. As the tape rolls and the transmitter beams your subversive messages and music over the city, you sit back, light up a smoke, and contemplate your handiwork. The adrenaline rush of fear and excitement you always get at the beginning of a broadcast dies away and turns into a delicious feeling of defiance. You start thinking about that big-ass transmitter kit you saw today in a pirate radio catalog: "For Educational Purposes Only." Yeah, right. It's time to pump some serious juice into this town.

KILROY WAS HERE!) The above pirate radio fantasy may be a bit overly romanticized, but not by much. On numerous nights of the year, from locations scattered across the planet, unlicensed radio broadcasters go through similar clandestine procedures to illegally surf the airwaves. Some pirates work out of permanent radio "shacks," confident that their government's communications enforcement group (analogous to the U.S. Federal Communications Commission) is not out to bag them. Others, in stricter countries such as the United States and Britain, roll through their neighborhoods in cars and vans customized as mobile radio stations, broadcasting on the run. Still others set up temporary shop on hillsides, rooftops, ships at anchor, and even aboard private planes. One shortwave station in the United States, operated by "Billy Joe Jack Daniels" and "Bob," claims to broadcast from an outhouse in the boonies.

Pirates come in all shapes and sizes, advancing all sorts of agendas. They can be found locally, on the fringes of AM and FM, or as part of global shortwave radio traffic. Reasons for broadcasting range from teenage pranking to political ranting and anti-government propagandizing. While a majority of pirates operate infrequently and clandestinely, some more evangelical anti-FCC broadcasters do regularly scheduled broadcasts, complete with call-in lines and mail addresses. These groups, such as California's Free Radio Berkeley and San Francisco Liberation Radio, exist to defy the FCC's corporate-friendly, high-dollar licensing policies and to make a point about the airwaves as public property. Most of these overt free radio broadcasters are currently fighting court battles with the FCC, risking fines from $10,000 to $20,000, in an effort to raise the public's awareness of the plight of small and community-based radio.

Most pirate radio is not so overtly political in its goals. Scanning the broadcast spectrum and the available pirate radio directories, a rather disappointing picture of the average pirate begins to emerge: They blip into the ether with a weak and staticky signal from a poorly tuned transmitter, run (and re-run) an obnoxious station identifier, play a couple of mainstream rock tunes and not-so-funny comedy bits, say a few nasty words of defiance at the FCC, and then disappear into static.

Far too much of pirate radio is basically devoid of content. For these stations, the entire point appears to be getting on the air to make farting noises at the FCC, the radio equivalent of "Kilroy Was Here" graffiti. For most DIY media—zines, cable access, cassette networking, etc.—passion for the content is the prime directive. For a large chunk of the pirate community, the fun comes in building the transmitter, getting on the air, and defying a crummy law. This, of course, is not the case for all pirate broadcasters. There are some pirates who obviously put lots of time and effort into making wildly creative programming and others who do a decent job of sounding like a professional station. Part of the problem seems to be that the threat of getting busted makes pirates too nervous to stay on the air for any length of time. The pirates who have significant content in their shows tend to be the ones that are politically motivated and willing to risk the fines should they be caught (or who have taken extraordinary security measures). Some pirates even publish schedules, broadcast regularly, and stay on the air long enough to actually say something. They are also frequently interested in helping others get on the air, hoping that if lots of people started to broadcast without licenses, the FCC wouldn't be able to prosecute everybody.

One of the more interesting aspects of pirate radio is the exchange of QSL cards. In all radio hobbies, QSLing is the act of a listener verifying a broadcast by sending a "reception report," a letter or postcard stating when, where, and on what frequency the broadcast was heard. The commercial station, ham radio operator, or pirate sends a QSL card (or letter) back to the listener, thanking them for providing the broadcast info and restating the time, location, and frequency that the listener reported. Receiving these reports help broadcasters learn how far their broadcasts traveled and other information that listeners provide on signal strength, sound quality, and content. For listeners, QSLing is a way of participating in a given radio community . . . and the cards are fun to collect.

In the pirate scene, QSL cards vary greatly in quality, from funky hand-drawns to professional-looking cards with station logos. Collecting pirate QSLs is exciting to radio geeks because pirate signals can be hard to find and because most pirates don't give out a mailing address on the air. To send in your reception report, after you've heard a pirate, you need to look up the station in one of the published pirate directories or the Black Book, an electronic directory posted on the Internet. Listed in these books are pirate mail drop addresses. After mailing the report to the mail drop, you might have to wait months before your card comes back. The rarity of these QSL cards makes them precious to radio geeks and pirate radio supporters.

One Nation, UNDERGROUND
The following is a sampling of PIRATE radio stations profiled in Andrew Yoder's *Pirate Radio: The Incredible Saga of America's Underground, ILLEGAL Broadcasters.* **These are only a FEW of the stations COVERED, but this listing gives you an IDEA of the DIVERSITY of pirate broadcasting over the nation's AIRWAVES during the past DECADE.**

∧ RADIO DOOMSDAY
QSL card

PLANETARY RADIO) In reading contemporary books about radio, such as *Radiotext(e)* and *Wireless Imagination*, one is instantly struck by the promise and power that early developers and exploiters saw in harnessed radio waves. The idea that wireless communications could go just about anywhere, traveling through the ether, inspired all sorts of wild ideas and utopian speculations. Avant-garde artists like Marcel Duchamp and the French surrealists saw radio as a medium for creating a new kind

[**C H G O** : Normally, pirate radio stations don't announce their exact locations, but CHGO was an exception to the rule. Throughout 1989 and early 1990, CHGO was very active with a progressive music format of blues, classical, jazz, and older "acid" rock with announcer Long John Silver. In early April 1990, the station was raided by the FCC in Chicago, Illinois. Although the station remained off the air, Long John Silver verified old reception reports and even signed them using his real name.

[**C S I C** : Throughout the 1990s, CSIC has been one of the most prominent and influential North American pirates. Its programming is a creative mix; rock music and comedy common, often with a Canadian focus. Also, the station has been one of the biggest sources of pirate relays in North America. For several years, CSIC had one of the best signals in North America, covering most of Canada and the eastern half of the United States with good signals. CSIC has sent out over 500 QSLs to its listeners, and it is one of North America's most widely heard pirate stations of all time. The station awards a rubber chicken QSL to every fiftieth listener who reports the station.

of revolutionary sound art. Theosophists considered the possibility of an electronically disembodied voice with mystical powers. Politicians and propagandists quickly realized the power of radio to reach and influence the great numbers of impressionable minds tuned into the new technology. Radio changed the nature of warfare, offering point-to-point communications in the field, air, and over the seas, and allowing field communication and decentralized decision making. Populists focused on the great democratizing potential of the medium. Radio was breathtaking, cutting-edge technology. Radio was revolutionary.

For many of us today, radio is little more than drive-time distraction, filled with obnoxious and condescending Top 40, equally distasteful shock jocks, and right-wing rabble-rousers. Little is left, it seems, of radio's earlier, utopian ideals. The world seems to have moved on to sexier new technologies. Radio has become marginalized.

But radio offers all sorts of opportunities for media hackers, both as an alternative source of news and information and as a broadcast medium. Radio is neither the behemoth rock stations that overwhelm the airwaves, nor the cheap plastic portable in your kitchen that receives them, nor the stodgy rules on the FCC's books. Radio is a gift of nature (as electromagnetic waves), an incredibly inexpensive and exploitable technology and a globe-spanning communications medium. It is a potential waiting to be applied. Most of us have only been exposed to a few of its more obvious commercially driven possibilities.

It's a well-worn complaint in the United States that news programming (on network television, mainstream radio, and in the newspapers) leaves much to be desired. The Left claims the news is too narrow and straight, intent on maintaining the status quo. The Right says it's clearly skewed in favor of its largely liberal ownership. Intellectuals say the news has been deep-fried into McNews nuggets, salty little fast-food sound bites with little nutritional value. Those in the vanguard claim that the news organizations in this country have become old and unresponsive to the complex and fast-moving realities of our time. They're still living in a post-WWII reality while the planet is spinning headlong into a global and wired twenty-first century. It seems as though there's no common ground to this dilemma. But, for the adventuresome of all political stripes—those who don't care to be fed premasticated news—there is a tried-and-true alternative: shortwave.

For the unenlightened, shortwave is the part of the radio spectrum that falls between AM (540 kHz–1.6 MHz) and FM (30 MHz–300 MHz). Unlike the radio waves above and below this spectrum, which are "line-of-sight" and travel a relatively short distance, shortwave signals travel skyward until they bounce off the ionosphere and return to Earth. Hitting the ground, they bounce back up to the ionosphere, and so forth around the planet. Higher shortwave frequencies can bounce, like a Superball trapped between two spheres, all the way around the globe. This potential global reach allows shortwave broadcasters, even low-powered pirate ones, to send their programming thousands and thousands of miles away from their point of origin. To access this global radio net, all one needs is a halfway-decent shortwave receiver.

Andrew Yoder, co-author of *The Complete Shortwave Listener's Handbook* (McGraw-Hill) and author of *Pirate Radio* (HighText), has been a shortwave junkie since he was a teen. Growing up in a rural part of Pennsylvania, Yoder found shortwave a way for him to reach outside his small frame of

[DOWN EAST RADIO:
Down East Radio is one of the few regional stations that helps to retain the culture of its particular area, in this case, Maine. Announcer Oscar Guggins, who has a noticeable New England accent, programs a rock format from an announced location in Maine. In addition to the music, Guggins airs comedy recordings about Maine, sends out Maine postcard QSLs, and sometimes even issues red plastic lobsters. DER has been sporadically active since taking to the airwaves in August 1992.

[FOURTH OF JULY RADIO:
Jett Johnson irregularly operated Fourth of July Radio between December 1989 and the summer of 1991. The programming was somewhat typical: rock music and talk; however, in some of the last programs from the station, Jett discussed and criticized various aspects of the shortwave pirate scene. Although Fourth of July Radio was rarely active and the broadcasts were always brief, the FCC was waiting when the station broadcast from its usual location on July 4, 1991. In less than thirty minutes, Fourth of July Radio was closed down and the operator was fined $1,000.

[FREE RADIO ONE: During the summer of 1989, Free Radio One was wildly active, making more than forty broadcasts on 4005 and 7415 kHz. Unlike most pirates, the station was bordering on the clandestine; nearly all of the programming was a talk-show format with interviews with various dissidents. The political stance was very conservative, with emphasis on "Christian patriots"—somewhat like popular American politics in the mid-1800s. Free Radio One had newsletters, books, and T-shirts available, but few people received the products that they ordered. In spite of the desire to have one transmitter in each of the fifty states, Free Radio One disappeared after less than a year of activity.

reference. While many of his shortwave-listening buddies turned to computers as they grew older, Yoder continued to focus on radio. "Computers always seemed so sterile to me, so I stuck with radio," Yoder writes, ironically, in an email interview. For him, shortwave radio was, and still is, an excellent way of accessing a broader range of perspectives and of reaching beyond the limited sensational, sound-bite journalism of the mainstream media. "It's one thing to have someone on a network newscast tell you what a country thinks, and it's another to hear the national outlet from that country speak for itself. Some of the things I've heard have an intangible importance. One of the most moving examples of this difference recently came from a Radio Canada International broadcast on the eve of the vote on the Quebec referendum. It had several hours of interviews with tons of people from Quebec. It ended with a collage of telephone answering machine calls people had left in the previous few days. It was extremely moving and the kind of thing you probably wouldn't hear from a local news source."

Besides the alternative news and information that can be sucked into your antenna as the radio waves bounce through the atmosphere, there's also a global media community clustered around shortwave. Yoder writes: "Because there are not that many people in the United States who listen to shortwave, those who do begin to know each other. The sense of community is strongest within each of the small niche areas of listening: pirate, long-wave radio, radioteletype listening, etc. Shortwave is the ultimate in niche broadcasting. There's a lot of 'patriot' and right-wing programming on shortwave. These programs might not attract a wide audience on a 5 kW AM station, but on shortwave, they can pull in like-minded people from across the United States and beyond. On the other extreme is the left-wing such as Radio for Peace International, which has the same type of following. I hope that there will be more low-power broadcasters on shortwave in the future. I think that shortwave has a huge potential to be the underground/niche radio area, in addition to being a home for huge international government outlets."

MYSTERIOUS SIGNALS *and* BLACK PROJECTS)

Anyone who's a fan of progressive electronic music, with its aesthetics of sampled media feeds, bleeps and bloops, and re-purposed noise, would feel right at home listening to a late-night radio feed coming through a short-wave receiver. It's a bizarre sonic territory filled with unintelligible, creepy signals; hazy jargon-laden chatter from troops on the move; propaganda broadcasts from ex-patriots of countries you've never even heard of; and monotonously read, continuous lists of numbers alleged to be spy codes and ciphers. Listening to this bizarre mélange is a unique media experience that has to be experienced to be fully appreciated. Enthusiasts of this fringe radio listening are called DXers, after the radioteletype abbreviation for *distance*. People pursue DXing for lots of reasons. For some, it's a hobby filled with puzzles and needle-in-haystack investigations—a game of unraveling encoded mysteries. For others, it's a way of monitoring law enforcement, the world's military, and amateur radio traffic. For others still, it's nothing more than a interesting way to pass a dull Saturday night. Real DXing geeks will some-times have a number of autoscanning radios going at once, with voice-activated tape recorders poised to capture the disembodied voices and odd sounds as they crackle through the speakers. They often keep detailed logbooks and share their information with other DXers, through zines, corre-spondence, over the Internet, and via ham radio. While Internet evangelists talk incessantly about the wild frontiers of cyberspace, this older, equally fascinating and lawless, frontier of communication is largely overlooked.

[HE-MAN RADIO:
Since first broadcasting on April Fool's Day 1991, He-Man Radio has become one of the most-listened-to pirates in North America in this decade. Besides the humorous put-on macho attitude and comments from He Man, the station also delivers a whopping signal across most of North America. In the four years that the station has been active, they have sent out approximately 500 QSLs to listeners in North America and Europe. Typically, He Man, He Man Jr., and Boy Roy host an entertain-ing program of talk, '60s rock, sports clips, and bagpipe music— all in upper sideband (USB), "the manliest of all modes."

[KGUN AMERICA:
More notable for jamming pirate stations and making harassing or threatening telephone calls to radio hobbyists, KGUN America only made a few broadcasts in the early 1990s. These programs were not widely heard, but the quality ranged from rambling to well produced. The station disappeared after July 4, 1991, when it jammed other pirates in the name of patriotism, and after another pirate announced what was said to be the actual name and address of KGUN's operator over the air. Later, pirate listeners mysteriously received fake verification letters from KGUN with the actual name and address of the operator. The station has continued under the guise of WJTA and (the fake) Radio USA with rambling, malicious programming.

[**K N B S :** KNBS is one of those niche stations that is usually mentioned when people discuss the variety of pirate programming. Unlike many pirates that broadcast on a wide range of topics, KNBS features a very narrow format about marijuana. KNBS (after cannabis, the active ingredient in marijuana) is operated by the California Marijuana Cooperative, which advocates the decriminalization of what has long been the biggest agricultural revenue producer in that state. Since the station began broadcasting in early 1985, it has been heard regularly, but infrequently; usually, KNBS rears its head several times per year in the 41-meter band, although 13900 kHz has also been used recently.

[**K X K V I :** Between 1990 and 1993, KXKVI operated as a somewhat eerie and mysterious voice on 7415 kHz. As their slogan "Interplanetary Radio" suggests, KXKVI features light space music with professionally produced IDs that often incorporate rocket and science-fiction sound effects. One of KXKVI's favorable traits has been its booming signal strength and high-quality audio. On the other hand, the station had a nasty tendency to sign on over other pirate station signals.

For over fifteen years, Steve Douglass has kept his ears and eyes to the sky in search of what others don't know exist or flatly deny. No, he's not a UFO nut—Douglass is a radio-monitoring fanatic who specializes in military transmissions. From his home in Amarillo, Texas, he's turned a lifelong hobby into a profession. With his wife, Teresa, Douglass publishes a zine for other "public intelligence" gatherers (called *Intercepts*) and operates the Reporter's Edge, an information gathering service for the media. He's also the author of *The Comprehensive Guide to Military Monitoring* (Universal Electronics, Inc.), the bible for radioheads who specialize in keeping close watch on the U.S. military.

Armed with consumer electronics—scanners, shortwave radios, camcorders, home computers—Douglass and his cohorts have been "ear witnesses" to conflicts across the globe. They followed the movements of armies that amassed before the Gulf War showdown in 1991. When bombs began to fall on Baghdad, radio snoopers heard about it firsthand, hours before the rest of us. Monitors also listen in on the president and other VIPs flying on Air Force One, Air Force Two, and other international flights using the VIP Mystic Star communication frequencies. Their main target is black projects—super-secret military projects conducted by the government.

THE DAWN *of* **NET.RADIO)** The future of noncommercial radio may be on the end of a wire, not over the airwaves. The Internet has been a boon to so many forms of amateur media, and radio may prove to be no exception. Although the current network technology, especially for personal computers connected to the Net, is still not sophisticated enough for delivery of digital radio, the basic components are already in place, and both commercial and noncommercial broadcasters (dubbed "netcasters" or "cybercasters") are already starting to create Net.Radio programming.

Radio first popped up on the Internet in the spring of 1993 when journalist and Net evangelist Carl Malamud began netcasting a professionally produced half-hour audio show called "Geek of the Week." Using National Public Radio as a model, the show was produced in a conventional sound studio and mastered onto digital audiotape. The finished programs, interviews with notable members of the Internet community, were then uploaded to several computer servers for distribution to other points on the Net. Users directly connected to the Net could play back the audio files. Users connected via modems could download the massive audio files, if they wanted to bear the expense and the long download time. The system was awkward by all accounts, but it did demonstrate the potential for radiolike programming in cyberspace.

Since these humble beginnings, Net.Radio has recently begun to come into its own. Programs such as RealAudio and Xing allow users to listen to audio programming while it's being transferred (instead of having to download it first) using a technology called *streaming video*. This nascent technology turns your PC into a radio with the audio quality of a cheap AM unit with wavering reception. Further technical innovations and faster Net connections will make netcasting an attractive alternative to both commercial and noncommercial radio programmers. An increasing number of radio programs, from NPR to local FM stations, are creating their own Web sites and making their shows available for listening in "real-time," using streaming audio or for downloading and later playback. So far, owing to the rather low quality of sound technology over the Net and through the home PC, most of this programming is spoken word, not music, but this will change with the next generation of Net and PC sound tools.

[9 X 2 V : 9X2V, "the Voice of 1932," was a strange little spoof-type station that operated in 1990 and 1991. It played scratchy records from the 1930s and announced that it was broadcasting from various hotels. Whenever anyone would write to the station, they would receive yellowed verification letters that were dated 1932, and the station operator would incredulously ask how someone from the 1990s could have heard his station! Evidently, the time warp closed in 1991 because 9X2V hasn't been heard since.

[NORTH AMERICAN PIRATE RELAY SERVICE (NAPRS): North American Pirate Relay Service is the North American version of the European pirate relay stations that are active at any given time. It is difficult to cover the personality of the NAPRS because the station almost never airs any of its own programming. After beginning its broadcasting career in mid-1992, station operator Richard T. Pistek has made the NAPRS one of the most active pirates in North America, and he has relayed dozens of pirates from North America, Oceana, and Europe.

[R A D I O   A N A R C H Y: Compared to Anarchy 1 and the Voice of Anarchy, Radio Anarchy is the most angry and music-based of this present genre. Charged with the slogan "an enemy of the state," Radio Anarchy features hard-core punk rock and verbal political attacks on some governmental leaders. As with other West Coast pirates, many of their broadcasts go unreported because of the lack of West Coast shortwave listeners. Since it began broadcasting in 1990, Radio Anarchy has a history of disappearing for as long as eight months at a time, then making a flurry of broadcasts before disappearing again.

[R A D I O G A R B A N Z O: Radio Garbanzo, with veteran cast Fearless Fred, Harry P. Ness, Buck McMoney, and Hugh G. Gough, is a very heavily produced comedy station that is somewhat like a 1990s version of the Voice of Laryngitis. But rather than the drier, more DX-oriented approach of the VoL, Radio Garbanzo is fast and crass—sort of like a morning FM shock DJ cut loose on a pirate station. Although Garbanzo was first heard in 1987, it was not widely heard until 1989. During that year and in 1990, the station was somewhat regularly heard and new programs were often being produced. Since 1990, the station has rarely been heard; when it has been on the air, it's usually via relay.

Although there are few instances of pirates using netcasting, it does offer a legal alternative to the airwaves. For the type of pirates who're involved in the illicit hobby because they fantasize being radio DJs, netcasting offers them a similar opportunity, minus the legal risks. They could tape their programs like they do now and then digitize them for distribution over the Net. And unlike radio broadcasting, where you either have the limited local range of AM and FM, or the limited audience of shortwave hobby listeners, on the Internet you have a potential global audience. The type of pirates who are unlikely to substitute airwaves for computer nets are those who are involved in pirating as a way of aggravating the FCC and fighting for the rights of noncommercial broadcasters and community radio. They're unlikely to want to leave the field of battle for the easy life of Net.Radio. Even for those broadcasters who want to stay on the air, the Net offers them a secondary means of distribution. It will certainly be interesting to see how the Internet co-evolves with the radio community and how it becomes, at least in some instances, a substitute for it.

IF PIRATES HAD THEIR WAY)

Because most of this chapter on radio has already dealt with piracy, I thought it might be fun to imagine what would happen if pirate radio went legit. What would happen if the FCC finally decided to let broadcast amateurs have a tiny slice of the radio spectrum? What questions would need to be answered before such a thing were possible? Keep in mind that the chances of this happening in the United States are about as likely as the legalization of drugs and the implementation of a flat tax.

Where Would Amateur Broadcasting Fit into the Radio Spectrum?)

If the Feds were sprinkled with fairy dust tomorrow and decided to make room for local "micro-broadcasters," what frequencies would they allocate? Most of the radio spectrum is already crowded with stations. Micro-broadcasting frequencies would have to be put someplace where a large number of listeners had access to them, but where they didn't end up interfering with existing commercial stations. The FCC and licensed stations get bent out of shape when anyone steps on their signal. Chunks of the expanded AM band might be a possibility, or perhaps by squeezing more stations into the current FM band.

And what about shortwave frequencies? Yoder and other radio hobbyists don't think that there's any chance for legalized AM/FM micro-broadcasting, but they point to open slots on shortwave. The 11-meter broadcast band (26 MHz, near the CB band), for instance, has almost no stations on it currently. Also, the low-frequency broadcast bands (the 120-, 90-, 60-, and 49-meter bands) are open during the day in North America (for the most part) and would not be audible outside of North America (because these low-end frequencies wouldn't bounce very far).

Who Would Get to Use the Available Micro-Broadcast Spectrum?)

If micro-broadcasters were given some airwaves, who would decide which amateurs could use them and when? There would have to be somebody to oversee and schedule the amateur frequencies. This could possibly work in the same way that cable-access broadcasting is now coordinated. You might join a local amateur broadcast network, take a short course, and then sign up for the next available broadcast slot. Besides basic traffic control, an organization like this could help with the technical aspects of getting on the air and with maintaining quality control.

[VOICE OF BOB: Since its initial shortwave broadcast in July 1984, the Voice of Bob has attained legendary status in the pirate radio hobby. This station— the radio voice of the Church of the Subgenius in Dallas, Texas— features talk about J.R. "Bob" Dobbs, a cartoon-faced man with an omnipresent pipe. The Bob Cult has been present in the American underground culture for decades, where it began as parody of religious cult kitsch. Voice of Bob programming is extremely fast-paced, and is very confusing. Bob's virtues are extolled through rock music, skits, and testimonials. Unfortunately, the Voice of Bob is only audible approximately once per year.

[WJLR : Rather than noodle around with mere mono shortwave audio, WJLR ("John Lennon Radio") pulled out the technical manuals and put a stereo signal on the air. In the past decade, a few North American pirates have used a sort of manual stereo—the left channel on one transmitter and the right channel on another transmitter. WJLR, on the other hand, modified a transmitter to broadcast in DSB (double sideband—both USB and LSB) and modulated each channel in an independent stereo configuration. Although this system received rave reviews from the few who tuned in to the broadcasts in stereo, the system was dropped after several tests because of listener confusion. Most hobbyists couldn't figure out how to tune it in; two receivers were actually needed to hear it in stereo. The format on WJLR is classic rock music and some light talk from Captain Crook and Dave Stone. In 1994, WJLR made what was announced as its last broadcast.

[**W R A R** : Along with WCYC, WRAR ("We Rock and Rap") is another of the survivors of the so-called baby pirate trend from 1992. The station's announcers are pre-teen or early teenage boys. Because of Lad and the Voice of the Night, the term *baby pirate* has negative connotations amongst most listeners, but WRAR broke away from the stereotype and was generally well received. Main announcer Funky Chunk aired a variety of rap, comedy, "alternative" and heavy metal music interlaced with the reading of listener letters and features.

[**W X Z R** : Main announcer Klaus began broadcasting his brand of alternative pirate radio late in 1989. The term *alternative pirate radio* might seem redundant, but the musical format of WXZR (*"Meontological Research Radio"*) was mostly industrial music with a touch of punk rock tossed in. Some of the promos were audio collages and many announcments were intentionally confusing. The overall effect was bizarre and the station was widely heard until it suddenly disappeared in 1990.

How Much Broadcasting Power Are We Talking?)

To be able to make a micro-broadcasting system work, the range of the broadcasts (or power of the station) would have to be local enough to allow for the greatest number of micro-broadcasting regions and so as not to interfere with commercial stations. Perhaps each neighborhood (up to some x-mile radius) would constitute a local amateur broadcast network. If you had some frequencies that were far enough away from commercial concerns and a good system for organizing access, you might be able to get by with a higher power/greater range.

Could Micro-Broadcast Stations Be Commercial?)

Amateur implies nonprofessional and noncommercial. If micro-broadcasting became legal, could it also become commercial? Would stations be able to seek advertising? Or would it make more sense to keep it all noncommercial like public-access TV is now? It's unlikely that commercial microradio would be possible. The stations would quickly be bought up and used by special interests.

Would Pirates Want to Fold Up the Ol' Jolly Roger and Go Legal?)

If the FCC created this new micro-broadcast category, like citizens band and ham radio, would pirates convert or would they continue to operate outside the law? A lot would depend on the type of requirements imposed by the FCC and restrictions. If the requirements were reasonable and didn't cramp the pirates' style, it's likely that many illegal broadcasters would seek licenses. Such a new category would undoubtedly create an increased interest in micro-broadcasting. You'd probably be able to go down to your local electronics store and buy a commercial-type transmitter (or kits, now available only through a few fringy companies).

One big question concerns censorship. If the FCC (or other regulatory bodies) were responsible for micro stations, they would have to enforce state and federal obscenity laws, like cable-access providers do now. Would this scare away the pirates who now enjoy unbridled freedom of speech? Given the flexibility that cable shows currently have (thanks to the lack of a clear censorship body), it's possible that licensed micro-broadcasting would likewise be able to push the envelope, at least a little. One way to entice former pirates to go legit is to make legal micro-broadcasting attractive (cheap fees, good training and resources, camaraderie), while raising the penalties for, and increasing enforcement of, unlicensed broadcasts.

Right now in the United States, pirate broadcasting is more of a nuisance to the FCC than a serious threat. Before a legal micro-broadcasting category would be considered by the Feds, pirating would have to be more of a threat and/or there would have to be a serious lobbying effort on the part of citizens. Given the unfortunately marginal interest in community radio, and the new potential for radio broadcasting over the Net, it's unlikely that such a category will ever be seriously considered. Because any type of licensing/legitimizing would mean that pirates have to clean up their act, legal micro-broadcasting might not even be desirable. What would be desirable is more lenient laws, lower fines, and better opportunities for local communities to be able to start radio stations with reasonable licensing requirements.

[**W Y M N** : **WYMN** ("Women's Radio" or "Testosterone-Free Radio") began operating in December 1984 as one of the few outlets for all-women radio. Since that time, the station has only featured announcers Pirate Jenny and Pirate Cindy along with songs (primarily folk music) that are always fronted by female singers. The programs are normally well written and produced, but the station only has appeared (on average) little more than once or twice per year.

(Reprinted with permission of the author and publisher.)

A RADIO USA QSL card

RADIO RECHARGE INT.
BP 130 92504
RUEIL - CEDEX
FRANCE

RADIO RECHARGE QSL CARD >

THE RADIO HACKER'S STARTER KIT

Getting Started **)** The first thing you'll want to do as a budding radio explorer is to learn more about radio and the low-power/pirate scene. There are a few books on the subject, some Internet FAQs, and an annual *Pirate Radio Directory* (see Resources below). Magazines like *Monitoring Times* and *Popular Communications* have columns covering the various areas of niche radio activity: scanning, clandestine, pirate, shortwave, etc. Getting a few issues of these mags will quickly bring you up to speed on fringe radio. Owing to the illegal nature of some radio activities, the landscape changes quickly.

There are basically four areas of pirate/fringe radio we'll be talking about here:

1) **Pirate/Clandestine Listening**—Anyone can be involved with "pirate" radio, as a listener and/or supporter. Some people listen in solidarity with the pirate ethic and the content of particular broadcasts, while others just listen because pirate signals are out there for the catching. A fair number of pirates issue QSL cards, which are fun to collect. Pirates can be found all across the broadcast spectrum, AM, FM, and shortwave. Clandestine broadcasts, from political exiles, dissidents, and propagandists, are mainly heard over shortwave.

2) **Scanning**—If you enjoy snooping and sleuthing (and killing lots of time listening to static and funny noises), scanning is definitely worth checking out. It's not really active media, but there's a wealth of overt and covert chatter you can tune into with a VHF/UHF radio scanner. Police, fire, military, intelligence, emergency, NASA, newspaper and TV reporters' radio, as well as private cell phones, can all be monitored. While most scanner hobbyists simply like the vicarious thrill of listening in on law enforcement and emergency communications (i.e., they have no life), others take monitoring law enforcement and the military seriously. Trying to assemble information on military "black projects" such as the Aurora plane are an obsession with this type of radio snoop.

3) **Pirate Broadcasting**—Pirate/free radio is a small movement of radio amateurs who operate unlicensed radio stations using small-power, often kit-built, transmitters. Some do it solely for fun and to be naughty, while others are on a mission to make the airwaves (or at least a part of them) free for the public's use. Pirates can be sparsely found on AM, but more often on FM and shortwave. They usually operate sporadically and from clandestine locations. A number of stations, such as Free Radio Berkeley and San Francisco Liberation Radio, operate in open defiance of the law.

4) **Internet Radio**—This new wrinkle in radio is not really radio at all. Radiolike programming is broadcast over the Internet. Higher-speed modems and freely available software like RealAudio and Xing (audio) are making this type of legal free radio possible. Some Internet radio is actual radio programming, either commercial or pirate, that's been broadcast over the airwaves and then digitized for subsequent netcasting. Internet radio is likely to become more common in the future as access and connection speeds increase, and given the relative ease with which one can produce, digitize, and distribute audio material over the Net. For those who are interested in getting into amateur audio broadcasting without the danger of unlicensed radio broadcasting, Internet "radio" is a viable alternative.

Warning: Running an unlicensed radio station is against the law. If you are caught, you could be fined from $10,000 to $20,000. The information on pirate broadcasting in this book is for educational purposes only. The author and publisher bear no responsibility for the illegal application of any information provided here. It's not against the law to build the type of radio equipment described here, only to operate it without a license. For more information on what's legal and what isn't, contact the Federal Communications Commission (202-418-0200 or www.fcc.gov).

There are other radio hobbies, like ham, CB, packet radio, and amateur satellite building and tracking, but we won't cover them here.

Radio Tools and Equipment **)**

What radio gear you'll need depends entirely on what type of radio you want to get in to. If you want to become a pirate radio listener, you can tune in to local ones on your regular AM/FM radio. You'll probably want a decent shortwave receiver so that you can listen to pirate broadcasts throughout the country (and even the world). If you want to monitor law enforcement, the military, and other government radio traffic, you'll need a UHF/VHF scanner. If you want to start your own pirate stations (and are willing to assume the legal risks), you'll need a small pile of equipment. Let's consider each of these.

SHORTWAVE RADIO

There are many models of shortwave radios. Retail electronic outlets have a number of inexpensive models. Trouble is, for listening to shortwave pirates you need a shortwave radio that's got some spunk to it. The inexpensive radios will only reel in the most powerful international broadcasts. You can squeak by with a mid-priced model and a decent antenna and/or an antenna amplifier (I have the Sangean ATS-803A [a.k.a. the now-discontinued Radio Shack DX-440]). Check hamfests, want ads, and Usenet newsgroups like alt.radio.swap and you might find a used one. The shortwave newsgroup *(alt.radio.shortwave)* is a great place to find information on

---

Building and tracking miniature satellites is a growing hobby, an educational pursuit, and a small growth industry. If you're interested in learning more, contact AmSat—North America (www.amsat.org) and check out the superb book Micro Space Ships by Rick Fleeter of AeroAstro (www.newspace.com/aeroastro), a Virginia-based small satellite manufacturer. Rick started out as a satellite hobbyist who decided to make it a vocation.

good, low-cost shortwave sets and advice on the type of radio you'll need. For good reception—good enough to hear pirates—a decent external antenna is essential. They don't cost that much, but it does take some tree and ladder climbing and wire stringing.

Scanners)

Scanners basically come in three flavors: base, mobile, and handheld units. The walkie-talkie-like handhelds are great because you can take them anywhere. Three common scanner brands are Radio Shack, Bearcat, and Cobra. Rumor has it that all of these are made by Uniden. There are lots of bells and whistles on the various models, but the basic important difference is the frequencies they cover. Obviously, the more frequencies available the more chances you have of hearing a broader range of interesting communications.

In the wake of the 1986 Electronic Communications Privacy Act, it is now illegal to listen in on cell phones, portable phones, and pagers. Scanner makers are no longer allowed to manufacture units that can scan these frequencies. So, if you're looking to snoop the cell phone spectrum, you'll have to buy an old scanner that covers that range, or do one of the many modifications (or mods) that are available to allow access to these frequencies. Again, ham meets, want ads, and radio newsgroups are great places to shop for used scanners. Many of them will specify "with cell!," "minus cell," or "cell mod capable" to indicate whether the model for sale has the cell phone frequencies or can be modified to receive them.

When buying a shortwave radio, make sure it covers the entire shortwave spectrum, from 1.6 to 30 MHz; has an external antenna jack and an AC adapter; has BFO pitch adjustment/Single Sideband (SSB) capability; has RF Gain control to pull in weak signals; and is connected to a decent (ideally outdoor) antenna. An audio-out jack is a bonus.

P I R A T E R A D I O R I G

To get started in pirate radio, one needs the following:

1) **Transmitter (TX)**—Kits for low-power transmitters are readily available from places such as Free Radio Berkeley and Panaxis (see Resources). Five-watt FM models are commonly used. You can also find used transmitters for sale in radio mags and at ham meets.

2) **Audio input(s)**—Something to feed into the TX since you can't go on the air if you have nothing to broadcast. You'll probably want to create your show in a home studio and then use a portable tape player (such as a Pro Walkman) to play the show over the air. If you want to broadcast live, you'll need a mixing board and microphone.

3) **Power supply**—12 volt lead acid batteries are a common power source, or you can buy an inexpensive AC-operated DC power supply.

4) **Antenna**—Can be made from a kit or constructed from scrounged parts following plans that can be bought or found online or in radio books. You'll also need a spool of 50-ohm coaxial cable to run to your aerial.

5) **Miscellaneous tools and equipment**—An output filter (used to avoid interference with other broadcasts), a dummy load and a frequency counter (used in testing and tuning the transmitter), a VHF power meter, an electronics tool kit, enclosures and carrying cases for all the gear.

6) A friend or two armed with walkie-talkies and posted as lookouts.

If this all sounds expensive, it isn't. Let's go shopping in the Free Radio Berkeley catalog and see what all of this would cost:

5-WATT TRANSMITTER KIT..............	$55
ENCLOSURE FOR TX.......................	$18
OUTPUT FILTER KIT........................	$8
DUMMY LOAD KIT.........................	$10
SLIM JIM ANTENNA........................	$15
(also requires pipe and wire)	
POWER SUPPLY.............................	$29
POWER METER..............................	$35
FREQUENCY COUNTER....................	$80
COAXIAL CABLE............................	$25
CASSETTE PLAYER	
(everyone's got one of those already)	
MIXER AND MIKE	
(optional for live broadcasting)	
TOTAL ESTIMATED COST	$325

Basically, a pirate can get on the air for under $500 (even less if you are already a wirehead and are willing to scrounge for parts). You'll need a moderate amount of electronics skill to build the above micro-station, but if you're up to the challenge, there are folks at FRB and on the Net who are happy to assist. If you don't have electronics experience and you still want to try building a station, find someone who does. For them, building these kits wouldn't be difficult. A reasonably experienced electronics person could put the above rig together in under ten hours.

INTERNET RADIO

To access Internet radio you need a basic multimedia-capable computer (with sound card, etc.), a PPP/SLIP connection (or better), and a high-speed (28.8 or higher) modem. For real-time playback, you'll need a program such as RealAudio or Xing. If you want to download audio files first and then play them, all you need is an audio playback application such as Wham for the PC or SoundMachine for the Mac. All of this software is available over the Net as freeware/shareware. If you want to be a netcaster, programming your own Net.Radio, you'll need standard recording equipment and the capability to transfer the analog recordings to digital. Most modern multimedia computers already come with the hardware and software to do this (at least for basic audio). You'll also need a considerable amount of storage space on an Internet server computer to store all of your audio clips.

Production)

If you decide to do a pirate radio broadcast, you'll need to put together a show. This seems to be an afterthought for far too many radio pirates, which is unfortunate. One of the cool things about pirate radio is that you get to be a DJ, without training or a license. *Lots* of people have DJ fantasies. So if you decide to risk breaking the law, why not take the time to create something that's truly worthwhile to broadcast?

First, you'll need to decide whether you're going to broadcast live or use a pre-produced tape. The live approach is more risky, and undoubtedly more exciting, because you're basically making it up as you go along (even if you have a script you're working from). Lots of pirates go with prerecorded material so that they can keep watch (for the Feds) and be more relaxed at the broadcast site while the show is on the air. By using tape, you can spend the time in a home studio polishing the material, the segues, the sound quality, etc. If you decide to do the show live, have a script prepared. It doesn't have to be word-for-word, just a workable outline for the show. You can still have prepared spoken material on cassette (not just music) to mix in.

For the sake of your listeners, try to move beyond the typical pirate transmission of a badly recorded station ID, a few mainstream rock songs, and a not-very-funny comedy bit. Why not play music that you can't readily hear on commercial radio, interview interesting, controversial personalities, or offer uncommon news and opinions? Do something interesting!

Distribution)

The first question regarding distribution of your broadcast will be answered once you decide on the type of radio transmitter (AM, FM, shortwave), how powerful it is, and what antenna you'll use. All these factors (and your location) will effect the penetration of your broadcast.

Some pirate shows are re-broadcast by fellow pirates in other locations (called *pirate relays*). This is not widespread, but common enough to be considered another potential way of getting your message out there. There are even several "best-of" shortwave shows that feature segments from pirates worldwide.

So how much FM broadcast power is allowed by the FCC? Not much. Under Part 15 of the FCC regulations, you can use (without a license) a transmitter "not to exceed 250 microvolts/meter at 3 meters." That's less than 1/1000th of a watt. This will basically allow you to broadcast from one end of your house to the other. One watt will reach about a mile, ten watts a few miles. A lot depends on your antenna and your location. Part of the naughty fun of playing with low-watt transmitters is seeing how much mileage one can cover with different locations and clever antenna designs.

The Internet can also be used as a means for distributing your show. You'll need to have the audiotape digitized and loaded onto an FTP site or, ideally, a Web page where you can provide additional information on your program.

You can also skip the unlicensed radio part altogether and just distribute your audio program via the Net. To do this, you would simply create the show in a home studio, have it digitized, and then load it onto an Internet server. At this point in the evolution of the Net and the modem, it's probably a good idea to divide the show into small segments. That way, people wishing to download can choose only those parts they desire. You can have one audio file containing the whole show for those listeners who will be using streaming audio programs such as RealAudio and Xing.

Promotion and Advertising)

As you might imagine, there isn't a lot of promotion and advertising going on in pirate radio. Pirates usually go out of their way to keep secret their true identity, whereabouts, and broadcast schedules. A few more bold stations publish schedules or at least broadcast at similar times on the same frequency.

Once you start broadcasting and put yourself on the radar of fringe radio listeners, you're likely to get listed in a pirate directory or Black Book (see Resources). These listings are likely to include known broadcast times/dates, frequencies, technical information, a description of programming, and a mail-drop address. Getting in these directories is a great way to create "a buzz" about your show. If you want to establish a mail drop, you can write the various mail drops listed in a directory and ask if you can list them as your mail-drop address. Once you have a drop, you can give that address over the air so listeners can send you reception reports and fan mail.

Sending out QSL cards is a great way to find out who your broadcast is reaching and to encourage repeat listening. QSL cards usually include a form to fill out with the reception information you get from listeners (UTC time, date, frequency, reception quality, etc.) and any other information you wish to convey. If you're truly lazy and don't care to design a QSL card, you can buy generic ones on which you just fill in your station name and the other info. But why not show some style and create something cool and collectible. Again, if you're gonna take the risks of pirating, why not do something noteworthy.

As a pirate radio listener, you'll be looking to collect these rare QSL cards. Here's the basic procedure one follows in preparing a reception report and seeking a QSL response:

How to QSL a Pirate Station:

1) Listen for the mailing address on-air or use addresses listed in pirate logs or directories (see Resources).

2) Send a "reception report" (a simple letter or postcard) containing your location, when you heard the broadcast (in Greenwich Mean Time/ Coordinated Universal Time), and the frequency you heard it on.

3) Tell them what you thought of the broadcast, both in terms of technical quality and content.

4) Send return postage, IRC coupons, or some money with your QSL request. Pirates are operating without a budget and need all the financial support they can get. It's also time-consuming to mail out the cards, so make sure you're nice to them and thank them for their time and effort.

5) Also, it doesn't hurt to ask for any other information they may have available. A few stations send out periodic newsletters.

Words of Wisdom)

Andrew Yoder (author of *Pirate Radio: The Incredible Saga of America's Underground, Illegal Broadcasters*)

Tips for listening to pirates:

: Buy a decent receiver with SSB reception or a BFO—otherwise, you will miss more than half of the pirate broadcasts in North America. It doesn't have to be a great, semiprofessional monitoring receiver, but it should be decent. Check the reviews in books such as *Passport to World Band Radio* (IBS, 1996) and *The World Radio TV Handbook* (Billboard, 1996) for ideas. Some of the receivers sold at Radio Shack will do fine for hearing pirates. But if you're on a budget, you're better off checking with a radio company that sells used receivers, such as Universal Radio.

: Connect a decent antenna. An antenna can be almost any piece of wire. The key isn't to build a theoretical engineering masterpiece, but simply to hear signals better. A great antenna is fantastic, but a simple 30- to 100-foot piece of wire will vastly improve signals.

: Learn a little bit about shortwave. It's helpful to understand how signals "bounce" into your region from hundreds or thousands of miles away. And it's a lot of fun to experience it firsthand, in front of your radio. Understanding the band allocations helps, too. "Is that station a pirate or the internal service of Radio Beijing fading in?" "Is that funny sound a jammer or a legitimate weather fax station?" and "Are those voices pirates talking to each other or a group of military amateurs (MARS) or unlicensed fishermen?" The list goes on and on, but understanding a few basics will keep you from constantly "running into walls." A subscription to a good shortwave magazine or a copy of a good background book, such as *The Complete Shortwave Listener's Handbook* will answer questions from most beginners.

: Keep abreast of recent activity. The pirate radio scene never stops; pirates broadcast on different days, times, frequencies, etc., and different stations become active or inactive each month. The only way to stay informed is to read books, and especially magazines and newsletters (such as *The ACE, Monitoring Times*, and *Popular Communications*). Making friends with other listeners and reading/contributing to the alt.radio.pirate newsgroup on the Internet also helps.

: Listen over weekends and especially holidays. Most pirates broadcast during these times. So few pirates broadcast during the week that it's usually a waste of time to listen then.

: Listen to the radio. It sounds silly, but it's the only way to hear pirates. Some people begin to listen for pirates by tuning the radio a few times and then giving up because they haven't heard anything. If the listener checks the best times and frequencies, and actually listens, chances are that a pirate will soon be heard. An even better method of listening is to turn the radio on to the main pirate frequency (currently 6955 kHz) and do other things while the radio is either at a low volume or completely turned down. When a pirate fires up on the frequency, you will either hear the signal or see the meter level go up.

Joop ter Zee (FRSH, Holland)

Notes from a Dutch radio pirate:

: First, we do not have all the concerns for "safety" and breaking regulations like you do in the United States. We operate from sites in Belgium and Italy. These countries leave us alone, as long as we don't cause severe interference. But, then again, one should always take care not to interfere. The worst countries for illegal broadcasting in Europe are Germany and Britain. Ireland, like Belgium and Italy, is also easy on pirates.

: In the early days, we broadcasted from a forest. This allowed us to:

    Hang our antennas as high as we liked (from trees), in a relatively easy way.

    Be far enough away from houses and other development to prevent jamming from ground waves.

: Some European-based pirates use several autoreverse cassette decks. This way, the equipment can be installed, turned on nonstop, and checked every eight hours or so.

: Another method used by FM pirates is a VHF link to the site. The radio program is produced live elsewhere and then beamed to a hidden site where the actual transmitter is located. Of course, the Dutch PTT (read: FCC) get smart to this after a while.

: In 1994, I visited a museum in Den Haag (The Hague) where you could see all the confiscated pirate radio sets (including one of ours!). There was a wide range of transmitters: hidden in cars, vacuum cleaners, television sets, etc. One nasty Dutch pirate even used a snake to protect his transmitter site. As you can imagine, this story hit all the newspapers.

: In the '80s, when the pirate scene in Holland was at its high point, one of the classier things a broadcaster did was put a bottle of wine near his site with a congratulations note on it for the RCD, should they find it. (RCD stands for Radio Control Service, a department of the PTT . . . which, BTW, stands for "post, telephone, telex.")

: The popular Dutch pirate stations in the '80s were Radio Decibel (Amsterdam), Radio Hofstad (De Hague), and Keizerstad (Nijmegen). There were basically *no* safety precautions taken by these stations. When their equipment was confiscated, they just switched to another site and the station went back on the air. Fines were minor. The stations were also very popular among the local population (another reason why the PTT left them alone). But then things changed when newer, stricter laws came into force.

: There are almost no pirate stations on FM anymore because of strong regulations, heavy fines, and the introduction of local and regional radio (government controlled). The shortwave scene is now low-key as well (FRSH is a shortwave station). In Europe, the shortwave stations are mostly popular in Sweden, Germany, Finland, and Italy. It all depends on the radio scene in a given country, the number of choices you have. In fact, it's a trend you can see all over Europe. Since the introduction of regional radio and TV, the pirates are sadly disappearing. Interestingly enough, most of the local/regional stations, such as Radio Sun in Portugal, Radio Veronica in Holland, and Radio One BBC in England, are all former pirates, or at least many of their employees are.

U.S. Time Zone Chart

When filling out pirate reception reports, you're supposed to use **Greenwich Mean Time (GMT).** *Here's a handy chart to help you translate your time zone into GMT.*

GMT	PST	PDT MST	MDT CST	CDT EST	EDT
0000	4 PM	5 PM	6 PM	7 PM	8 PM
0100	5 PM	6 PM	7 PM	8 PM	9 PM
0200	6 PM	7 PM	8 PM	9 PM	10 PM
0300	7 PM	8 PM	9 PM	10 PM	11 PM
0400	8 PM	9 PM	10 PM	11 PM	12 AM
0500	9 PM	10 PM	11 PM	12 AM	1 AM
0600	10 PM	11 PM	12 AM	1 AM	2 AM
0700	11 PM	12 AM	1 AM	2 AM	3 AM
0800	12 AM	1 AM	2 AM	3 AM	4 AM
0900	1 AM	2 AM	3 AM	4 AM	5 AM
1000	2 AM	3 AM	4 AM	5 AM	6 AM
1100	3 AM	4 AM	5 AM	6 AM	7 AM
1200	4 AM	5 AM	6 AM	7 AM	8 AM
1300	5 AM	6 AM	7 AM	8 AM	9 AM
1400	6 AM	7 AM	8 AM	9 AM	10 AM
1500	7 AM	8 AM	9 AM	10 AM	11 AM
1600	8 AM	9 AM	10 AM	11 AM	12 PM
1700	9 AM	10 AM	11 AM	12 PM	1 PM
1800	10 AM	11 AM	12 PM	1 PM	2 PM
1900	11 AM	12 PM	1 PM	2 PM	3 PM
2000	12 PM	1 PM	2 PM	3 PM	4 PM
2100	1 PM	2 PM	3 PM	4 PM	5 PM
2200	2 PM	3 PM	4 PM	5 PM	6 PM
2300	3 PM	4 PM	5 PM	6 PM	7 PM

Resources)

____BOOKS

Citizen's Guide to Scanning

LAURA QUARANTIELLO
TIARE PUBLICATIONS
P.O. BOX 493, LAKE GENEVA, WI 53147
800-420-0579
$19.95 PLUS $2.00 SHIPPING

> An excellent well-rounded guide to scanning. It includes basic introduction to the pastime, description of scanner jargon, and a frequency guide.

The Complete Manual of Pirate Radio

ZEKE TEFLON
SEE SHARP PRESS
P.O. BOX 1731, TUCSON, AZ 85702-1731
1993, 47 PAGES, $5

> Most everything in this slim guide can be found for free in Radio Is Our Bomb (see Net Sites below), but it's such a classic it's almost a shame not to have it on your shelf. It includes stories of Teflon's pirate days along with a basic run-through of getting on the air and staying on the air (read: "duckin' the cops"). It concludes with sketchy plans for several FM transmitters and some antenna designs.

The Complete Shortwave Listener's Handbook, 4th Edition*

HANK BENNETT, DAVID T. HARDY, ANDREW YODER
TAB BOOKS/MCGRAW-HILL
BLUE RIDGE SUMMIT, PA 17294-0850
1994, 321 PAGES, $19.95

> A comprehensive guide to shortwave that will appeal to both amateur and veteran listeners. It covers the basics on receivers, antenna designs, QSLing, a tour of the shortwave spectrum, a continent-by-continent briefing on available programming, VHF/UHF scanning, and access to clubs and resources. Yoder has also written *Build Your Own Shortwave Antennas* (Tab Books, $16.95), which makes a great companion volume for the serious shortwaver.

The Comprehensive Guide to Military Monitoring*

STEVE A. DOUGLASS
UNIVERSAL ELECTRONICS, INC.
4555 GROVES ROAD, SUITE 12, COLUMBUS, OH 43232
1994, 280 PAGES, $19.95

Military-monitoring guru Steve Douglass has spent over fifteen years keeping tabs on the military. He's turned a part-time hobby into a full-time profession, publishing his findings on military "black projects" and other activities of the Pentagon. This book bundles together years of Steve's monitoring wisdom and hard information. It covers the basics on monitoring (gear, antenna designs, a tour of the bands), military shortwave and UHF/VHF frequencies, major military installations (with maps!), code words and acronyms, "black projects" background, and a lot more. If you're interested in military monitoring, you need this book.

The Pirate Radio Directory (1997)*

ANDREW YODER AND GEORGE ZELLER
TIARE PUBLICATIONS
P.O. BOX 493, LAKE GENEVA, WI 53147
800-420-0579
1997, $12.95

An annual guide to pirate radio for the past seven years. It includes a brief paragraph on each known station with frequency information, times of broadcasts, QSL verification address (if known), and a rating of how good the station is at responding to QSL requests. You'll also find a brief intro to pirate listening, successful QSLing, and a list of additional resources.

Pirate Radio: The Incredible Saga of America's Underground, Illegal Broadcasters*

ANDREW YODER
HIGHTEXT PUBLICATIONS
P.O. BOX 1489, SOLANA BEACH, CA 92075
800-247-6553
$29.95 PLUS $4.00 SHIPPING

A book/audio CD combo that provides a history of the pirate scene for the last few decades and an introduction to pirate radio as a broadcast medium. It includes lots of resources, how-to instructions (selecting a radio, QSLing), and other useful information for the pirate listener and would-be broadcaster. The attached CD contains excerpts for fourteen pirate broadcasts. While some of these are interesting (and funny), they're all short and the whole CD is over much too quickly. It should have included at least twice as many examples.

Radiotext(e)

SEMIOTEXT(E) #16
NEIL STRAUSS WITH DAVID MENDL, EDITORS
SEMIOTEXT(E)/AUTONOMEDIA, 1993, 352 PAGES, $12

A varied (and varied quality) exploration of the spirit, history, politics, and possibilities of radio. It includes everything from early radio manifestoes to alternative histories of radio to the far fringes of radio (radio from outer space), as well as essays by Walter Benjamin, Upton Sinclair, Kurt Schwitters, Hakim Bey, Negativland, and Abbie Hoffman.

Wireless Imagination: Sound, Radio, and the Avant Garde

DOUGLAS KAHN AND GREGORY WHITEHEAD, EDITORS
M.I.T. PRESS, 1992, 452 PAGES, $35

A beautifully-produced collection of essays on the interplay between art, noise, experimental music, and technology in the twentieth century. While some of the essays are academically fussy and impenetrable, this is, overall, a highly illuminating exploration of a little-known area of art history. The most fascinating revelations concern the early days of phonography and radio and how avant-garde art movements (Futurists, Dadaists, Surrealists) fantasized about creating new forms of human/machine art with the new technology.

(MAGA)ZINES

Free Radio Press (formerly Radio Resistor's Bulletin)

P.O. BOX 3038, BELLINGHAM, WA 98227-3038
EMAIL: Mbrauns1@passage.net
WEB: www.rootsworld.com/rw/feature/rrb.html
$14/YEAR

Free Radio Press is a paper and electronic zine covering all aspects of noncommercial radio ranging from "professional" community radio to the micro-radio movement and radio on the Internet. Regular features include reviews, publication reviews, station updates, and contacts. *Free Radio Press* grew out of a battle in Bellingham, Washington, to assure community access to the campus station at Western Washington University and to preserve its eclectic free form.

Intercepts Newsletter

P.O. BOX 7176, AMARILLO, TX 79114-7176
EMAIL: webbfeat@arn.net
WEB: www.perseids.com/projectblack/
$20/YEAR *(check payable to Steve Douglass)*
SAMPLE COPY FOR A SASE

Steve Douglass's bimonthly newsletter on military monitoring. It includes up-to-date info on shortwave and VHF/UHF military frequencies, call signs, and code words as well as monitoring equipment reviews, news, and updates on "black projects." See also Douglass's *Comprehensive Guide to Military Monitoring* in Books section.

Monitoring Times

P.O. BOX 98, BRASSTOWN, NC 28902-0098
704-837-9200
WEB: www.grove.net/hmpgmt.html
$24/12 ISSUES

A monthly magazine covering shortwave, scanning, ham and pirate radio. Its departments cover aerospace, military, government, and public safety communications, broadcast, satellite, and long-wave radio. Each issue also includes product reviews, technical articles, and projects for radio hobbyists. Selected articles from the magazine are available on the Web site.

Popular Communications

76 N. BROADWAY, HICKSVILLE, NY 11801-9962
516-681-2922

The other popular monthly magazine dedicated to all types of radio hobbies. Regular columns cover cell phones, ham, shortwave, scanners, pirates, clandestines, communications satellites, and radio nostalgia. It is chock full of ads for all the major (and minor) radio and electronics parts and equipment companies.

CATALOGS

EEB (Electronic Equipment Bank)

323 MILL STREET N.E., VIENNA, VA 22180
800-368-3270
EMAIL: eeb@access.digex.net
BBS: 703-938-3781

A store crammed full of the latest in radio gear: shortwave, scanners, amateur, spy gadgets, GPS, metal detectors. This place is radio-geek heaven! The general EEB catalog offers a healthy sampling of all they have to offer, plus there are separate, smaller catalogs for specific interests (Shortwave, Mobile/2-way, Gift catalog, etc.). EEB's prices are usually competitive.

Free Radio Berkeley*
(see Organizations below)

FRB offers a complete line of kits: transmitters, amplifiers, power supplies, antennas, and other tools of the trade. The kits are reasonably priced and have a fairly good reputation for being reliable, and are shipped with complete instructions. Since the FRB folks are free radio crusaders, they are also willing to assist you in building your rig and getting on the air.

Pan-Com International

PANAXIS PRODUCTIONS
P.O. BOX 130, PARADISE, CA 95967-0130
916-534-0417
$1 CATALOG

An excellent catalog of kits, books, and other resources of interest to radio hackers. They carry everything from transmitter kits to ham, CB, and shortwave devices, as well as basic science and electronic projects.

Progressive Concepts

P.O. BOX 586, STREAMWOOD, IL 60107
630-736-9822
EMAIL: 102475.3010@Compuserve.com
(free catalog)

A small catalog of broadcast electronics. They carry several transmitters, amplifiers, frequency counters, power supplies, and components.

Radio Shack

$3 CATALOG *(from your local outlet)*

With all the consumer electronics, toys, and such, people might forget that the Shack was originally all about radios. They carry a well-respected line of scanners; several decent shortwave radios; and a line of ham, CB, and walkie-talkie radios. And for all those quick-and-dirty electronics projects and repairs, you can't beat the Shack's "around-the-corner" availability.

Universal Radio

1280 AIDA DR., REYNOLDSBURG, OH 43068
800-431-3939
(free catalog)

A fat and sassy catalog of scanners, shortwave radios, ham gear, antennas, books, and other goodies. The prices are not fantastic, but they have frequent sales. The catalog descriptions are more detailed than many catalogs, making it useful even if you end up finding the gear cheaper elsewhere. I got my shortwave receiver (on sale) from Universal and was more than pleased with the process and the product.

ORGANIZATIONS

A*C*E*

THE ASSOCIATION OF CLANDESTINE RADIO ENTHUSIASTS
P.O. BOX 11201, SHAWEE MISSION, KS 66207-0201
MEMBERSHIP IS $20/YEAR IN THE UNITED STATES;
$27/YEAR WORLDWIDE

The A*C*E is an association of individuals interested in pirate, clandestine, and covert radio communications. A*C*E's monthly newsletter reports on pirate, clandestine, covert, and unexplained broadcasts. Regular features include the latest in pirate loggings, pirate QSL news, a directory of pirate mail-drop addresses, Euro-pirate reports, and columns on covert and clandestine broadcasts.

Free Radio Berkeley/Free Communications Commission*

1442-A WALNUT ST. #406, BERKELEY, CA 94709
510-464-3041
EMAIL: frbspd@crl.com
WEB: l0pht.com/~hotrod/frb.txt

Anytime you talk to someone who knows anything about pirate radio, Steve Dunifer and Free Radio Berkeley will eventually enter into the conversation. Steve and his cohorts have been openly broadcasting in the Berkeley and Oakland, California, area since 1993. FRB is frequently on the news and the topic of discussion in cyberspace because of their open defiance of the FCC (which got them slapped with a $20,000 "Notice of Apparent Liability"). So far, there's been a legal standoff, and in the meantime FRB has stayed on the air. FRB puts out a newsletter (*Reclaiming the Airwaves*) and a catalog of radio kits and accessories.

NET SITES

Chris Smolinski's Radio Pages

WEB: www.access.digex.net/~cps/radio.html

Shortwave, pirate, links to other radio pages and Chris's own Macintosh software for radio applications.

The Free Radio Network*

WEB: www.frn.com

FRN is pirate radio central in cyberspace. There's news, how-to guides, the latest version of the Black Book, and lots more. There's also a massive link list to just about every fringe-radio related site on the Internet. I can't recommend this site highly enough.

Glen's Pirate Radio Site

WEB: www.speedline.ca/~glen/

Billed as "Canada's only Web page dedicated to pirate radio," this site has pirate audio clips, tips, link to pirate-related e-zines and sites, pictures of some QSL cards, late-breaking news, and more.

Monster Radio Link Site*

WEB: itre.ncsu.edu/radio/

It covers shortwave, AM, FM, digital, ham, Net.Radio, pirate, scanning, satellite, hardware, software, organizations, zines, catalogs, station Web pages—you name it.

Packet Radio Home Page

WEB: www.tapr.org/tapr/html/pkthome.html

It contains a packet radio primer, the packet FAQ, and links to a number of other valuable resources related to this corner of the amateur radio hobby.

Radio Is Our Bomb

WEB: www.dojo.ie/active/bomb.htm

An e-text version of a popular pirate radio guide looking at pirate radio from the U.K. perspective. It includes information on the U.K., getting started yourself, and full technical plans for building a transmitter.

Usenet Newsgroups:

alt.radio.pirate
alt.radio.swap
rec.radio.amateur.homebrew
rec.radio.amateur.space
rec.radio.info
rec.radio.scanner
rec.radio.shortwave

Media PRANKS
[CHAPTER SIX] and Art
HACKS

A CICADA CORPS BILLBOARD HACK,
photo by Pedro Carvajal

A friend of mine, a particularly eccentric chap who wears outlandish costumes in public with the express purpose of turning heads and triggering snickers, wears a big button that says: "Why be normal?" A rarely asked question, when you think about it.

Another friend, an M.D. who travels the corporate lecture circuit speaking on stress management, argues that "normal" is actually unhealthy; our intense anxiety over trying to fit in, to keep pace (so as not to lose face) with our neighbors, is making us all sick (not to mention insufferably dull).

All of the pranksters and process-oriented artists in this chapter are dedicated to offering antidotes to media mesmerism. The commercial media are undoubtedly the biggest cultural hypnotists of them all. Everything is cordoned off into neat little compartments and labeled like guests on a daytime talk show. Diversity, ambiguity, and complexity do not exist long in the mediascape before they're wrestled into a category, relegated to a sound bite, and sold back to us as the flavor of the week.

Get someone from an OUT-OF-STATE newspaper to run a story on something sight UNSEEN, and then XEROX that story and include it in a second mailing. JOURNALISTS see that it has appeared in print and think, therefore, that there's NO NEED to do any further RESEARCH. That's how a SNOWFLAKE becomes a SNOWBALL and finally an AVALANCHE.

—Joey Skaggs,
media hoaxster

Poetic terrorism is the term coined by anarchist Hakim Bey for media pranks and art hacks that poke fun at consensus reality and being "normal." An act of poetic terrorism can be as simple as paying for the next few cars behind you at a tollbooth or as elaborate as a full-blown media hoax. For the poetic terrorist, anything that says "Wake up! Think for yourself! Life isn't your annual vacation!" is a life-enhancing act. *Cultural jamming*, a term coined by the art collage band Negativland to refer to billboard alteration, is often used in a similar, although usually overtly political, context. Mark Dery's *Open Magazine* pamphlet *Culture Jamming: Hacking, Slashing, and Sniping in the Empire of Signs* has become something of a manifesto for those looking to make political statements through media sabotage and guerrilla art.

In our wired age, the media has become a great amplifier for acts of poetic terrorism and culture jamming. A well-crafted media hoax or report of a prank uploaded to the Internet can quickly gain a life of its own, passing between BBSes, email, newsgroups, and Web sites. Print and TV newsmedia are always looking for "human interest stories" or sensational ratings-grabbing subject matter. Anything that's out of the ordinary or worthy of a sound bite will find its way into the local and national media (albeit shoved into a little suffocating compartment). This has helped inspire a whole new generation of media pranksters and artists who use the media as a vehicle for their activities (or at least as a powerful means of documentation).

GI JOE GETS A GENDER adjustment. From the BLO video.

NEW! GENDER-BLENDER BARBIE!) In December 1993, obedient consumers who were buying Barbies for their little girls and GI Joes for their little boys got a bizarre surprise. **Barbie's voice box no longer chirped "Let's plan a wedding" or "Can I ever have enough clothes?"**

Instead, the perky blonde barked warrior phrases ("Eat lead, Cobra!") with a timbre reminiscent of Linda Blair in *The Exorcist*. Burly Joe, on the other hand, was suddenly sounding a lot more in touch with his feminine side. Imagine Rambo talking about the trials of doing his hair.

This particular model of Talking Barbie had sparked some protest before. Feminists and educators complained about one of her preprogrammed phrases. When Barbie spouts "Math is hard," they said, it reinforces the negativity that young girls already have about math, and discourages them further by reinforcing stereotypes about women and science. Mattel took that phrase out of Barbie's repertoire, but left in the others regarding shopping, etc.

But this was the first time that Barbie protest had moved to the level of unauthorized Barbie hacking. The retooled dolls were the handiwork of the San Diego–based Barbie Liberation Organization (BLO). This group of "culture surgeons" spent nearly $10,000 of its own money to purchase the Mattel and Hasbro toys, transfer the voice boxes, and return them to store shelves, unbeknownst to the manufacturers or the doll's retailers. The transubstantiation came to the attention of the media when consumers bought the altered dolls and brought them back, bewildered. The gender-blender dolls showed up on store shelves on both coasts, in places as diverse as Albany, New York, and Walnut Creek, California. The BLO claim to have altered over 300 of the popular plastic icons. They say they have a membership as diverse as media hackers, gender warriors, and Holocaust activists who are appalled by the bloodthirsty GI Joe.

Needless to say, Mattel was not amused. As M.G. Lord points out in her book *Forever Barbie*, this type of cultural critique becomes more highly charged when it involves corporate property. She places the Barbie alterations in the context of other doll-oriented artworks, but it is more profitably considered in the agitprop tradition. Mutilating Barbies and reissuing them into the consumer food chain is an act of subversion that harks back to the Yippie demonstrations at the New York Stock Market in the 1960s. The Barbie Liberation Organization may not have yet succeeded in liberating Barbie, but they did tweak the market's sensibilities and added an element of the surreal, if not the dangerous, to an icon most Americans take for granted.

THE JOYOUS SOUNDS
of CACOPHONY)

A few years ago in Los Angeles, a series of strange flyers began popping up in some of the skankier coffeehouses and clubs around the city. Like demented garden club calendars, they listed upcoming events for a mysterious entity calling itself "the Cacophony Society." One week they would be dressing up like cave people and roaming Rodeo Drive, the next they'd be off touring cults around L.A., or pulling pranks at a UFO convention. This didn't look like the latest outbreak of pretentious performance art; it had the odor of something different: a group of eccentric souls who were sponsoring wild and wacky stunts that other people only dreamed about (if they were possessed with twisted imaginations).

> LA CACOPHONY BUSINESS CARD

All this served to signal the arrival of the L.A. branch of the Cacophony Society, a loose-knit network of groups originally from San Francisco and now boasting chapters in L.A., Seattle, and Portland. Though perhaps best known for their involvement in the desert party extravaganza "Burning Man," each Cacophony chapter reflects the interests of its members. While a smaller project may only involve the core members, some of the larger events can draw hundreds of attendees.

REVEREND AL'S FLYERS

On first glance, it looks like the kind of ordinary baby-sitting flyer you might see tacked up at the supermarket or library. A wholesome fresh-scrubbed man, identified as Dr. Leonard Stynch, offers "free baby-sitting in my home." The bottom of the flyer is fringed so you can tear off the phone number for handy reference. But when you look at the details, a different, unsettling picture begins to emerge. Dr. Stynch uses "electrically-assisted learning procedures" to build character in kids and "clear their heads of all that Nintendo crap." He offers "garage playtime" and "solid foods . . . upon request."

Clearly, this is a hoax, and for anyone with children, a particularly creepy one. Welcome to the twisted world of Los Angeles Cacophony member "Reverend Al," who's also the author of other flyers promoting mass burial services (handy for industrial accidents and genocide), psychic car repair, and searches for animals of indeterminate species, possibly freak research escapees. Al compiles some of the responses he gets on his voice-mail and shares them with friends. He even had local TV stations call him up inquiring about the body of a "large tailless ape" he was advertising as having found. He still bemoans the fact that he didn't have the forethought to create a life-size dummy of the creature for the cameras.

Pushing the Envelope
'til It Tears, by Stuart Mangrum)

No force on Earth can stop one hundred Santas. I kept chanting this mantra as I hung from a handrail on the Geary Street line, trapped like a rat on a double bus with fifty other fools in cheap red suits. Somewhere behind us was a second bus full of lost-weekend Santa thugs, every bit as drunk and scared as we were. Cop cars trailed both vehicles like hungry lampreys. It was a tense, low-speed juggernaut; like the movie *Speed* but really slow. Like O.J. in the Bronco chase, but with no burger breaks. Acting on a complaint from the security staff at the Emporium, a downtown department store, The Man was after Santa, and He was out in force. He didn't care how many video cameras Santa had, or how it would look on the eleven o'clock news. He tasted Santa ass. He smelled Civil Disobedience. Santa was not playing by the rules of the game. Santa was screwing up Christmas for the merchants. And for that, Santa was goin' down.

When the idea first came up, I had refused. Not because it was dangerous and stupid, but because it was a retread. A year before, the Cacophony Society had hosted a cheap-suit Santa event the week before Christmas, and it had unfolded so magically that I was convinced we could not come close in a second attempt. Thirty Santas had run amok with impunity, swilling booze from Pine-Sol bottles and stopping traffic in downtown San Francisco, shuttling from one ugly spectacle to the next in a chartered bus. It was the stuff of legend, an event so shamelessly over the top that it was clearly irreproducible. Why bother?

But I already owned the suit, so I went. Duh. And for some reason my wife, hammered as she was by influenza, couldn't bear to miss it, either. Cacophonists were mobilizing up and down the coast to be part of Santa II, and the phones were ringing off the hook at Omaha's Oriental Trading Company, purveyor of the absolute lowest grade of $25 one-size-fits-none Chinese prison–made polyester-blend Santa suits. One Hundred just seemed like a magic number. It sounded like critical mass, and if Santa was gonna blow, we were going to be right there at ground zero.

By the time we made it over the Bay Bridge there were already close to a hundred Santas assembled by the Embarcadero skating rink, drunk and rowdy and looking for something to tangle with. I'm not making this up. A hundred rowdy Santas! Close your eyes and imagine. I passed out song sheets with our twisted carols from the previous year along with candy canes and 600 "Kris Kringle Institute" business cards I had hastily printed up with the Cacophony phone number. Santa J., one of the organizers of the event, had asked me to help out; I found him at the rink giving last-minute instructions through a bullhorn. He had a police scanner in one ear, and was hooked up to at least three other Santas with radios. One of them, Santa M., was patched by cell to the Cacophony phone line, from which he was able to give position reports to last-minute arrivals and stragglers. Seeing that security was in capable hands, I quickly relaxed and started drinking. Every other Santa had a hip flask or a joint.Ho ho ho! The column started to move, surging through the streets like a red tide.

Santa went to many of the same spots as the year before—the department stores Emporium and Macy's, the hotels Fairmont and St. Francis—but this time most of the event's good humor seemed to give way to fist-shaking. Santa did a lot of angry shouting, hurling *Ho*! around like a threat. Children seemed more frightened than amused. In the hotels, Santa helped himself to other people's booze and food, and in the department stores he screamed incessantly at the shoppers to *Buy! Buy! Buy!* and *Charge It!* Whenever someone stepped onto a balcony to look at the Santas in the street, Santa chanted *Jump*; and when Santa J. was hanged from a lamp-post (another retread idea from last year), the crowd got especially viscious, chanting *Die, Santa, Die!* and whacking at the soles of his dangling boots with oversized candy-cane clubs.

One hundred was indeed a magic number. It turned out to be the point at which a crowd turns into a mob. We were out of control, and mob rule quickly eclipsed common sense. In a word, Santa got ugly. Other than a brief spin through the restaurant Planet Hollywood, where the tourists cheered, Santa was not received well. At the Mark Hopkins hotel, there was a scuffle with security for control of the elevators. People kept asking, "What are you protesting?" The Santas replied with swear words and extended fingers, because of course they weren't protesting anything, just running wild. Not making a statement, just screaming. Doors began to be bolted in the Santas' path. Children began to cower behind their mother's skirts. And security guards began to call in the cops.

At first, the blue suits just trailed the red suits, watching and waiting. Then word went through the crowd that one of the Santas had been carrying a starter's pistol—it was to have been used in a mock Santacide—and the gun had somehow fallen onto the sidewalk and been retrieved by a cop. The Santas were on foot this year due to their numbers; this time there was no chartered bus to whisk us out of harm's way and onto new adventures. Stopping at a Muni stand, the Santas were quickly surrounded by a half-dozen patrol cars and a paddy wagon. A tense standoff ensued. Some of the more skittish Santas, particularly those new to Cacophony and the ones with outstanding arrest warrants, shucked out of their suits and tried to fade into the night. The hardier fools, self included, scoffed at the police and laughed out loud at their little paddy wagon. Even with defections, Santa was still strong. There is no force on earth, I reminded myself, that can stop one hundred Santas. When one hundred Santas link arms and go limp, what are the cops going to do? Bring out the gas and truncheons? Okay, make that eighty Santas. Maybe seventy. Across the street, I saw two cops putting on their riot gear. And on the scanner, Santa J. heard the blue suits call for four more paddy wagons.

J., a veteran of many near misses and a few direct hits with the blue suits, chose this moment to bravely cross the street and initiate a parley with the on-scene commander, a dour old division chief with a gray buzz cut and very little patience. "I was pretty sure they'd just arrest me," he confided to me later. "But somebody had to do something." J.'s years of experience paid off, and the order for paddy wagons was canceled. Explaining that we were *not* protesting anything (this seemed to be their biggest concern), he portrayed us as simply a big party that had gotten a little out of control. We were on our way to a new venue, he explained, a private party on the other side of town to which we had all been invited. Of course, there was no such party—unless you counted the *Chronicle's* Christmas bash at the Palace of the Legion of Honor, which we planned to crash—but for some reason the blue suits seemed to accept his story and let us get on the bus.

The next twenty-five minutes seemed to take forever. Would they bust us all? Would they let us go? Santa was running scared, pale and sweating under the hard fluorescent bus lights. Santa A., an artist, tried to raise everyone's spirits with an off-color Jackson Pollock joke. Nobody laughed. He started to explain who Jackson Pollock was. Again, nobody laughed. Santa J., usually confident to the point of cockiness, was as nervous as I've ever seen him. "This is bad," he said to me at one point. "You might want to think about getting out."

A good idea, but where? A few Santas managed to lose their suits and get off the bus with the normals, but my wife, in her Mrs. Claus outfit, would have been next to nude if she'd tried to lose the costume. And I, for some perverse reason, was determined to see the event through. Earlier that night, when the run had degenerated into dumb slogans and drunken bullying, I had thought about leaving, but now things were finally getting interesting. Of course, I had no desire to be searched—Santa was "holding"—but ultimately even that wouldn't have mattered. I had to see the whole wretched thing through.

Finally the red lights spun up and the bus was pulled over, and the Santas filed out the front doors and into an impromptu lineup. Two Emporium security guards fingered the Santas they thought were responsible for some damage in the store; these two unlucky souls were cuffed and hauled away, and the rest of us were set free.

Free, or at least reasonably priced. Whipped, we shuffled up the hill to the Palace of the Legion of Honor, a sorry lot of broken Santas too tired to raise hell. When the staff asked us to leave after a few minutes at the hors d'oeuvres table, we hung our heads and went quietly, not wanting to cause any more trouble.

The Santa Two, as our prisoners were quickly dubbed, were charged with attempted strong-arm robbery of Christmas decorations, and bail was set at an exorbitant $15,000 apiece. According to newspaper reports, a female Santa was also arrested and charged with exposing her flaccid breasts to small children at the Emporium's rooftop kiddie carnival, but none of the Santas I talked to knew anything about that.

Legal aftermath: Flasher-mama Santa was cited and released. The two "strong-arm" Santas had their charges reduced to obstructing a business and public intoxication, and were released on their own recognizance. Initial media reports (radio and the two dailies) were rather negative, but the weeklies came out shortly after and our media posture improved.

THE "RAY BATADO" PRANK **)** "It all started when we were in Palm Springs hanging out with Les Baxter," Joe Seahee says in his gravelly voice. His partner in crime Patrick Tierney adds: "We'd been at this joint Combustible Edison/Esquivel record release party and they had this video interview with Esquivel on his deathbed. It was so sad. Like . . . here's this guy being exploited to sell their cheesy records. It was just wrong, so we thought it would be funny to create a fake Esquivel of our own."

Tierney and Seahee had a right to want to mock the latest bachelor pad music wannabes. They'd been two of the premiere proponents of the genre for years. Tierney had even made a pilgrimage to Hawaii to interview Martin Denney and Seahee's roller blading lounge extravaganzas to draw L.A. hipsters like a high-power magnet.

Another friend, Joe Altruda, had just completed a record of musical exotica and asked Seahee to help with the publicity. "This became the natural starting point for the prank, but we saw it as more than just a publicity stunt. We also wanted to bring Chris Douridas down a few pegs and make a statement about hubris," says Tierney. Douridas was a DJ at KCRW, a much-vaunted public radio station in L.A. and the host of a show called *Morning Becomes Eclectic*. They had an acetate made of the CD, slapped on an old RCA test pressing sticker from the 1950s, and placed it in a weathered record jacket. They sent it off, specifically addressing it to Douridas, a supposed world musicologist. He bought the shenanigans wholesale, playing cuts off the record repeatedly, even reading aloud from the press kit that detailed Ray Batado's exile from Cuba, his friendship with Hemingway, and his hoped-for comeback. Pushing the prank as far as they could, Tierney and Seahee arranged for Douridas to do a phone interview with Batado and hired an actor to play the part.

"Then things kind of started to get out of hand," says Seahee. The actor didn't show up, so the interview was done with Tierney's friend Mario Acuna, sporting a Cuban accent that any *I Love Lucy* fan would recognize as farce. He discussed the Hemingway connection again, and explained to Douridas the meaning of the record's name, *El Pistato*. "After Pat said that it meant 'fried brains,' there must have been the longest pause in the history of radio," chuckles Seahee.

With the prank exposed in all its deviant glory, Douridas was furious. He first banned Seahee (who releases records himself) from the KCRW airwaves, then demanded that the two give an on-air apology (which they did). The best part for Seahee was not attacking Douridas but the thrill of pulling off such a well-executed prank: "It always feels good to get away with something at this level. I don't know why more people don't try it."

CICADA CORPS BILLBOARD HACK, photo by Pedro Carvajal

THE ART *of*
BILLBOARD LIBERATION)

On January 16, 1996, Bay Area journalist Brad Wieners accompanied the notorious San Francisco's Billboard Liberation Front on one of their hits. The following "field report" offers a rare inside look at how billboard "improvers" go about their mischievous business.

BLF Field Report, by Brad Wieners)

Like any joke, a bad prank can be worse than no prank at all. This is especially true when the goal of the prank is to create a spectacle that will attract media attention and extend, through the looking glass of commercial media, the message of the prank. Acutely aware of this, the San Francisco–based Billboard Liberation Front, or BLF, has distinguished itself for twenty years in the field of "outdoor" media piracy by adhering to certain principles as they go about "improving" billboards. They even went so far as to publish a primer on the subject a few years back, a pamphlet entitled *The Art and Science of Billboard Improvement*, published by Los Cabrones Press, also reprinted in *Processed World* magazine.

As 1996 began, word spread that the BLF would be attempting their most elaborate billboard alteration ever: hacking of a neon sign. Having written and interviewed BLF members previously, I asked if I might report the entire operation, start to finish. On the grounds that I protect their identity, they agreed. They also permitted me to quote liberally from their pamphlet so aspiring media hacks everywhere might know the method to their madness.

The hit that went down—or rather up—on January 16, 1996, began several months earlier, when Jack Napier, one of three founding members of the BLF (and the only active cofounder), expressed his desire to do something in neon, and, in particular, to deploy a red neon skull he and L. L. Fontleroy, another BLF operative, had fashioned.

The BLF favors strong, easily recognized symbols like skulls, happy faces, swastikas, or radiation/biohazard warnings as a way to catch the attention of passersby. This affinity for striking symbols stems partly from the fact that ads—especially billboards—become visual white noise through repetition. One of these symbols, the BLF contends, will often force a double take. But it's also a philosophical issue. Whereas some billboard hacks, such as New York–based Artfux or the Guerrilla Girls, create their own billboards and paste them over existing ones, the BLF (as well as New Jersey–based Cicada Corps), prefers the economy of altering the existent advertisement— editing it rather than replacing it.

Napier brought up his desire to see his Jolly Roger skull flashing in the neon wilderness with the BLF's acting minister of propaganda, Blank DeCoverly. DeCoverly, in turn, expressed his desire to do something about Joe Camel. Specifically, he wanted the BLF to express solidarity for Joe Camel, as he would later explain in a press statement:

"The Billboard Liberation Front has undertaken this action as a gesture of public support for the heroic executives of R. J. Reynolds in their valiant struggle against the dark forces of regulatory oppression. By dramatizing the plight of Joe Camel, outdoor advertising's most endangered species, we express our outrage at those who would plot Joe's extinction, and vigorously proclaim our solidarity with RJR . . .

"We must remain strong. Government must not be allowed to filter the pure essence of Joe Camel. To us, he is a class-A hero, with more clout than the surgeon general and a hell of a lot more style . . . He has a life of his own, firmly embedded in the fabric of popular myth and adored by children everywhere. Smooth, sexy, and oh so cool. We are disgusted by the FDA's proposals to limit outdoor advertising to black-and-white text. Is not the urban landscape already bleak enough? Joe Camel is a dash of color, a splash of savoir faire in an otherwise dull and dreary world. More importantly, he is . . . more than just a cigarette spokescamel; he's the high-living, high-stepping voice of a generation. A Mickey Mouse for our times, symbolizing all that we hold dear: the fast life, the good life, cool sax music, and pocket billiards.

"Joe lives! Long live Joe!"

In conversation, the BLF plays down their ideology. To be sure, their politics defy easy categorization. They are committed primarily to satire and feel that other midnight billboard editors not follow their ideological cues so much as take to heart that, whatever the message, it's best not to express it destructively. As Napier says, "If you just climb up on a board and fuck things up, all those who see it will think, 'what a bunch of assholes.' But if you concentrate on the quality of your work, people will react to what you have to say."

Neon and an arch defense of Joe Camel—that much was settled. Now began the search for a target board. The BLF takes this next stage of their preparation quite seriously. As they note in their pamphlet, "in most instances, it should not be necessary to use the elaborate—even obsessive—precautions that the BLF has resorted to for an individual or group to get their message across. A can of spray paint, a blithe spirit, and a balmy night are all you really need."

Nevertheless, the BLF has something of a reputation and no one knows for sure what the statute of limitations is for billboard improvement. In the hands of the wrong deputy district attorney, it could qualify as criminal trespassing, a felony. What's more, a couple of BLF members work professionally in advertising. It just wouldn't do for them to get caught.

Preparing for a hit, the BLF first takes into account the accessibility of the targeted billboard. A location scout asks herself, "How do we get up on the board? Will we need a ladder? Can we climb the support structure?" Preparing Camel's new lights, L. L. Fontleroy, Napier, and DeCoverly identified a few possibilities, settling on one located above a market and roadhouse parking lot that faces Bayshore Boulevard. Bayshore is a sea-level, three-lanes-in-each-direction avenue parallel to U.S. 101, the main north-south artery leading into San Francisco. Because the board had neon lettering, the hit would take place during the day, in plain sight, when the board was "dark."

The scouts realized immediately that they would not be able to conceal their actions and so would have to present themselves as a legit sign company. The BLF called around and found a friend with an unmarked van. Then, they came up with two pair of coveralls, and waist belts so the operatives on the board would appear to be pros. The first scouting expedition finished with a search for places to plant lookouts. Three or four lookouts with walkie-talkies would keep an eye out for "wilburs" (cops), and warn the operatives on the board if it appeared any wilburs had noticed them. Three locations were settled on for the lookouts: one, John Thomas, would lie down, in the guise of a passed-out bum, on the pedestrian overpass over the 101 freeway. The overpass afforded him a bird's-eye view of everything but the board itself. L. L. Fontleroy and Modesty Blaisé would hang at a bus stop and be mobile if anything needed fetching. Mister Szabo would keep an eye on the intersection of Oakdale and Bayshore.

The week before the "hit," the BLF executed a trial run. This was not merely a rehearsal, but a second scouting expedition. To get the effect they wanted, they needed to obtain precise measurements, to match the colors with signage already in place, and to ascertain the power sources for each of the neon elements so they could hijack them. The lookouts, meanwhile, would test their positions and their handheld two-way radios. Winslow Leach and Jack Napier pulled into the parking lot beneath the sign and immediately three other vehicles pulled away. (The parking lot appeared to be the site of other clandestine actions.)

Napier and Leach brought their own ladder to the bottom of the sign, reached the sign's ladder, and climbed up onto the board. As they made their measurements and figured out the wiring, a freelance photographer, Nicole Rosenthal, and I went in search of the best location to document the hit. On the slope between U.S. 101 and Bayshore Boulevard, we stumbled through a thicket of trees, bushes, and garbage and eventually into a muddy homeless encampment, a blur of shanty and latrine. In addition to our unintentional invasion of privacy, we failed to find a unobstructed view of the billboard. We, too, would need a new plan if we were to get a clear angle on the alteration-in-progress.

The day of the hit arrived. Even though I was primarily a witness, a granny knot of anxiety tied up my intestines. The photographer and I picked up a model, a friend of mine, Csilla. Wanting to get photo documentation of the entire process but not get the BLF busted, we brought the model so it would appear we were photographing her and not the BLF's handiwork. We set up Nicole's tripod and camera on the median, smack in the middle of Bayshore Boulevard.

The timing for the hit couldn't have been better. The San Francisco Forty-Niners football team were in a playoff contest with the Green Bay Packers at Candlestick (3Com) Park that afternoon, so the cops in the area had greater concerns than billboard pirates. Also, the game meant that at sundown Bayshore would fill to capacity with football fans headed back into the city—a captive audience for the new, improved Joe Camel.

As they climbed up on the billboard, thirty or more feet above the parking area, Napier and Leach looked for all the world like repairmen sent to fix something on the board (and, in a way, they were). They first switched off the power on the letters "C" and "E" in the word "CAMEL," as well as the words "Genuine Taste." They then affixed a new piece of neon over the "Genuine Taste" that read "Dead Yet?" in the exact same purple as the ad's neon border, wiring it into a transformer they brought with them. But then they got spooked.

A man sitting in his van munching McDonald's takeout directly opposite the billboard had, to Napier's mind, taken too keen an interest in their work. Leach radioed the four BLF operatives assigned to surveillance, and asked one of them to check him out. Meanwhile, Napier and Leach disappeared. A half-hour later, the man drove away and Napier and Leach resumed their improvements, lowering a clear sheet of Lexan Plexiglas—the foundation for an as-yet-unlit neon skull over the cartoon figure known as Joe Camel. Growing more rapid in their movements, they next masked the bottom half of the letter "L" in the word "CAMEL" so it registered as an "I." They then placed a twelve-pack of Miller Genuine Draft and the following note, which Steven Shin of Gannett Outdoor faxed me later. Shin failed, however, to mention the beer.

Dear Sign Men:

We apologize for any inconvenience to you or your company and hope that your workday is going well.

We have altered the message on this billboard. During the alteration process, we have gone to great pains to be sure that no part of the existing signage has been damaged. It shouldn't take you very long at all to restore the board to its original state.

You will find when you turn on the power to the neon and floodlights that some letters are out. If you switch on the disconnect switches on the letters themselves, they will turn back on.

The new units of neon glass that you will find over the "Genuine Taste" letters are tied to the existing units with tie wire and can be removed with a few snips of your sidecutters. The large image on plastic over the Joe Camel section is held in place with ropes, and two men can easily lower it. The two neon transformers are in metal cans and just unplug from the electrical panel.

Once again we are sorry for any inconvenience to you or your company. We have nothing at all against billboards. We actually like them. We just don't happen to own any, so we've taken this opportunity to display a slightly different message on this particular board. We hope you view it in the same spirit in which we meant it.

Sincerely,

The Billboard Liberation Front

Then they climbed down and got the hell out of there.

As dusk and the Niners fell, traffic thickened on Bayshore Boulevard. Across from the board, I waited with Nicole. Lights up and down the block flickered to life. And then *voila*! The billboard illuminated. It read, in brilliant neon, "Am I Dead Yet?" with the skull glowing red over Joe Camel's profile. Dejected football fans, packed in their cars, could be seen pointing, laughing, and giving the neon improv a big thumbs-up.

An hour or two later, a pickup truck with "Gannett Outdoor" painted on the side pulled into the lot beneath the sign. The driver, in a huff, found the property owner and had him unlock a gate to the fenced-in area beneath the sign. In what seemed an attempt to turn off the electricity to the entire board, the Gannett man switched off only the floodlights on the bottom of the board, which only made the neon glow more intensely against the darkened sky. By Sunday, however, the sign had been restored to its original state. That is the nature of BLF's work: "A board like that—they had to be proud of," Napier said. "It had three different light sources, all well designed and well crafted. We *liked* the board, too. That's why we choose it. We just thought the message could use some help."

Over the next few days, the BLF sent out press releases and 35mm slides claiming hundreds of such hits up and down the state so the short-lived hack might live on, as it does here, in *media res*.

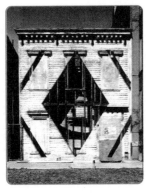

A VISIT FROM ART ATTACK, photo by E. Bowen.

THE *REAL* DECONSTRUCTIONISTS)

You're driving down a road in suburban Arlington, Virginia, late at night, just a grenade lob from the Pentagon and a shoulder rocket away from CIA headquarters. Passing the lot at 4749 Old Dominion Drive, you do a flashback double take at what used to be an old abandoned farmhouse. The structure you now see is like something out of a bizarre dream. The front yard is covered in water, with the ceiling of the front porch floating upside down in it. The facade of the building appears to have slipped, as if it had been rolled down like a car window. The revealed upper floors are cantilevered in different directions; a radiator slides across one of them. The staircase that once went from the first floor to the second now starts from the second and punches its way through the roof and towards the stars. From a room on the ground floor a low rhythmic clanging can be heard as a piece of wire cable flails the guts of a piano. Window panes, freed from their frames and suspended by monofilament, bang around as fragile chimes that shatter as the wind gusts.

Hakim Bey's instruction to create phony alien landing sites as acts of poetic terrorism is old news to the members of Art Attack, a collaborative art posse that's been mutating the commons for years with their public art hacks. Since 1979, it has altered the urban landscapes of Los Angeles;

Washington, D.C.; New York; Berlin; Linz; Austria; and elsewhere. The group started in Los Angeles as an outlet for process-oriented artists with free time and good ideas who wanted to do anonymous guerrilla art. Over the years, Art Attack has become more established and above ground, opting to trade anonymity and the thrill of clandestine art making for a bit of notoriety and the ability to create more complex work supported by donations of material and equipment (and, all too infrequently, money). The group has always worked as a team, not simply a group of artists contributing individual work. "The group as prosthesis . . . that's how I see it . . . the superorganismal artist," says Alberto Gaitán, a long-term member. "Art Attack is an experiment in human cybernetics, working with process, feedback, and the inevitable chaos to transform something that's been given to us." "We've always been committed to bringing art into everyday lives," says founder Lynn McCary. "Our work is site-specific, temporary, and not for sale." Another interesting feature of Art Attack is its multidisciplinary cast of characters. Arts administration, architecture, music, video, metal sculpture, painting, graphic arts, cabinet work, performance art, film, and pyrotechnics are just some of the disciplines that long- and short-term members have brought to the table. "Having a lot of different types of artists involved gives each of us an opportunity to share our expertise with others and to learn about theirs," offers Gaitán.

On college campuses, "building hacking" is the art of finding hidden rooms, passageways, and sealed basements of old buildings. Art Attack is a group of literal building hackers, deconstructing existing structures before they succumb to the wrecking ball. Besides *Dominion Dum* (the apparition described above), there was *Vessel*, another Arlington attack where the group filled the basement of a house with water and cleaved the garage in half. For *427 Massachusetts Ave., N.W.* in downtown Washington, D.C., it cut a diamond shape out of the building's facade and used the removed exterior as a mobile that freely turned inside the structure.

Although building hacking is a big part of what Art Attack does, it's not the only thing. *For Demarkation*, a site work in east Berlin, it erected five mysterious-looking aluminum posts in vacant lots with no explanation of their meaning. In 1985, it created the *Used War Lot*, a meditation/provocation on war, in an abandoned used car lot. An inversion of the Vietnam Memorial was erected and covered with pages from the Washington, D.C., phone book. Then-member Jared Hendrickson (now with the band Chemlab) paraded around like a crazed car salesman with a bull horn, hawking the contents of the installation, which included dirty needles collected from the inner city war zone where the site was located. "People were outraged, especially when they found their own name, address, and phone number on 'the wall'" says McCary. "Somehow, having that information posted in this environment was unnerving to them, even though it was readily available at any corner phone booth."

With the exception of the more boisterous *Used War Lot,* Art Attack's work has a subtlety about it. There are many clever little hacks and visual jokes that exist within the larger deconstructions. The big changes draw you in, but the little things make you pay attention. There's a haunted feeling of connection with the lives of the people who once inhabited these spaces. What would they make of this? It's as if the building was experiencing one more bright burst of light and heat, one last hurrah before it implodes to dust. It's probably no accident that water (a symbol of reflection and memory) is an Art Attack leitmotif.

MAIL ART *and the* SANDWICH MAILED *'Round the World*)

IMAGE BY J. COHEN, "dude," the sticker dude

Doctors get the weirdest mail and free stuff from drug companies and others vying for their business. Years ago, a doctor friend gave me a notepad that looked like a sandwich. It had wheat-colored foam-rubber bread that hinged opened to reveal a thick tricolored pad of paper. It was an elaborate ad for a new kind of cholesterol-free, reduced-calorie mayonnaise. We had a running conversation about bizarre doctor "swag," so he was showing this to me as the latest goofy example. As soon as I saw it, an idea popped into my head. I was heavily involved in mail art at the time and was always on the lookout for new materials to work with. The next day I wrote up a description of a mail art project on a napkin, put the sandwich in a lunch bag, and addressed it to the A-1 Waste Paper Company, the pseudonym for a mail art couple in Britain. The instructions were simple: Decorate as many pages as you like, mail a postcard telling me who the sandwich will be visiting next, and then mail it there. When the pad is filled, mail it back to me (the last page had mailing instructions). I didn't really have any expectations that I'd ever see the sandwich again, but I was interested in how long it would stay circulating and if I could track its whereabouts. The postcards came back for about six months and then stopped. I was convinced that my traveling sandwich was lost and soon forgot about it. One year later to the week, a package arrived from England. Inside was an impressively tattered and torn lunch bag festooned with addresses, rubber-stamped images, and stickers. Inside that, now bulging with mail art goodness, was my sandwich. I can't describe the thrill. It was like throwing a message-in-a-bottle into the ocean, and one year later, receiving dozens of replies in the same bottle. The notepad had traveled through nine countries and had been worked on by sixteen different people. There were hand-drawn images, rubber stamps, stickers, eraser carvings, poetry, fiction, photos, shards of glass, string, yarn, scrabble letters, foreign money, and a key chain. Most of the work was not overwhelming by any traditional art standards, but it was the process that was so exciting. People from around the world had participated, adding a little piece of themselves, and then passing it on. Each person was invested enough in the project to keep it going. In response to the project, I printed up a sheet of documentation and returned it to everyone who'd been involved (if they left their address).

This is just one example of the playful, diverse, and democratized world of mail art. Within this world there are countless forms of expression: eraser-carved stamps traded as images; collage art (done either individually or collaboratively) and mailed to other collage artists; themed projects where everyone sends work to one person on a particular subject and the curator sends documentation back to all; or where each participant sends a certain number of copies of their work (say 100) and the curator collates them and sends a mail art "kit" back to all of the participants. Some mail artists specialize in pushing the limits of the postal system, mailing three-dimensional objects, currency, three-foot-long letters, etc. The basic credo of mail art is: everyone can play (everyone has an artist within them), mail art is noncommercial, and the process is at least as important as the product. Mail art has also been called the proto-Internet, a form of international networking that allows people from different cultures and walks of live to share art, ideas, and information through the postal system.

Ray Johnson (1927–1995) is often credited as the father of mail art (but, in fact, mail art stretches back to the Dadaist and Futurists). In the 1960s, Johnson, of Black Mountain College in North Carolina and the New York avant-garde art scene of the '60s, created what was dubbed the New York Correspondence School. Anyone who sent art correspondence to Johnson was made an instant member. Johnson was best known for his numerous phony fan clubs (Shelly Duval Fan Club, Paloma Picasso Fan Club), his cartoon bunny multiples (which looked like crude mutant Mickeys that celebrated the "stars" of mail art and pop culture, and prefigured the works of Andy Warhol and Keith Haring), and his "Ray Johnson 1927–1989" sticker prank. Johnson's interest in conceptual art, word games, puzzles, junk culture, pranks, and his fascination with flavor-of-the-month pop culture set the tone for much of the mail art that has followed.

Mail art grew as a response to an increasingly commercial art marketplace that deified a few artists and relegated their work to gallery and museum walls. Mail art was (and still remains) largely conceptual and ephemeral art that defies easy categorization and commodification. Like punk music and zines, mail art is about being spontaneous, raw, and unfiltered. It's about sharing yourself and your passions with little regard to widely accepted notions of beauty, artistry, or taste. Although the growth of the email, fax networking, and the Web has lessened activity in postal art networking, there is still a healthy international community of artists who participate. Many have embraced the Web, email, and fax as other channels for disseminating their work and announcing upcoming mail art events.

Somebody recently gave me another notepad. This one looks like a six-foot paintbrush with a colored notepad where the bristles would be. I think I feel another mail art project coming on. Time to paint the planet!

THE PRANKSTER'S STARTER KIT

Getting Started) Like all forms of media hacking, pranks are usually content-driven: You have something to say and you decide what media channel to send it down. There are, of course, situations where the medium itself is the proverbial message—pranks designed to call the media's attention to itself and its predatory nature.

Sometimes, opportunities present themselves that just beg to have a prank built around them. Several years ago, a Washington, D.C., artist was walking around the Mall, marveling at the patriotic overbearingness of the many statues: white men on oversized steeds rearing up and galloping through the city's squares like they own the place. When he brought this up later in the day at a gathering of fellow artists, an idea for a prank immediately popped to mind. By the end of the night, after bantering around lots of possibilities, the plan was set to dress the statues up like clowns—adding giant rubber noses, Day-Glo hair, giant goofy shoes (on both the human and the horses) for the upcoming Presidents' Day. At first, there was no real message, but after the clown concept gelled, and someone mentioned the proximity to Presidents' Day, the full prank emerged. A lot of lively discussion followed: What would people be told the action meant? Would a phony group name be used? Would the pranksters attach their name to the action or remain anonymous? How would people react to it? What sort of trouble could they get into?

The prank never happened, but it made for a fun evening of scheming, arguing, and marveling at the potential for making media-amplified art. It seemed certain that if it had been pulled off, it would almost certainly have made the evening news and the next day's paper (which, in D.C., is the globally distributed *Washington Post*). Of course, the press would have been tipped off beforehand to make sure that they were on the scene.

This example illustrates several infectious aspects of pranks: They're almost as much fun to conceive as they are to actually do. They can be so satisfying to brainstorm—especially among a group of seasoned and good-humored pranksters—that there's a danger of getting lazy about bringing such spectacles into the real world. Fear of getting caught and of getting arrested can sometimes shackle the pranksters, encouraging them to keep the prank safe in the realm of fantasy. Luckily, real pranking has a thrill to it that makes it worth all the risks, as any performer of media pranks and acts of poetic terrorism will tell you. Pranks, both real and imagined, are also therapeutic. They act as an antidote to the helplessness, anger, and frustration that comes with full critical awareness of the insidiousness of mainstream media. For those who feel hustled, brainwashed, talked down to, and marginalized by mainstream media (and media seems to be synonymous with culture these days), pranking is a way of fighting back, through parody, humor, and absurdist gestures.

Planning)

Once you've figured out what kind of trouble you want to get into, careful planning of your prank is the next step. Don't underestimate this. While you don't want to overplan and lose the spontaneity, thinking through all of the logistics, safety considerations, likely impact, and how to get the biggest media bang for your buck will almost always pay off. Not every prank is intended to be done before the big eye of the media, but for most pranks discussed here, it's an essential part of the equation.

Let's look at each of these aspects:

1) **Logistics**—Pranks are almost always intended for public consumption. Sure, there are private pranks and practical jokes, but what we're

considering here is the kind of shenanigans that produce public reaction. To pull off such feats, you need a sensible plan of attack. In the above example of the clown statues prank, the group of artists was planning on first scouting out all of the statues, even going so far as to take pictures and measurements. The group would have likely divided itself up to handle different tasks (fabricating the props and costumes, preparing media materials, researching the legal risks, etc.) and spent many hours discussing all of the relevant details. In some situations, you'll even want to go so far as to "case the joint" to get some idea of traffic (people and vehicles) and other conditions surrounding the site.

2) **Safety**—If your prank involves breaking the law (such as trespassing), you'll want to plan extra carefully to ensure that you don't end up behind bars. In scouting out a site, you'll want to appear inconspicuous, even to the point of dressing the part. For instance, if you're planning on going onto the grounds of a business to snoop through their trash, you might want to wear a little something that "says" service personnel. For years, computer hackers have used "social engineering" (usually, impersonating someone else) to gain information they need to go where they're not invited. You can use similar techniques for getting information that can be useful in pulling off pranks.

With an illegal prank, it's a good idea to post lookouts who can tip you off if law enforcement shows up. Some cheap walkie-talkies can come in handy for this. In doing any sort of orchestrated event that covers a lot of ground, mobile radios will save a lot of excess legwork.

In discussing the practical aspects of media pranks, guerilla art, and acts of poetic terrorism, I've simplified things by lumping them all together here as "pranks."

Naughty pranks that push or break the boundaries of the law should be undertaken with full knowledge of the consequences. Find out beforehand about applicable laws and likely penalties. And don't kid yourself into thinking that you're not going to get caught. If you can't afford that risk, don't do anything illegal. Make a plan for what to do if any of the participants get arrested. If you're really slick about it, you'll already have a lawyer standing by should anyone get arrested.

Besides being able to pull off a prank without getting caught, you have the physical safety of the participants to consider. The naughty enthusiasm and sense of danger that comes with some pranks is a big rush, but it can also be dangerous. You can forget what you're doing and not look where you're going. The adrenaline that's generated during a prank can make you more daring. Everyone should be reminded to keep their heads and not doing anything stupid.

3) **Impact**—Obviously, you can't predict the outcome of a prank. Once you let it loose into the cold cruel world, it'll unfold by circumstances beyond your control. But you can gauge, to some extent, what the impact of the prank might be. If there is any way you can make contingencies for likely outcomes, do so.

For instance, if your goal is to alter a billboard, you should expect some local media exposure and an investigation by the sign company into who messed up their sign. It is unlikely that the impact will go beyond that. On the other hand, if you plan on marching naked with a group of anti-fur protesters through downtown Manhattan, it's likely that you'll . . . er . . . arouse quite a bit more attention, draw a crowd, stop traffic, and get arrested. If the arrest is part of the impact you're seeking, you might at least want to plan on stashing clothes near the likely arrest site (unless you want to be hauled off to jail nude). If you don't want to get caught, you can use the crowd you're likely draw to your advantage. You can put on clothes that you've stashed beforehand and quickly blend into the crowd. If you plan on burning an American flag on the steps of the Capitol, you might end up getting assaulted by angry patriots. Contingency plans for how to get out of such a situation unharmed are a smart idea (unless, of course, getting the crap kicked out of you is part of your plan).

4) **Media Mileage**—Since most pranks are intended for media consumption, knowing how to exploit the media can make for a higher impact prank. If it's the type of prank that would benefit by having the media as a witness, you can send them press releases (by mail or email) or phone ahead of time. Put together a database of media contacts. Over the years, thanks to the various DIY media projects I've been involved with, I've established a considerable list of key people in the national and local media, in print, TV, radio, and now, cyberspace. Armed with such a list, a phone, fax machine, and a computer, one can quickly and easily send out enticing media bait.

Regardless of how clever your pre-event publicity is, don't expect the media to automatically show up. As you might imagine, they have lots of stories vying for their attention. Make sure you invite a photographer (shooting black-and-white film), and ideally a videographer, to your prank. Follow up the event with another release, and ideally photos. Even then, you can't guarantee coverage.

If you're doing a prank with a group, it's often a good idea to choose someone who's articulate and diplomatic to be your media liaison. This isn't to exclude anyone from talking to journalists, but in this world of sound-bite journalism, you might get more mileage if someone is particularly good at explaining your activities.

Execution)

How you go about executing your prank has a lot to do with what type of prank it is. Some events will need more planning and orchestration than others. If your prank involves breaking the law, you may want to not only plan the prank carefully but also go through a dry run so you'll know how long everything takes. For instance, platform jumpers (those daredevils who parachute from buildings, towers, and bridges) often use a team of helpers and a carefully planned and pre-timed scheduled to maximize safety, impact (ew . . . poor choice of words), and to ensure a successful getaway. Some platform-jumping groups have been able to pull off dozens of these very visible stunts (some in the middle of rush-hour traffic) without getting caught.

Documentation)

Anyone who's involved with performance art or other process-oriented forms of art will tell you that documentation is everything. Documentation, documentation, documentation. When I interviewed Lynn McCary of Art Attack, she lamented several times the fact that early "attacks" had not been recorded. Now the group is very attentive to documentation, and even collects artifacts from their installations. These events are fleeting, and while that's part of their charm, they can have a more lasting impact and greater reach if recorded. The more media antenna you can deploy, the better: cameras, video, tape recorders, written accounts, whatever.

Words of Wisdom)

Reverend Al (L.A. Cacophony Society):

: Pranks aren't reactive like acts of revenge. They don't punish, they provoke. They don't target individuals, they target ideals.

: Revenge is a science, pranking is an art.

: In certain situations, you may not be able to be there to savor the expression on the face of your "victim." It may be incriminating or impractical. But this shouldn't deter the prankster. Pranks are for the world.

: The true prankster pranks altruistically.

: An artful practical joke can be considered a prank; a prank that endures is a hoax; and a hoax that endures is reality.

Alberto Gaitán (Art Attack):

: Decide if you want to work legally or . . . ah . . . "extra-legally." But don't tie yourself to one way of doing things. Some projects are better suited for guerrilla tactics, others for more above-ground tactics. If you want to work illegally, accept the fact that your work will be very temporary (left to the whims of weather and authorities), and that you won't be able to reap any public relations benefits from it. ("…fakirism in vacuo does not fecundate!"—Ezra Pound). If you want to work legally, you may want to get yourselves a nonprofit corporation rating. This is a marginally helpful way of getting donations of money, materials, and services. Also, get permits, where possible, to work in public sites. This usually entails a visit to the local Department of Public Works.

: Keep your eyes open for trash or salvage heaps around construction sites and around town. It's always better to ask permission, where possible, even before taking trash. Visit dump yards regularly, especially those specializing in materials you like to work in (metal, for example). Remember the value of multiples of anything!

: Start planning early on your publicity/propaganda campaign. Don't wait until you finish a project before putting out press releases. Try to get as many people as possible to write about your work or to otherwise document it. Documentation is all you'll have left after a temporary piece is demolished. It is not only invaluable as a learning aide, it will also get you into many doors as lecturers, etc.

: Find collaborators that cover a wide set of talents. Get in contact with collaborative groups around the world. Correspondence with foundations and arts centers around the world can yield good contacts.

: Organize cheap happenings that can raise funds for operating costs. Research possible cultural grants internationally; apply to as many as you can, as often as you can.

: Remember that collaborative work is not the easiest way of working. If you have trouble letting go of "bad" ideas, or of letting your ideas get morphed by group dynamics, go back to your lonely studio. Leave as much of your ego at the door as possible and learn to be an advocate for ideas you care strongly about.

: Meet regularly, either in meatspace or cyberspace. Have a running agenda list that includes new prospects, materiel safaris, and development of modular (off-the-shelf) projects that can be deployed rapidly, in case the opportunity arises.

: Leave a significant amount of brainstorming for a project until you're on-site. Let the creative process become interactive with all phases of project development and materials acquisition.

Eternal Network: A Mail Art Anthology*

CHUCK WELCH
UNIVERSITY OF CALGARY PRESS
2500 UNIVERSITY DR. N.W., CALGARY, ALBERTA, CANADA T2N 1N4
1995, $39.95 (PLUS $3 SHIPPING)

Longtime mail artist and archivist Chuck Welch (who works under the pseudonym the Crackerjack Kid) has put together an exhaustive history, manifesto, and archive on mail art networking. *Eternal Network* includes essays by artists from around the world along with photographs and illustrations of mail art artifacts (letters and envelopes, stampoid sheets, posters, collages, artists' books, visual poetry, computer art, mail art zines, copy art, and rubber-stamped images). You probably don't want to spend too much time on the history of mail art (it's an immediate, democratic, and active art form), but as an artifact of art history this book is essential.

Happy Mutant Handbook:*
Mischievous Fun for Higher Primates

GARETH BRANWYN, MARK FRAUENFELDER, WILL KRETH, CARLA SINCLAIR, EDITORS
RIVERHEAD BOOKS, 1995, 205 PAGES, $15

Shameless Plug Alert: I co-authored this book. While it's not completely devoted to pranks and media hacks, there's a lot of interest here to the budding poetic terrorist. Herein are profiles of posterist Robbie Conal, media hoaxster Joey Skaggs, found footage filmmaker Craig Baldwin, the Cacophony Society, and the Billboard Liberation Front. "The Urban Absurdist Survival Kit" provides original artwork for stickers, coupons, and other signage that can be color-photocopied and cut out. There are head-scratchin' signs for the workplace ("CAUTION: Small Mind Sector. Displays of enlightenment may carry risks for individuals"), stickers to put on supermarket foodstuffs ("Bioengineered Food Product. Genetically Altered Through Combination with Human DNA"), and all kinds of other bizarre messages to confound and delight fellow humans.

Pranks! (RE/Search #11)*

JUNO AND VALE, EDITORS
RE/SEARCH PUBLICATIONS
20 ROMOLO ST. #B, SAN FRANCISCO, CA 94133
415-362-1465
EMAIL: research@sirius.com
1987, 240 PAGES, 164 PHOTOS, $19.99

An issue of the notorious San Francisco fringe culture "bookazine," *Pranks!* is an overdose of serious, twisted fun from RE/Search regulars Henry Rollins, Mark

Pauline, Monte Cazazza, Joe Coleman, along with Earth First!, Timothy Leary, Abbie Hoffman, Paul Krassner, Jello Biafra, Karen Finley, and others. Here are accounts of pranks great and small, plus essays on the significance of pranking for better cultural health. *Pranks!* cruises the spectrum, from practical jokes and prank calls to the classic countercultural pranks of the Yippies and Timothy Leary. Some of those interviewed recall pranks played on them by "ordinary" folks, like their garbage man.

(MAGA)ZINES

Adbusters/The Media Foundation

1243 W. 7TH AVE., VANCOUVER, B.C., V6H 1B7 CANADA
604-736-9401, 1-800-663-1243 *(ORDERS ONLY)*
WEB: www.adbusters.org/adbusters/
EMAIL: adbusters@adbusters.org
$18/ 4 ISSUES

> *Adbusters* is a Canadian-based magazine that critiques the media through essays and spoof advertising. Using these anti-ads (which they call "subvertising"), it makes fun of cigarette, car, clothing, and liquor ads and other forms of commercial propaganda. *Adbusters* is part of The Media Foundation, "a media activist organization counteracting those who would pollute our mental environment." It recruits culture jammers on college campuses and elsewhere, coordinates the annual International Buy Nothing Day, and runs Powershift Advocacy Agency, an anti-ad agency that has placed 30-second TV spots and print ads with CNN, the BBC, *Utne Reader*, and elsewhere. (See Videos below.)

Global Mail

MICHAEL DITTMAN
GROVE CITY FACTORY STORES
P.O. BOX 1309, GROVE CITY, PA 16127
EMAIL: soapbox@well.com
WEB: www.well.com/user/soapbox/eglobal.html
$3/PRINT ISSUE *(free on the Internet)*

> *Global Mail* is a massive listing of mail art and mail art events, along with zines, books, audio, video, and just about anything else editor Ashley Parker Owens hears about. *Global Mail* comes out three times a year in January, May, and September.

Twisted Times

STUART MANGRUM, EDITOR
BOX 271222, CONCORD, CA 94527
EMAIL: stumangrum@aol.com
$3/ISSUE, $10/4 ISSUES *(cash only)*

Stuart does an excellent job of putting together this digest-size fringe culture and prank zine. There are strange articles from the mainstream press, detourned ads, articles on all sorts of bohemian pursuits, and reports on pranks and Cacophonic events (Stuart is a member of the S.F. Cacophony Society).

ORGANIZATIONS

®Tmark (pronounced ArtMark)

EMAIL: artmark@hotmail

®Tmark is a secret organization whose goal is "to encourage the intelligent sabotage of mass-produced items." They describe themselves as "essentially a matchmaker and bank, helping groups and individuals fund sabotage projects." In the last five years the group has funded such projects as the Barbie Liberation Organization and the SimCopter prank, where a programmer for the Maxis game company put animations of kissing men into a helicopter flight simulator. The group has only recently gone public with their email address in an effort to recruit new culture jammers. Email them for more information.

The Cacophony Society

Offering "experiences beyond the pale," the Cacophony Society is a loose-knit network of groups located in San Francisco, Los Angeles, Seattle, and Portland. Each group has its own flavor, but they're all dedicated to offbeat pursuits and celebration of the unusual. All of the societies publish newsletters and maintain cool Web sites with event announcements, event reports, and pictures.

Cicada Corps of Artists

WEB: www.surfcap.com/cicada/home.html
EMAIL: cicada@escape.com

Cicada Corps is a small network of artists who are involved in various forms of culture jamming: billboard alteration, public service postering, exhibitions, subvertisements, and other media events. They also curate the "10 on 8 Windows Exhibition Space" (located on the corner of 53rd Street and 8th Avenue in New York City), which is viewed by some 15,000 people daily.

The Foundation for Convulsive Beauty

EMAIL: fcb@mailmasher.com

FCB is another secret organization dedicated to encouraging and funding pranks against the media, the advertising businesses, and consumer culture. The group has $20,000 to award "for the best act of creative subversion of any highly visible commercial product (mass-produced item, advertisement, television show, etc.)." The award rules, available at the email address above, specify that the subversive act "MUST NOT cause physical injury, MUST NOT gratuitously damage the product or company, and MUST NOT be an attempt by one individual or company to damage another."

Los Angeles Cacophony Society

P.O. BOX 291718, LOS ANGELES, CA 90029
213-937-2759, FAX: 213-666-4261
WEB: www.alumni.caltech.edu/~reynard/la_caco/la_caco.html
EMAIL: cacofony@address.net

> L.A. Cacophony publishes both a newsletter, *Tales from the Zone,* and a zine called *LOONIESIDE.* Sample issues of *Tales from the Zone* are available for free (send stamps). $10/year gets you *The Zone, LOONIESIDE,* prank flyers, religious tracts, plastic oddities, stickers, and whatever else Rev. Al and company feel like tossing into the envelope. For the special "Fanatic Rate" of $15, you get all of the above, plus more mailable weirdness. *Tales from the Zone* is also available from their Web site.

Portland Cacophony Society

P.O. BOX 25093, PORTLAND, OR 97225
503-727-2428
EMAIL: albob@zzz.com

> *Meaningless Madness* is printed and mailed at cost to the Cacophony faithful. Subscriptions are $9.95/year which gets you the newsletter and other goodies inside an artistically decorated envelope. *Meaningless Madness* is also available from their Web site.

San Francisco Cacophony Society

P.O. BOX 424969-W, SAN FRANCISCO, CA 94142-4969
415-665-0351
WEB: www.zpub.com/caco/
EMAIL: zpub@sirius.com

> S.F. Cacophony Society publishes *Rough Draft,* a periodic calendar and newsletter. Single copies are free (send stamps); a one-year subscription is $12.

Seattle Cacophony Society

923 27TH AVE., SEATTLE, WA 98122
206-251-1185
WEB: www.halcyon.com/anitar/cacoph.html
EMAIL: anitar@halcyon.com

> *Machination: Plots, Plans, and Schemes of the Seattle Cacophony Society* is the Seattle Cacophony Society's newsletter. Subscriptions are $10/12 issues. *Machination* is also available on their Web site.

VIDEOS

BLO Nightly News
BARBIE LIBERATION ORGANIZATION
3841 4TH AVE, SUITE 207, SAN DIEGO, CA 92103
1994, VHS, $25 *(make check payable to Igor Vamos)*

> A documentary of the Barbie Liberation Organization's now famous toy hack on Barbie and GI Joe. The video shows how the group made the alterations (a how-to!), and documents the event and the media aftermath.

The Culture Jammer's Video
(see Adbusters in (Maga)zines above)
VHS, 14 MINUTES, $35

> A series of 30-second spots created by the Media Foundation's "social marketing" arm, PowerShift. It includes "The Product Is You" (about couch-potato consumerism), "Obsession Fetish" (on the beauty industry), "Autosaurus" (on car worship), and "Buy Nothing Day" (a spot about their annual anti-consumer campaign). Culture jammers have shown these spots to groups, put them on the air, and even recorded them onto the ends of rental videos.

Sonic Outlaws
CRAIG BALDWIN, DIRECTOR
992 VALENCIA ST., SAN FRANCISCO, CA 94110
1995, VHS, 87 MINUTES, $30
(make check payable to Craig Baldwin)

> A dense montage "documentary" on culture jammers that grew out of an investigation into the lawsuit U2's Island Records filed against the audio collage band Negativland. Island accused the band of copyright infringement and "causing confusing in the marketplace" for their use of the title "U2" for one of their singles and the unauthorized use of a U2 song sample. The video covers other audio collage artists such as Emergency Broadcast Network, The Tape-Beatles, and John Oswald of Plunderphonics fame. Baldwin's other films *Tribulation 99* and *¡Oh No Coronado!* can also be ordered from him at $19.99 each.

CATALOGS

American Science & Surplus
3605 HOWARD ST., SKOKIE, IL 60076
847-982-0870, FAX: 800-934-0072
WEB: www.sciplus.com

> Looking for Israeli gas masks, "Police Line—Do Not Cross" tape, mini-Tesla coils, bags of neon-colored turkey feathers? American Science and Surplus has all sorts of bizarre junk and useful tools, materials, and supplies that can be used in pranks and art projects.

Archie McPhee

P.O. BOX 30852, SEATTLE, WA 98103
206-745-0711
WEB: www.mcphee.com
EMAIL: mcphee@halcyon.com

These self-proclaimed "outfitters of popular culture" sell plastic kitsch: toys, gags, and baubles that work like surrealist exaggerations of more mundane consumer items (bugs in a three pack, punching nun puppets, Torah Personality trading cards, quart jars filled with tiny gumball charms). Since many of these items sarcastically poke fun at pop culture and the media, they make good materials for pranks. I bought a quart jar of "Tiny Treasures" and had fodder for my mail art projects for years.

Paper Direct

1-800-A-PAPERS
(see more details in the New Media Hacker's Starter Kit)

This catalog is a gold mine for pranksters looking to work in print. They carry all kinds of laser- and copier-friendly sticker paper, posters, signage, certificates, etc. You could probably take over the world with the social engineering possible through phony documents made using the materials available in this catalog.

NET SITES

bOING bOING Online

WEB: www.well.com/user/mark

This is the Web site for *bOING bOING* magazine and the *Happy Mutant Handbook*. The content is slow to change, but there's some fun stuff here, including pieces on a number of media pranks.

Electronic Museum of Mail Art

WEB: www.dartmouth.edu/~emailart/

EMMA is Chuck Welch's Web site. There's a "gallery" of postal art, back issues of Welch's mail art newsletter, a directory of email artists, and information on his book *Eternal Network* (see Books above).

Goy Division

WEB: www.tezcat.com/~kritikal

Goy Division is an audio prank comedy group that targets fundamentalist and right wing radio talk shows. Their Web site has a number of essays and comedy pieces along with examples of their call-in pranks that can be listened to with the TrueSpeech audio player. The site also has a useful guide on how to get onto a radio call-in show and stay on long enough to deliver your message.

Guerrilla Girls

532 LAGUARDIA PLACE #237, NEW YORK, NY 10012
WEB: www.voyagerco.com/gg/
EMAIL: guerrillagirls@voyagerco.com

"The Guerrilla Girls are a group of women artists and arts professionals who make posters about discrimination. Dubbing ourselves the conscience of the art world, we declare ourselves feminist counterparts to the mostly male tradition of anonymous do-gooders such as Robin Hood, Batman, and the Lone Ranger. We wear gorilla masks to focus on the issues rather than our personalities. We use humor to convey information, provoke discussion, and show that feminists can be funny. In ten years we have produced over seventy posters, printed projects, and actions that expose sexism and racism in the art world and the culture at large. Our work has been passed around the world by kindred spirits who consider themselves Guerrilla Girls too. The mystery surrounding our identities has attracted attention and support. We could be anyone; we are everywhere. The Girls' Web site contains an archive of their posters, letters from friends and enemies, some diary entries on their travels, and a catalog of their books and posters.

Tabloid Trash

WEB: pages.map.com/rclark/

A Web zine dedicated to mail art, email art, eraser carving, and other forms of correspondence art. There are scanned images of eraser carvings, an email art gallery, a how-to section on eraser carving, and links to other mail artists Web sites.

Trolls, Media Hacks, and Pranks

WEB: www.nepenthes.com/Hacks/index.html

A huge link list of information, articles, and reports of media pranks and practical jokes. UFO hoaxes, prank callers to TV shows and email to corporations, P. T. Branum, phony virus scares, the Grunge Lexicon prank, Joey Skaggs, Crop Circles, Yippie actions . . . it's all here.

Usenet Newsgroups:

alt.shenanigans

A Usenet newsgroup devoted to pranks and practical jokes. There's a lot of dumb college dorm stuff here (putting saran wrap over a toilet bowl), but some clever pranks and media hacks as well.

Sociomedia and Publishing with ELECTRONS

> The technology that makes **VIRTUAL COMMUNITIES** possible has the potential to bring enormous leverage to ordinary **CITIZENS** at relatively little cost— **INTELLECTUAL LEVERAGE**, social leverage, commercial leverage, and most **IMPORTANTLY**, political leverage.
>
> —Howard Rheingold, *The Virtual Community*

Back in the bad ol' days of the Net, before URLs began appearing in television commercials and there was no such thing as junk email, communication was low bandwidth, plain-text only. There was no VRML, no Java, no cybercasting, no online soaps, and no virtual strip malls. Then along came the World Wide Web in 1993, and everything changed. The Web gobbled up the Internet at an awesome speed, morphing it into its own multimedia image.

The World Wide Web was originally created to help far-flung clusters of tossled-haired physicists exchange research papers and other electronic documents. The idea was to create a globe-spanning "universe of documents" where references in one document—say in a computer in Geneva—could be linked to the actual referenced document, even if it was located halfway around the planet. This system for interlinking Net documents in a hypertext web was conceived of in 1989 by Tim Berners-Lee, a researcher at CERN (a physics research facility) in Switzerland. The Web existed modestly for several years as a little-known corner of Internet geekdom. With the introduction of the graphical Web browser NCSA Mosaic (which begot Netscape) in 1993, the speed of Net development took an exponential leap, leading by Net years (now equal to dog years) to today's digital feeding frenzy.

What set the graphical browser apart from previous Web technology was that it provided a way of displaying more than just text-based information. It could display pictures, sounds, small movies, and variable typestyles, all in an attractive, graphic package. In short, Mosaic allowed the average netizen to put together information that looked more like the printed page than ever before. And like a lot of Net technology before it—emerging from university and research environs—Web server software, the Mosaic browser, and a suite of support programs (helper applications) were offered to the Internet community for free. This allowed anyone, from tiny zine publishers to Fortune 500 megacorporations, the capability of setting up shop on the Net.

The Web offers a remarkable opportunity for the fledgling small publisher. Though it's still possible (and sometimes preferable) to publish through emailing lists and FTP sites, the Web offers the opportunity to create full-blown magazines at a very low cost. One can also incorporate media not traditionally found in print: digitized videos, sound clips, animations, links to other related publications, and even interactive stuff like feedback forms,

When talking about the Internet and the World Wide Web, it can get confusing as to when to say Web and when to say Internet. They are often used interchangeably. Basically, the Internet is the all-encompassing network of networks that runs a set of standards called TCP/IP. The World Wide Web is a subset of this, a distributed system of multimedia documents (and the software to store, retrieve, and display them) housed on Internet computers throughout the world and marked up for display using a system of codes called HTML. Adding to the confusion are Web browsers that are increasingly becoming Internet platforms in and of themselves, allowing you to do email, access newsgroups and software libraries, conference, watch videos, run Java applications, and other functions, all without ever leaving your browser. The easiest way to think about it is that the Web is a suite of applications that run on top of the Internet (sort of like how Windows runs on top of DOS on a PC).

conferencing areas, and real-time chat. And best of all, your little media empire is accessible to potentially millions of people worldwide.

Internet publishing represents a new form of media, a metamedium, able to synthesize nearly every other media type. It's interactive, allowing publications to change to suit the moods and choices of producers and consumers. It's immediate—you can change your publication whenever you like—you're not constrained to a fixed publication. Though the Net is huge, this immediacy and interactivity seems to pull people together in ways that more traditional, solitary forms of media can't. Net publishing builds virtual community. People *participate* in online publications, coming together to read, comment on, critique, cajole, and contribute material, creating something that's truly unique. In fact, as Web technology develops, the whole idea of a publication in the print sense is becoming obsolete. Online publishers are starting to create information "spaces" that people ("readers," "members," "users," whatever you want to call them) can wander around and interact in. One term that's been suggested for this type of metamedium is "cyberstation."

The sociomedia of cyberspace is breaking down old relationships between media producers and consumers. In more traditional forms of media—magazines, newspapers, films, television, recorded music—the producer rarely gets a chance to interact immediately with consumers. On the other hand, the consumer of old media is presented with an unchangeable object, an artifact that represents a fixed point in time. Things may (and usually do) change after publication or broadcast, but the media producer cannot respond (until the next publishing/broadcast cycle). Web publications are fluid. Corrections and clarifications can be made on-the-fly, based on user response. Published pieces can grow as new material is acquired. And instead of ending up with a series of published artifacts (back issues of magazines, an archive of taped broadcasts), Web publications exist as a single growing entity that can be quickly and easily searched. There doesn't have to be any hierarchy or fixed points of access. One can enter anywhere and move in any direction.

But the World Wide Web has also come at a cost, perhaps with grave implications for noncommercial publishers and legitimate virtual communities. The incredible potential of the Web as a new form of media has caused a feeding frenzy among mainstream media producers, the entertainment business and product providers. Big media and the marketplace have discovered the Web big-time and would now like to retool it to meet their ravenous needs. The Internet population explosion is taxing the infrastructure of the network and siring a new generation of netizens who think the Net is synonymous with radio and television—just another broadcast medium. Wrong. Wrong. Wrong. In this headlong rush to deliver online shopping, TV-like programming, and advertisements masquerading as Web content, we're losing what's really special and powerful about the Internet: people communicating with each another. Being someone who's frequently called on to give my opinion on the future of the Internet, I'm often asked: "So, what are you most excited about now and in the near future?" My answer has remained relatively unchanged since the late '80s: "People are what drew me to the Net, and people are what will keep me coming back. People sharing ideas, expertise, stories, struggles, and creativity." It may sound corny, but it's the truth. The World Wide Web and all of the innovations that have come from it are wonderful and they provide an unprecedented opportunity for the media hacker and the virtual communitarian, but without warm bodies on the other end of the wires, you're just looking at more dancing baloney.

It's still too early to say exactly how the big media will influence cyber-space. Information gridlock is already a big problem and will get worse as streaming media, Web TVs, email pagers, and other bandwidth-gobbling technologies tax the system. It's also likely that future legislation and regulation will be friendly towards media conglomerates and less than magnanimous to the little people on the Net. As I write this, the Fox network has just sent a cease and desist letter to all Webmasters who run unofficial *X-Files* sites, saying that the consumer will be better served by officially sanctioned *X-Files* content on the Web. This is beyond clueless and a perfect example of how the mainstream media still doesn't "get it."

THE FOURTH WAVE
of ZINES)

Jerod Pore of *Factsheet Five* has called e-zines the fourth wave of zinedom. The first wave was the sci-fi fanzines of the '30s and '40s, the second was the underground comics and political publications of the '60s, and the third wave was the emergence of punk/disaffected youth zines of the '70s and '80s. He writes, in Issue #57 of *Factsheet Five*:

"E-zines can be as simple as the Internet-published versions of existing printed zines (*F5, Bust,* and *private line,* for example), or more complex publications that exist only on the Net. Like printed zines, e-zines will start in a mad flurry of enthusiasm, a couple of issues get produced, and then the publication vanishes. Unlike printed zines, though, an e-zine can either stay available to the public for years after the publisher has given up (such as *High Weirdness by Email*) or the zine can instantly vanish off the Net

BUST E-ZINE >
www.bust.com

when some snooping corporate or university geek happens to notice an unusually high number of hits to the Web server. Where printed zines can have reprints from other zines, sophisticated webzines can have actual links to other webzines—so you can be reading one zine, click on a button or tab down to a pointer and suddenly you're reading another zine—presuming it hasn't been yanked by the aforementioned geek."

The diversity and number of available e-zines is truly staggering. John Labovitz, who maintains the E-Zine-List Web site, has some 1,400 titles listed, reviewed, and hyperlinked. A quick spelunking through his database yields: *8-Track Mind*, a zine for 8-track tape "dead media necronauts"; *Chip's Closet Cleaner*, covering pop culture, sex, trivia, pranks, and fun; *The Circular File*, "the online guide to disposable culture with essays and criticism for people who can't keep their rooms clean"; *Fine Fishing*, a zine devoted to the art of angling; *Gearhead*, a zine about science fiction and high technology; *Gremlins in the Garage*, devoted to model kit enthusiasts; *Gutter Voice*, web fiction with a bad attitude; *Minerva*, a zine for politically progressive Catholics; *Proust Said That,* a zine for fans of Marcel; *Star Facts*, a watering hole for astronomy geeks; *Vagabond Monthly*, a small highways travel zine.

While most Web-based zines are still mainly text and graphics, some are beginning to add background and downloadable sounds, animations, streaming audio and video (i.e., no download time), and even conferencing and chat areas. But as Net technology becomes increasingly sophisticated, it'll become more difficult for the average netizen to keep up with the skills set needed to program a cutting-edge Web site. Already such languages as (high-end) HTML, VRML, and Java have leapt so far ahead of the original HTML that noncommercial users are being left behind. But at the same time, new meta-tools are being created that do all the heavy lifting so that publishers can use input boxes and menu items to create the applications they want. The other impediment to keeping up with these new technologies is that many of them require a full-time Internet connection, a cost-prohibitive proposition for most noncommercial media producers. This will not change until the next generation of Net connectivity options (cable modems, ADSL, and ISDN) become widespread and affordable to home users.

But ultimately, these high-end tech questions don't have much to do with DIY Net publishing. It's still all about content. One of the absolutely best e-zines out there is Brock Meeks's *CyberWire Dispatch*, a periodic emailed and Web-accessible zine about digital politics. It's nothing but text, and that's all that's needed. Meeks, a reporter by day, uses his dispatches to indulge his more edgy gonzo journalistic personality. All the Java scripts and VRML coding in the world wouldn't add much to what Brock has to say in these vitriolic screeds. Just as in the print publishing world, where scrawny little zines can sometimes hold their own against the content of a Condé Nast behemoth, so too e-zines are sometimes getting the scoop and setting the trends alongside commercial publishers. And sometimes, when the mainstream media gets it wrong, netizens rise up to make it right.

SOCIOMEDIA *in* ACTION) The July 3, 1995, *Time* arrived on newsstands and in subscriber's mailboxes with the face of a terrified child on its cover, bathed in the ominous glow of a computer monitor. Across it, splashed with a banner marked "Exclusive," the caption read:

^
HOTWIRED'S PARODY
of the TIME CyberPorn cover

"Cyberporn: A new study shows how pervasive and wild it really is. Can we protect our kids—and free speech?" Inside were other titillating images (including a naked man humping a computer monitor) and an article by Philip Elmer-DeWitt, a longtime, well-respected technology journalist. The article was principally based on a study of cyberporn that an alleged "research team" at Carnegie Mellon University in Pittsburgh, Pennsylvania, had given exclusively to *Time* and to the *Georgetown Law Journal* (where its findings were later to be published). The contents of the study, as reported in *Time*, were shocking. It claimed that not only was cyberporn on the increase, but that the images were getting more hard-core, more violent, more disturbing. The study team claimed that they "surveyed" 917,410 sexually explicit pictures, descriptions, short stories, and film clips, and that they discovered 83.5 percent of the pictures on Usenet newsgroups were pornographic in nature. The article, and the study it validated by its prominent coverage, goes on with even more alarming revelations.

Almost the instant the issue of *Time* hit cyberspace (the Sunday night before its Monday print release), it ignited a firestorm of controversy. On The Well BBS, where many journalists, civil libertarians, and cyber-pundits hang out, the Media conference fashioned itself into a crisis situation room. People who'd had dealings with Marty Rimm, the one-man "research team" who'd conducted the study, began offering their suspicions about the study and its oddly qualified, apparently lone, author (electrical engineering students usually don't single-handedly publish complex academic studies outside their field of study). An ad hoc investigative team quickly began to organize, with people volunteering to track down information on various aspects of the study and how it got legitimized by *Time*. Several academics, lawyers, and other netizens started deconstructing the Rimm study and putting together detailed critiques. Both people with a professional interest and those acting out of outrage and civic-mindedness began posting their findings: email messages that Rimm had written to various people involved in the study (and those whom he tried to sucker into endorsing it), Usenet postings, articles from other publications about Rimm's shady past (it was even discovered that Rimm had authored a small "how-to" book on marketing online porn!), and a mountain of other bizarre and revealing pieces of evidence. As Brock Meeks said in his *CyberWire Dispatch:* "Throughout this story you have to keep telling yourself: I am not in the Twilight Zone . . . I am *not* in the Twilight Zone." As information poured in on the many critical flaws in the study and Rimm himself, online journalists began cranking out columns and articles refuting the *Time* piece and the Rimm study. Within days, Internet researchers Donna Hoffman and Tom Novak had constructed a devastating point-for-point analysis that they published on their Web site at Vanderbilt University.

It was one of the most poignant, positive examples of sociomedia I have ever witnessed on the Net. The response on The Well, hundreds of lengthy postings per day, illustrated how quickly damage control can happen in cyberspace. The article came at a particularly sensitive moment, as Congress was considering passage of the Communications Decency Act (which would criminalize "obscene" and "indecent" speech over the Internet) as part of the Telecommunications Bill. During the arguments on the act, members of Congress and the Christian Right waved around the *Time* issue as the best argument so far (from the liberal media, no less!) for cracking down on an Internet clearly out of control.

The Communications Decency Act passed, but it was later overturned in a case in Philadelphia and is now awaiting appeal in the Supreme Court.

Clearly this was only the beginning of the fight over control of cyberspace. The world at large has discovered the Net, and it seems that increasing numbers of powerful moral, government, and corporate interests want authority over its future. Short of accomplishing control, these interests may seek to destroy it altogether. Given this sobering possibility, it was heartening to have witnessed an example of sociomedia taking on conventional media with impressive results. It gave me hope that the Net (or at least certain quarters of it) might be able to stem the tide of regulation and commercialization that certainly threatens it today.

FIFTEEN KEYSTROKES *of* FAME, *or* How to Become an OVER-NET SENSATION)

HOT GEEKS TRADING CARD, Tiffany Lee Brown, www.magdalen.com

The Internet is much more than a publishing medium or an information repository. It's a place where people can experiment with different styles of communication, even to the point of assuming different personalities . . . or just letting a shy personality out of the closet. Over the years, a small pantheon of well-known Net personalities has arisen, some adored, others despised. Most "enjoy" a degree of both. They've become "virtually famous," either for their bizarre beliefs and antics, their flamboyant personalities, or their ubiquitousness. This type of Net personality construct has become its own form of media: part entertainment (for both net.personality and his or her "fans"), part perzine, part self-help/self-therapy, and part art event. I asked my pal Mikki Halpin to track down one of these colorful online characters to find out what it's like to be a cyber celeb:

Some people can seduce you even in the limited text-only quarters of Usenet. "Wednesday" is a master of this art. I first ran into her in the *alt.slack* newsgroup, where I was intrigued by her rumored affair with the Cheerios Honeybee. I also found her in *alt.fan.devo, alt.wired.tired.tired.tired*, and *alt.society.neutopia*. Known throughout Usenet for her prolific posts, wry sense of humor, and withering honesty, she's instantly recognizable by her now-famous signature file, which exclaimed (tantalizingly) "Never Freeze Brie!" ("Brie is a soft cheese, and ice crystals will form, destroying the texture.")

Alternately ingenue, siren, poet, and sarcastic pop culture analyst, Wednesday started on the Net several years ago, originally posting anonymously to the *alt.abuse/recovery* groups, using an alias so her "egg donors" (parents), who are also online, wouldn't recognize her.

The first question is obvious: Why "Wednesday"? Wednesday's child is full of woe, indeed, but is there a deeper meaning? Lots of people first thought she was Christina Ricci (the actress who plays Wednesday in the *Addams Family* films) in disguise. Our Wednesday replies: "The appeal of Wednesday Addams is two-fold. For one, I think Christina Ricci is an incredibly gifted young actress. She already has an awesome screen presence. But more importantly, the character of Wednesday is very appealing to me. She's a child that grew up in a twisted, sick environment, yet she's embraced it rather than being warped by it and needing twenty years of therapy. The character (in the movies and cartoons, more than the TV show) is one of the strongest, greatest role models a child could have. She's an archetypal character, one who doesn't let anyone else define her behavior, or how she should look, or anything else. That's far more powerful than any role Julia Roberts ever played."

So how does she feel being considered a Net personality? "It's weird. I never expected anything like this. I don't know whether this is Warhol's fifteen minutes of fame or what. I don't know if it gets bigger—if it does, I'm a little afraid." Wednesday doesn't think being "famous" in cyberspace is materially different from being famous in the traditional sense. "It's just as real as any interpersonal environment, and you can be recognized just as personally as by your face. I'm an honest person, so I don't try to hide who I am when people ask." But when it comes to the Net, an issue that comes up over and over again is the possibilities for deception. Is identity a construct or a hack? "That whole reaction implies that there aren't possibilities for deception in real life," she offers. "I have been deceived on the Internet by a couple of people who've hurt me deeply . . . but generally I've had far more cases of people lying to me in person. Maybe it's the very fact that the Net allows some modicum of anonymity that propels people to come forward and be themselves. Given the chance to either finally strip bare a lot of social pretense and say what you really think, or to go to all the trouble of creating an elaborate fantasy and deluding people into believing that the fantasy is real, I think a lot of people will go for the former."

Is there anything bad about the Net and its possibilities? "Lately, with all the media hype, there's been a large influx of people who arrive with no clue about the space they are invading." While AOL has been the target of much net.wrath, Wednesday points out that the so-called September phenomenon (when freshmen arrive on campus and are given Internet access) has been a long-standing Net tradition. "I think anyone who gets a commercial account should get a FAQ in the mail, and they can't access the network 'til they read it. They arrive unprepared for the different social conventions of this environment. There's an established culture here. It makes me crazy when FAQs are disregarded. If people would take the time to educate themselves, 90 percent of all flame wars could be avoided." Ultimately, the clueless ones hurt themselves the most.

"If you don't want to connect with other people, then what the heck are you doing on the Net? I've formed many deep connections through this medium. The people I live with now, I met online, for example. Most of my closest friendships have been formed over the Net, in some capacity or another. And I try to use the Net to maintain these relationships as much as possible. It's a lot easier for me to break out of the "accepted social roles" online and actually strip myself bare (figuratively speaking!). It's possible to get intimate on any number of levels *very, very* fast. And as far as I'm concerned, those relationships are just as real as the ones maintained and/or originated in the so-called real world. I don't see this as hiding behind a computer, like lots of people do. I'd like to believe I'm not the only one throwing her real self into the virtual world, as opposed to creating a mask. People tell me there's little to no difference between the net.persona of Wednesday and the real one. Perhaps it's a naive view to take, but I wouldn't be comfortable with anything less than that kind of honesty. I've tried role-playing online and it doesn't really work."

What's the most common misconception that people have about Wednesday? "Oh God! I'm told I should answer with something like 'Huge hooters,' but then again . . . . [looking down at her chest] Nevermind! . . . I think the closest thing folks have to a misconception of me is that they tend to forget that I have my bad days, too. Wednesday has her occasional funks and grumps and off-moments."

geekgirl@logo >
logo
geekgirl motto by St. Jude >
geekgirl

GRRRLS *with* MODEMS) Sassy chicks everywhere are turning in their baby barrettes for modems, as geek chic reaches new heights. The bible of these female online hipsters is the thoughtful, personal *geekgirl* webzine from Australia. Put out by the inimitable RosieX, in seven issues *geekgirl* has established itself enough to be ripped off by *Details,* which tried to start a "Geek Girl" techno-advice column, much to Rosie's annoyance. Don't be fooled by pale Condé Nast imitations—the real thing can be found only at RosieX's Web site.

The *geekgirl* world is filled with fellow travelers in techno-feminism, as RosieX hooks up with covens of electronic witches, online support groups for Bosnian women, and theorists ranging from Sadie Plant (author of *The Cybernetic Hooker*) to the always dramatic Kathy Acker, interviewed at home alone in the bathtub. RosieX brings her personal interests and ideas to the well-researched interviews, calling Acker on inappropriate rape analogies, asking writer/filmmaker Jayne Loader for the lowdown on her long-standing friendship with Tim Leary, and talking to Hakim Bey about the Internet's and rave culture's adoption of the TAZ concept.

Each issue gets more conceptually and technically sophisticated as RosieX gains a greater command over her medium. A blast of racy political thought disguised as an easygoing conversation, *geekgirl* is a subversive signal amidst the endless noise and hype of the Web. Current estimates put the percentage of women online at 47 percent, a dramatic increase over just a few years ago. The old-boy network is giving way as more girls get wired and find their niche in cyberspace. RosieX bears their standard because grrrls need modems! Several years ago *geekgirl* was chosen as part of an exhibit of webzines at the New Museum of Contemporary Art in New York City.

AND NOW, A MOMENT *with* GEEKGIRL) *Dr. Sadie Plant teaches cultural studies in the U.K. She is interested in the issues attached to drugs, cybernetics, cyberfeminism, and machine intelligence and self-organizing systems.* This is an excerpt of an interview that appeared in the January '95 issue of *geekgirl*.

www.feminist.com >

RosieX: Why do you use the term *cyberfeminism?*

Sadie: *Cyberfeminism* to me implies an alliance being developed between women, machinery, and the new technology that women are using. It seemed to me a lot of women really love this type of technology, and because of the "toys for boys" complex it was curious that they did. I thought women should be encouraged to go with their desire. To start with, I simply used the word *cyberfeminism* to indicate this alliance. A connection. Then I started research on the history of feminism and the history of technology. It occurred to me that a long-standing relationship was evident between information technology and women's liberation. You can almost map them onto each other in the whole history of modernity. Just as machines get more intelligent, women get more liberated!

RosieX: Can I infer from your work that the term *cyberfeminism* implies that patriarchy is doomed?

Sadie: The interesting thing about this is that obviously a number of tendencies have developed. Tendencies of feminization exist economically, particularly in industry and employment practices. It's not happening because people are trying to make it happen—or even because feminist politics are driving these changes (although that is a part of it), but changes are occurring almost as an automatic process. This process is underway, and women do become more important, especially in advanced capitalist cultures. And it seems there is a shift happening right across the world.

In every sense, geographical shifts are occurring—from the center to the periphery. Sexual relationships are shifting as well. It's beautifully effortless, it's an automatic process!

RosieX: Do you think a paradigm shift is occurring? Say, an exchange from a decidedly male paradigm to a female paradigm in terms of who has power in the infotech world?

Sadie: I think the two start to converge. In a sense, women have always been the machine parts for a very much male culture. Women have been the means of reproducing the species, reproducing communications (secretaries, etc.), which is obviously similar to the role of machines and tools. So I think there really is a concurrent process: As machines get more autonomous, so do the women. I think women, once they start to make the connection, feel more comfortable with technology. And really the notion that it is all masculine is a convenient myth sustained by the present power structures. This myth is increasingly irrelevant and is an untrue picture of what's occurring. A lot of the new thoughts are being provoked by the whole cyberpunk movement—by which I mean not just the literature but the whole chaos/technoculture in which men participate in a feminine way or increasingly feminized way.

RosieX: But at the moment, generally speaking, only a few women have access to this power—are they capitalizing on these shifts? What about the gap between information-rich and information-poor women?

Sadie: It's important to realize that there is never an instantaneous change, but nevertheless, if you look at the historical situation and women's lib so far, you can begin to track future potential. Access to technology is widening. Even though we still have problems, it seems implicit in economic and political terms that these processes are automatic. The power structures with a vested interest, be they men or women in those power roles, won't hang on to them forever. The material processes underway totally mitigate against that. There is always a split between intentions and effects. I mean the intentions of the military or the power structures may intend the technology to be for them, but the effect is quite different. The more they (the military) want it for themselves, the more paradoxically they end up spreading it around. I mean, we are in the first wave of information technology, and of course, issues of access are important, but soon the issue will not be access but how to avoid it.

RosieX: Which are the major forces that will, or are, forcing a paradigm shift?

Sadie: Definitely economic. The software producers want to sell this stuff. It's not free, but it's getting very cheap. Prices are plummeting. We are witnesses to accessible technology via the market forces inherent within capitalism.

RosieX: Going back to your point about the construction of myths . . . You don't agree that girls are technophobic?

Sadie: Well, it's difficult. Generally, girls are brought up to avoid interaction with technology. Nevertheless, women's relationship with machines is more intimate historically than men's. Now, for instance, girls grow up with technology: It isn't new to them. Technophobia is increasingly becoming a myth. I think it's a shame that a lot of feminist theory buys into this notion of technophobia. It not only buys into it, it's keen to perpetuate it.

RosieX: Do you agree with Donna Harraway that technology is a deadly game?

Sadie: Only for the white guys.

(Reprinted with permission of RosieX.)

DIY METAWORLDS) There's a party goin' on. We're in the

hallway of a house, flirting, trading news, gossip, and non sequiturs. Someone is thirsty for beer and keeps asking about it. Another is shouting, "WHERE'S THE MUSIC? I WANNA DANCE!" People are filing in and out, moving to and from the upstairs, the first floor, the basement, and the outside of the house. It *feels* like a regular party, but there are some notable exceptions. I, for one, am a furry white gerbil crawling upside down along the ceiling (I'm also the one who's been yelling about music). Gene Simmons's head is floating in the corner, his legendary tongue flicking in and out as his eyes flash and multicolored threads snake through his hair. Tank Girl is standing in front of the bathroom carrying on a conversation with a large, orange female head with buck teeth. The robot from Lost in Space—whose head has temporarily changed to an old guy with white hair—is the one thirsting for the booze. As we talk, cartoon balloons appear over our heads. The only sound is an occasional giggle, car crash, or phaser blast.

Welcome to the Palace, the latest chat sensation in cyberspace. While IRC (Internet Relay Chat) and other forms of text-based chat have been around for years, The Palace, and other programs like it, offer graphical chat with sounds and animation. The "rooms" of our party house (called The STIMuVERSE) are pictures of rooms that appear on each participant's computer screen. The on-screen conversants are computer-generated characters called avatars. Each person has a customizable menu of avatars and props (hats, food, booze, flowers, weapons, groucho glasses, anything that can be created on or scanned into a computer). Text typed on each person's keyboard appears as cartoon balloons over their avatar's head (if it has anything resembling a head). An alternative interlinked network of over a thousand such Palaces has popped up in cyberspace in the last few years.

The Palace is the brainchild of Jim Bumgardner, a programmer at Time Warner who wanted to create an alternative to the more bandwidth-intensive VRML (which creates navigable three-dimensional environments that can be accessed over the Net). "We realized that for interaction between people, 3-D VR was overkill," Bumgardner says in a discussion conducted on the Minds Palace. As he talks, the 40-odd member audience (including Tinker Bell, a huge human eye, Alfred E. Neuman, a can of Spam, and dozens of other diverse creatures) is mesmerizing by his swirling vortex avatar. "We know that the social interaction is what most people were looking for. The Palace was kept simple so that lots of people could easily create their own environments." Besides the simplicity, another great thing about the Palace is that it's free (in generic guest mode, anyway). You can even create your own Palace. When you download the Palace client software, it also comes bundled with a personal server so that you can set up a Palace on a Mac or Windows machine. It also comes with a set of prefab rooms, the same rooms used in Time Warner's Palace. Custom rooms can be created in a graphics program and then saved as GIF image files. Once the rooms are created, they can easily be "wired up" with doors, workable light switches (to dim the lights when that romantic mood hits you), small animations, sounds, and links to other Palaces and Web sites. A sophisticated scripting language (called "Iptscrae") allows Palace creators to customize the environment and visitors to customize what their avatar can do. Even people on home computers with temporary Internet connections can create a publicly accessible Palace. When you fire up your connection and launch the Palace server software, your location is registered in a database at the Palace Web site. People can then check these listings to see if you're open for business.

Graphical chat is not only playtime fun. Meetings (albeit surreal ones) take place in chat rooms, interviews are conducted, performances and even weddings are held. This technology is in its infancy but holds promise for creating a new type of social niche in cyberspace. One of the things that originally generated such enthusiasm for the Web was that creating home-pages was so easy. Building virtual worlds with Palace software is equally simple. And also like the Web, Palace technology is sophisticated enough to allow a creator's Palace to grow with their desire to improve it. The Palace also allows hyperlinks to Web content so that a Palace can be integrated into a Web site. Future plans for the Palace include the ability to exchange data and MIDI audio files, and more advanced use of animation.

PIRATES *in* CYBERSPACE)

All of the issues surrounding copyright infringement, intellectual property, and out-and-out commercial theft come to a head in cyberspace. The digitalization and global distribution of media through the pipelines of the Internet has greatly muddied issues of property, piracy, and fair use. Pirating a perfect copy of a video, song, or "book" becomes as simple as issuing a command to replicate its ones and zeros. Uploading an article to a newsgroup is as easy as cutting and pasting it from one computer window to another. Displaying copyrighted graphics on an unauthorized Web page is as easy as entering the Web address of the material into an HTML tag (without moving it from its "home" computer). If you maintain a noncommercial Web page for fans of a TV show and display the show's logo and images from the show using this method (so that the images are not stored in your computer files), are you breaking the law? Is linking to a copyrighted Web site without permission a violation? If you view illegal material on the Net and have such material temporarily stored in your computer's memory, have you stolen it? The recent National Information Infrastructure Copyright Bill, which has been postponed indefinitely, suggested that all of these would be copyright violations. The entire NII Copyright Bill is a stunning example of government and industry fear over how the Internet is changing the rules of the game. It would have eliminated the sorts of fair use rules that now allow one to make copies of material for personal use. "This bill would be like arresting a mother for sending a clipping from the newspaper to her child," argued one online critic. The bill would also have turned Internet service providers into Net cops, making them liable for illegal transfers of copyrighted materials through their servers.

As the digital age marches on, old copyright laws are being stretched to fit this intangible world of information that now blankets much of our planet. Debate over whether old laws can be effectively amended or whether entirely new approaches are needed has divided many communities. As government and industry try to legislate, regulate, and police the datasphere in the service of existing ideas of ownership, new and often radical ideas are being proposed. It is certainly understandable that creators of content want to be paid for their work. The question is, what's the most workable method of compensation, one that also takes into account the fluid realities of cyberspace?

In the 1980s, the software industry got a harsh lesson in their efforts to curtail software piracy. The copy-protected disks that they manufactured, which made it impossible for users to make backup copies, were unpopular with consumers. Software vendors who ignored this copy protection scheme got the public's business, eventually ending the practice of copy protection. The idea may have looked good on paper, but it didn't square with the reality of how people actually use software. Similarly, in the commercial development of the Web, content providers want to start charging for access, but so far that proposed arrangement has proven to be very unpopular with consumers. There's just too much content out there. If one provider decides to charge, people will move elsewhere. Esther Dyson, writing in an article in *Wired* 3.07, suggests that intellectual *value* will be sold online rather than intellectual property. In other words, content will be devalued (and therefore given away for free) because of its oversupply, while services (tech support, content filtering, community, assurance of quality, brand identity, real-time events, etc.) will be more highly valued (and therefore purchased). We can already see this in companies such as Netscape, who give free versions of their Navigator software to the public but still make huge amounts of money selling supported versions, manuals, and especially software and services to the business community. The key to the success of any approach to Internet commerce will be gauging public response. If government and industry act out of fear (as they seem to be doing now), ignoring the realities of the technology and of how people use it, they could create something that the public will not accept. The genie is already out of the bottle. If we spend all of our time arguing over how to get him back in, we will forget the wishes he is capable of granting.

The other issue surrounding Internet piracy is the question of hackers. These computer junkies who like to go where they're not invited have become mythologized and demonized in a manner similar to terrorists—they are feared in gross disproportion to their actual menace. Sure, the threat of computer intrusion is real, and yes, there have been instances of break-ins and data heists, but media and law enforcement overstate the danger, as if there were dark-side hackers lurking in every corner of cyberspace. People are frightened to send sensitive data over the Internet, not because someone in their office or the system administrator will read it (a far more likely proposition), but because they're afraid some wily hacker is waiting to intercept their data packets. Almost every time there's a news report on data piracy, the media revisit the hacking of Craig Neidorf, Kevin Mitnik, and a few other high-profile cases, but only casually mention (if at all) white-collar computer crime, which is far more prevalent. The other thing they fail to emphasize is that most of these hackers are not interested in stealing things. It's true that Kevin Mitnik stole a file of credit card numbers from Netcom, but he never did anything with them. In hackerdom, the point is not thievery. It's getting access and taking some evidence that you were there (to brag to your friends). If these guys are pirates, they're pretty inept.

ASCII ART
by Jim Leftwich

THE NET PUBLISHER'S STARTER KIT

Getting Started) Online publishing can be a bit bewildering at first, especially if you're new to the Internet. Let's take a look at some of the basics you'll need to consider before venturing into the world of online media.

There are basically three types of electronic publications:

[**TEXT-ONLY E-ZINES** : These are the easiest and cheapest to produce, but they suffer from being visually unexciting. Graphics can't be used because they can't be sent through regular email, which is how most text e-zines are distributed. It is possible to send attached media with email, but handling it is difficult for many users. The only design elements you have are the characters on your keyboard (known as ASCII characters). Text zines are a reasonable choice if you're on a budget or putting out an e-zine that doesn't require images (such as a news or literary zine). If you want to get started right away with a simple online publication, a text-only zine is a great way to go. There's even some creative stuff that can be done design-wise with ASCII characters. By looking at other people's e-zines, you can get ideas. There are even programs that translate various types of graphic formats into ASCII-based art. But go easy on the ASCII art, my friend. Due to its slight hokeyness, its association with geeks with too much time on their hands, and a practitioner's tendency to use it in saccharine-sweet ways, ASCII art is like Barney the Dinosaur of cyberspace: to be joyfully loathed. Although text zines are usually emailed, they can also be posted to bulletin boards, newsgroups, and made available for downloading from file libraries on the Internet (such as FTP sites).

[W E B Z I N E S : Zines published on the World Wide Web allow you to combine media (text, graphics, sounds, videos) and include connections (called "hyperlinks") to other places on the Net. Webzines can be similar to print publications, using only text and graphics, or they can be very complex and very unlike print media, with audio, video, animation, input forms, chat areas, and even navigable environments. Obviously, the more media that's used, the more time and money you'll need to invest. Also, the more space your publication takes up (sound and video take up a lot), the more you'll pay in monthly storage fees to your Internet service provider. It is possible to run your own Web server, if you want to have a 24-hour Net connection, or if you want to serve up your Web pages only at certain times. This gets even more expensive and will turn you into an Internet administrator, with security concerns and the hassles associated with running an Internet service. Unless you already have such a direct connection, you're better off renting space at an existing service.

[**S P E C I A L F O R M A T E - Z I N E S :** These are digital publications that are made using non-Net "authoring" software such as HyperCard, Director, or a page layout program. People download the publication from a site on the Internet and then either view it online, using a "plug-in" or "helper application" and a Web browser, or offline, using the appropriate viewing software. A common way of distributing a special format e-zine is in PDF format. PDF ("Portable Document Format") is a technology developed by Adobe. Using their Acrobat program, you can convert a document that was created in page layout software (such as QuarkXPress or PageMaker) into a PDF file. To read it, the file is downloaded from a Net site and then opened using Acrobat Reader, which is readily available *(www.adobe.com/)* for free. Common Ground is another document converter/viewer program.

One advantage of publishing a special format e-zine is that you can create the document in one program and then publish it on paper, floppy disk, CD-ROM, online, or in other electronic media. The disadvantage is that fewer people have the appropriate software for viewing your publication. Publishing on the Internet already limits your audience to those who are wired—a special format zine limits them even more.

Hardware and Software)

First, you'll need a decent computer. This doesn't have to be the latest cutting-edge system. If all you want to do is publish a text e-zine, you can get away with a very modest computer and modem. You don't need color capability, a sound card, or high-priced software.

If you want to do any sort of Web publishing with graphics and sound, you'll need a more sophisticated machine. You should get a system that can display color, with enough horsepower to run essential graphics programs, and lots of hard disk space. A 486/66 MHz DOS/Windows machine or a Quadra 605, if you prefer Macs, are entry level machines for Web publishing.

For any type of online publishing, you'll need a modem. Modems are rated by how fast they can pump data through a phone line. You can get away with 14.4 (that's 14,400 bits per second), but a 28.8 is highly recommended. Emerging technologies like ISDN and cable modems will make connectivity much faster, allowing you to add more audio, video, and other media that takes a lot of time to transfer using slower modems.

If you're using a Mac LC-series or higher, the hardware required to do sound is already built in. If you have a Windows machine with a sound card, chances are you're all ready to go. For doing video on a Windows or Mac system, you need to have a special video card. A/V Macs come with a video-card already installed. If you don't mind funky low-resolution quality, a company called Connectix makes the QuickCam (for both PC and Mac), a cheap digital video camera that plugs into the back of your computer and allows you to shoot video on the desktop. Black-and-white and color versions are available.

As for software, the choices are varied. For a text e-zine, the only publishing software you need is a word processing and a modem program. If you plan on doing anything with sound, video, and graphics, it gets more complicated. For graphics, you'll need software for creating, editing, and converting graphics (such as Paint Shop Pro for the PC and GIF Converter for Mac). For sound and video, the choices are limited only by the type of hardware you have and the size of your credit line. For Web publishing there are a number of software tools available for automating HTML (see Design and Production below), converting graphics, creating animations, and other tasks. Luckily, many of these tools are free or very low priced.

Finally, you'll need a connection to the Internet. The big three commercial information services—America Online, CompuServe, and Prodigy—are OK if you're putting out a text zine through email. If you want to do a full-blown Web publication, you're going to want to get an account with an Internet service provider (ISP). Check the newspaper or phone book for a listing of providers near you. Make sure that they allow users to put up their own Web pages. Many ISPs offer small Web space as part of their standard monthly fee or for an additional fee based on how much space your publication takes up. Shop around to find the best price and don't be afraid to ask already-wired friends and associates for advice on the best services. One hint about finding an Internet home for your zine: Don't tell the provider that you want to put up an online publication or they may hit you with an inflated commercial rate. You can also try to find a friend who has a Web site and sweet-talk them into letting you put your pages up there. As long as your zine is small, you can probably find a cubbyhole in cyberspace to stash it for free, but as it grows, you'll likely have to start paying.

Design and Production)

In considering the design and production of our three types of zines, only webzines need to be discussed in any depth. As pointed out above, text zines are limited to ASCII characters, so there's little that can be done in terms of design. Special format zines are designed and laid out in conventional layout programs or stand-alone multimedia programs such as Director. For more on non-Net multimedia zines, see chapter 3.

In considering a webzine, one challenge is figuring out how to combine all the different media and hypertext into a coherent whole. The best webzines are carefully designed so that their information unfolds in a logical (or at least interestingly illogical) manner. Getting "lost in hyperspace" is a real danger with webzines, because readers can (and often will) follow hyper-link after hyperlink, soon ending up in link limbo. To avoid this, you'll need to carefully plan your webzine. Decide what parts you want to link, why they should be linked, and always make sure to provide, on each page, a way for the reader to get back to the beginning.

Graphics, sounds, digital movies, and animations can all be used to keep things interesting and to communicate ideas using several media. However, producing multimedia requires special programs and skills that not every-one has. Just remember, with each layer of media you add, you add a new layer of design and production skill. If you don't have much experience, you can start off with something simple and then expand as you develop new skills. This flexibility of Web publishing is one of its special attractions.

To produce your webzine, you'll have to learn something called Hypertext Markup Language (HTML). HTML is the code that tells the viewer's Web browser how to display your publication on-screen. Font codes (how the text appears), link codes (for attaching media and hypertext), and format codes (for page layout) are sent over the Net along with the text and other media that make up your zine. Once they arrive in the viewer's machine, the browser translates the HTML and combines everything to produce the page the viewer sees. HTML sounds more deep geek than it actually is. To give you an idea of how it works, here is a short sample:

```
<H1><Font Color=Red>Jamming the
Media</Font Color></H1><BR>
<B><I>A Citizen's Guide</I></B><BR>
<IMG SRC="cover.gif"><BR>
<BLINK>Order Now!</BLINK>
```

If viewed in a Web browser, you would see the headline (<H1>) *Jamming the Media* in red (<Font Color=Red>) and the line *A Citizen's Guide* in bold (<B>) and italic (<I>). A picture of the book's cover (<IMG SRC>, which is in the common GIF graphics format) would appear as the page loaded. The words *Order Now!* would blink on and off instantly. The <BR> tag is used to mark a line break. That's basically how HTML works. As you add more design elements, media, and interactivity, the coding gets more complicated. Luckily, there are HTML editor programs that let you design pages by selecting menu items and clicking buttons that generate the HTML code for you. (Suggestions for HTML books and programs can be found in the Resources section below.)

When you're finished creating your HTML documents, you upload them to the Internet server computer where your zine is stored using something called an FTP (File Transfer Protocol) program. Current Macs and Windows machines that support "drag and drop" allow you to simply drag your HTML pages from a folder on your hard drive and into a remote folder (or directory) on your ISP's computer. And that's the basics.

Distribution)

How you distribute your e-zine depends on the kind of publication it is and the best way to reach your target audience. There are basically four types of distribution channels to consider:

```
> emailing lists
> Usenet newsgroups
> Online libraries
> the World Wide Web
```

If you're doing a text-only e-zine, mailing lists are usually the main means of distribution. To publish, all you do is upload each issue to your Internet account and email it out to your subscribers list. The simplest way to do this is to maintain the list yourself, and "gang email" it to your readers. As your subscriber base grows however, this can get rather tedious. For a bigger list, you'll need to set up an automated mailing list using list management software that runs on your service provider's host computer (or your own if you have a full-time Net connection). List management software acts as an automated email address database and can also be set up to act as a reflector, sending whatever anyone posts to the list to everyone else on the list, automatically. Because everyone on the list can talk to everyone else, mailing lists are a good way to build a community of readers. Ask your Internet service provider about what resources they have available for setting up mailing lists. If your provider does not have a list service available, there are other sites that will rent you mailing list services (usually based on the amount of traffic on your list), or even give them to you for free.

Strictly speaking, Usenet isn't exactly part of the Internet. Instead, it exists as a parallel network set up like a giant, worldwide bulletin board system. It's divided up into "newsgroups" devoted to topics on everything from angst to zoophilia and everything in between. When you post a message to a Usenet newsgroup, it's "published" to the group such that anyone logging on can read it, comment on it, or send you private email comments about your posting.

If you're publishing a text or reasonably small special format zine, you can post it to appropriate newsgroups. There are several groups devoted to zines, including *alt.zines* and *alt.binaries.zines* (for posting multimedia or PDF files in binary format). It's a common practice to use appropriate newsgroups as a place to "publish" zines. Before you post your zine to a group, however, make sure that you've spent some time there and gotten a feel for what's appropriate and what's not. Newsgroups have different personalities. Some have few rules of "netiquette," while others like to stick tightly to established guidelines.

Because it's a global, basically anonymous, system, Usenet attracts an extremely broad range of humans. And because no one needs to know your name or your face in cyberspace, Usenet also seems to foster "flames," nasty messages from know-it-alls and kooks out to pick a fight. You may encounter this when you first start poking around, and may even get a few flames from self-appointed critics after you post your zine for the first time. Learn to develop a thick skin if you want to hang out on Usenet.

FTP sites (and other Net-based libraries such as Gopher and software libraries on information services such as AOL and CompuServe) are another way to distribute your zine. These sites are basically places where you can upload your zine so that others can download it. This works great for text, PDF, and multimedia zines. Library sites are available twenty-four hours a day, unless the host computer (called a server) goes offline. All you have to do is announce where people can find your zine, put it online, and sit back and wait for feedback.

If you want to put your zine on an FTP site (the most common type of Net library), there's two ways to go about it. First, you can set up your own FTP directory on your Internet service provider's host machine and let people come to you to snarf up your handiwork. The one advantage to this is that you have total control over how you set up the site, how long you keep materials available, etc. And if you want to make changes to the documents, you can easily access them. The problem is that, unless your ISP is known as a place to go looking for zines, you could languish in obscurity, with no one coming by to download the latest issue. Fortunately, there are several FTP servers devoted to distributing zines from all over the world. Since people regularly come to these sites, putting your pub there is a good way to get wide exposure. In addition, many of these sites regularly publish a list of all the new zines they've received—it's like free advertising.

Webzines, like zines stored on FTP sites, are available twenty-four hours a day, seven days a week to anyone with a Net connection and a browser. You really don't have to work at "distributing" it. The trick is, because the Web is such a humongous place, letting people know where to find it. Which brings us to our next subject: promotion and advertising.

Promotion and Advertising)

The Net has grown exponentially in the last few years. The World Wide Web, the latest revolution in cyberspace, has mushroomed in the last few years. All the other types of Internet services such as FTP, Usenet, email, conferencing, and chat can now be linked to Web pages and viewed with browser software. These services aren't actually on the Web, but the distinction between all of them has been blurred. While the Net/Web offers a tremendous medium for amateur publishers, its vastness makes it a challenge to promote and advertise electronic zines.

If you post your e-zine solely to one or more Usenet newsgroups, you don't need to promote it. You have placed it dead smack in the middle of heavy, global Net traffic, where it can potentially be seen by thousands of users. It does help to give your zine a descriptive and attention-grabbing title so that people are more likely to view it when they encounter it in their list of available newsgroup posting (called "articles"). "New Flaming Sock Puppet Review Will Rip Your Eyeballs Out!" will probably get more readers than "Puppetry zine."

Even if you don't post your zine to Usenet, you can use newsgroups as a way of promoting your work. If you have your zine on an FTP site or Web server, try posting an announcement to any and all relevant newsgroups. Besides a spiffy description, make sure that you give the appropriate instructions on what people need to do to access it. These days, URL format (Uniform Resource Locator) is the way to go, whether your zine is on the Web, an FTP, or a Gopher site. URLs are a standardized format for Internet addressing. For example, if your publication is on the FTP server *zines.com* in the directory */pub/zines/socks* and is called *flamingsock1.txt*, then the URL would be *ftp://zines.com/pub/zines/socks/flamingsock1.txt*. If your zine is Web-based, the URL might look something like this: *http://www.website.com/socks/flamingsock1.html*. (Check out some of the Net guides in the Resources section below for more on the rhyme and reason of URLs.)

If your publication's on the Web, besides posting an announcement about where to find it on Usenet, you may want to submit it to the many of the Web indexes that are available. These indexes, also called search engines, allow users to search the World Wide Web for pages on whatever subjects or keywords they specify. This means that when a person wants to find out about something, they go to the search engine, type in a few choice words, and the search engine returns a list of all the Web pages that match that description.

Another trick for creating incidental advertising for your e-zine site is to put a small description and the URL in your Signature file (or .sig file). The .sig file is a small text "banner" that can be automatically attached to the bottom of your email and Usenet postings. Most email and newsreader programs have a feature that allows you to create and store your .sig file. Every time you send an email message or a newsgroup posting, the .sig file will be amended to the bottom of your message. A typical .sig file for a zine publisher might look something like this:

```
---------------------------------------------------------------------------

Joe Kafka                      Email: joe@socks.com
Editor                         URL: http://www.website.com/socks
Flaming Sock Puppet Review     Mailing list: info@socks.com

***Exploring the World of Hardcore Puppetry***
==============================================================
```

Since the Web is really a big interlinked universe of documents, you can also promote your zine by asking other people who have Web sites if they would add a link to your page. That way, anyone who accesses their site can just click on a link and go to yours. It's considered neighborly, if someone agrees to add your site to their link list, that you do the same for them on your site.

Finally, don't overlook advertising your e-zine in print. A lot of people are getting used to seeing URLs in magazine ads and newspapers, and it might be a good way to reach an audience that you wouldn't otherwise reach if you just stuck to online advertising. *Factsheet Five* (see chapter 1) now includes a review section for e-zines.

And it might not be a bad idea to crank out a press release about your new publication and fax it (and/or email it) to your local (and even national) newspapers and magazines. Editors these days are still pretty gaga over anything related to the Net, and you might even get someone's juices flowing enough to write a story about you and your intrepid little endeavor.

Pricing)

At this point, the majority of content on the World Wide Web is free of charge. Most of the zines on the Web (and in FTP and Gopher directories, etc.) are also free and noncommercial (no online advertising). This is changing, as technology is being developed for the secure transfer of credit information over the Net. Two of the first online commerce systems are called First Virtual and CyberCash. Instead of sending credit card info over the Net to purchase something, the buyer sends only a preregistered account number. With First Virtual, buyers sign up for the service via email and then provide First Virtual with credit card information over the phone. No credit info is sent over the Net. First Virtual then pays the vendor and bills the buyer. Vendors either offer the First Virtual payment service on their Web site or post their wares at First Virtual's InfoHaus, a commercial information market. To find out more information on being a vendor or a registered buyer, check out *http://fv.com/*. To get more information on how CyberCash works, go to *http://www.cybercash.com/*. At this point, you shouldn't expect to charge anybody anything for your e-zine. If you become successful and get lots of traffic at your site, you might be able to sell "banner ads," which are small strips of advertisements that run along the top and bottom of Web pages, or seek a sponsor for your site.

Words of Wisdom)

Chip Rowe (*Chip's Closet Cleaner*)
: Think small. People's attention spans are getting shorter and shorter.

: Just because you have access to a scanner doesn't mean you have to use it. You'll lose a lot of readers if they have to wait for lots of graphics to download long after the words have arrived.

: Choose images carefully. Words have more weight when you don't have too many illustrations to distract your reader.

: Test, test, test. There's nothing more frustrating than Web links that don't work properly.

: Don't sign someone up for a subscription to your email zine without asking them first. And don't take it personally if they decline.

: The Internet is never as easy as you think it will be.

: They call it the Web because it can ensnare you.

: The easier your e-zine is to digest, the more diners you'll have.

: Paper has its charm. You can't stuff an e-zine in your back pocket (at least not yet).

: Don't get addicted to "hits" (number of times your webzine is accessed). How many people visit your e-zine isn't as important as how many come back.

: Links from your Web page are valuable; be prudent.

Todd M. Kuipers (keeper of E-mail Zines List):
: Doing an e-zine is just like doing one in print, minus the paper and distribution costs.

: Figure out what drives your publication: information or visuals (or both).

: Publishing on the Internet does make distribution different: You have to do most of the distribution/advertising yourself.

: Establishing a presence on the Net can be hard work, sometimes as hard as producing the zine itself.

: Promote your e-zine by:

> publishing information about your zine to Usenet newsgroups (such as *alt.zines*, *alt.etext*, or *alt.culture.saudi*, if applicable).

> finding other Web sites that have the same socio-political, literary, or informational bent and have them place info about and links to your e-zine.

> If you're a webzine, set up an emailing list for announcing that a new issue has been placed on your site.

> If you're an email zine, find a list server you can use. Hundreds of these exist on the Net and a lot of them are free.

RosieX (*geekgirl*)
I feel somewhat odd giving generic advice about setting up a Web site and an e-zine. Zines, dead tree or alive, are highly unique and usually very focused on a particular idea or thread.

I also assume every country has its own peculiar bent on what Internet service providers charge for storage, bandwidth etc. And no matter how the arguments or discussions about "form follows function" in the digital jungle turn out, everyone I know (except the lamers) has a desire to create their page or zine, as a statement and reflection of themselves. Personalities, hopes, desires, fantasies, and in some cases anguish and torment are the catalysts for production. The e-zines that work best are highly individual, creative, and focus on content and style. And they keep up-to-date on tools and resources. Here are the basics:

: Firstly, you need to get familiar with the Net, especially the World Wide Web, and learn some basic HTML (hypertext markup language).

: The trick is to check out other sites you like, bookmark them, and most importantly, use the capabilities of your browser (like using the "document source" or "source" menu choices to see how someone else has constructed their page). Seeing HTML code demystifies what many fear, that a Web page is difficult and the sole terrain of geeks and nerds. It ain't. But you will need to create order forms and other nifty things that require "scripting."

: The beautiful thing about HTML is that you can practice offline. If you have a Windows machine, for example, and a browser such as Netscape, toggle back and forth between that and Notepad and watch a blank screen come alive with your pages.

: Tweaking: making adjustments; placing images; creating backgrounds; deciding on links, document sizes, colors, font sizes, etc. Tweaking is what you will spend an inordinate amount of time on.

: Now, I could write a whole book on this stuff, but others already have. For those keen on buying a good book, try a feisty HTML author such as Laura Lemay (see Resources below).

: For those who want to know about costs, it very much depends on what arrangement you work out with your service provider, and whether it will be able to handle a lot of traffic (if your site becomes really successful, like mine).

: I have found that "content is queen" and independent producers are giving the corporate players a major headache as more and more of their market is supporting and preferring independent product, particularly with online publishing.

: Which means: Go after and use fresh material. Include comments by those who have something to say. Generate feedback, provoke debate. The medium is the massage, so you wanna knead that massage and deliver it in one powerful package.

: Decide if you want a lot of text, sound, and/or graphics. Your decision will be extremely important in determining how much time you will to spend on your e-zine and how often you can refresh it.

: Be very sure that you have the time to answer all email inquiries about your site. And avoid being rude if people make constructive criticisms. Do not use form letters to respond to mail. Many of us know the frustration and the annoyance of waiting weeks for a human response to email; this practice is detrimental to establishing a relationship with your audience. So be there for them!

: Creating a bit of merchandise such as T-shirts, stickers, CD-ROMS, etc., is a good way to gauge if people like what you do and are willing to support your online zine. Let's face it, all that fantastic info you are producing (unless sold to a media buyer) is free. If you want to make an e-zine your living, then work out some kind of fair exchange with your audience. Don't get carried away and produce everything from e-zine coffee mugs to fridge magnets (on second thought. . .); until you get extremely popular, do a couple of sample items such as a T-shirt to see if they will sell. If not, they'll make great Xmas presents. To expedite purchases, set up a convenient and secure way for people to leave credit card info.

: In terms of promoting your site, you have to combine snail mail with email or utilize available posts in Usenet groups. Always check if it's okay to post info about your zine if you are intending to make "profit." And don't pinch other people's mailing lists and assume it's okay to post to strangers.

: Use any form of shameless self-promotion with the media, which includes the invaluable support networks fostered within the online zine community. Check out as many e-zine sites/directories/archives, etc., and leave a brief request for the site manager to include your new listing. A brief description of your e-zine helps, too.

: It's worthwhile, if you have a hard copy and online version of your zine, to try traditional cross promotion. Write nice letters to people such as R. Seth Friedman of *Factsheet Five*. And, very importantly, send PR to journalists working for (free or profit) radio, TV, and print who compile "surfing the Net guides" or cool new site listings. Be focused.

: You need to decide if your zine is a hobby or a whole new career and big lifestyle change. You need to buy, or have access to, a good ergonomic chair, a computer and modem, a scanner, videocard, and some money for connectivity and the phone bill. If you're serious, raise enough capital to pay wages to yourself for at least a year. If you want your e-zine to be a hobby, then I salute you!

: If you don't have the skills of a journalist, good communicator, and designer, and lack geek knowledge (or computer skills), you may want to: 1. take courses or 2. work in a collective or co-op situation. If you choose the latter, be completely sure you can depend on each other and have a similar vision in mind. Working on a zine can be like playing in a band—lots of egos and no free beer.

: Don't treat the zine community online like you are such hot shit that you don't know how they survived without you. Make sure your site is warm, friendly, and easy to navigate. Don't create an awesome tangled web or labyrinth of information. Keep your site neat and fun. More people will appreciate it and tell others about it.

: Run contests or other things that will keep visitors coming back.

: Themes are great for zines. They allow you to concentrate on an issue that you may want to research, and also ensure a niche audience and regulars every time.

: How often your e-zine is published is completely up to you (daily, weekly, monthly, etc.).

: And last but not least, a very old adage: "Enjoy what you do!" Otherwise, you'll get burned out, bitter, and bored.

Resources)

SOFTWARE

I have done my best to choose shareware and freeware programs. Shareware grew out of the early days of personal computing when software development was still largely experimental and noncommercial. Lots of programs were distributed on compilation disks for a small fee, through users' groups and at conventions. Users would try out the programs (some of them clearly not worth wasting money on) and then send a modest shareware fee to the creators of programs that they found useful. Shareware today is pretty much the same except the Internet has become the main distribution channel. Although shareware has not proven to be profitable for many of its developers, the Net has allowed good shareware to be more widely distributed so that its creators can, at the most, make a decent return on it, and at the least, show off their skills to potential clients. There is a lot of excellent freeware on the Net as well. Many of the browsers, email programs, newsreaders, and Net utility programs are freeware. Besides weekend programmers and university students, freeware is developed and distributed by software companies to get you to try their software in hopes that you'll purchase commercial versions with more features and tech support. Some of this freeware is "crippleware," meaning that it will expire after a certain number of days or amount of usage. If you look around, you'll find share/freeware that is as good as comparable commercial programs. It might not look as slick or come in a big fancy box, but you won't have to pay $300 for it either. Shareware fees range from under $10 to not more that $50.

Building Your Own Web Conferences (Windows)*
O'REILLY SOFTWARE
CD AND BOOK/MANUAL
$59.95

Creating a place for sociomedia to take place on the Net is not easy. Many of the Web-based conferencing systems are clunky, slow, and they get in the way of people talking to each other. O'Reilly's WebBoard 2.0 software changes all that. For $60 you get a conferencing system that can handle two separate bulletin boards, up to twenty conferences each, and unlimited topics in each conference. The features of WebBoard are amazing: the ability to post in HTML and attach files, a spell checker, a Java-based real-time chat client, a place for users to set up their own homepage, a directory of users, and lots of other nifty stuff. It's all very customizable and a cinch to use. I can't recommend this program highly enough.

Chat Software:

There are so many ways to talk to people over the Net. Besides email and bulletin boards, there's also real-time "chatting" using text and images. On the Web, you can link your pages to chat software so that you and those accessing your site can talk to each other on Internet Relay Chat (IRC). Think of IRC as the CB radio of cyberspace. Anyone with a Net connection can log into an IRC chat channel and respond to what's being said. Having scheduled chats on the topics covered in your zine is a great way to get feedback from your readers and to build a small "community." To incorporate IRC into your site, everyone has to have IRC software and you need to have a chat channel somewhere. You can set up your own IRC server if you have a full-time connection, or you can get someone with such a connection to set you up on their machine. There are also many chat servers on the Net that anyone can dial into and join (or start up) a temporary channel. If all of your talks are scheduled, you can just tell people beforehand which channel to punch up. Global Chat is a popular chat client program that runs on both Mac and Windows machines. It's shareware and available from Quarterdeck *(www.quaterdeck.com).*

There are also graphical chat programs such as the Palace *(www.thepalace.com).* Anyone, even with a temporary modem connection, can set up a Palace server. I help run a Palace for STIM (see Net Sites below). We have a link to our Palace on the STIM Web site so that people reading the magazine can hop right into STIM's funky little house in cyberspace. Although all of the Palace software is free, to be able to use advanced features (such as user scripts and animation), each user has to register their client software for a fee. A basic Palace can be up and running in a matter of minutes. If you're interested in adding a hang out space to your Web site, you might want to check out the Palace.

Internet Access Software:

Most computers sold today have Internet software already installed on them. On Windows machines, it's called Dial-Up Networking. Macs use something called MacPPP, FreePPP, or Open Transport. Some ISPs and online services such as AOL have their own software that they provide for free. For Web publishing, you'll also need an FTP program to upload new files to your file directory on your ISP's site (called a "remote directory"). There are a number of great shareware FTP programs such as CuteFTP for the PC and Fetch for the Mac.

Mailing List Management Software:

If you want to maintain a mailing list on your own computer, you'll need a mailing list program such as Majordomo (Mac) or ListServ (for Unix and Windows). Again, unless your computer is always connected to the Internet, you're better off finding or renting space on someone else's list server for your mailing list.

Web Server Software:

If you're interested in serving up Web pages from your own computer (as opposed to storing them on someone else's fully connected machine), you'll need Web server software. There are a number of shareware and demo programs available for downloading over the Net. WebCompare reviews all of these server programs at *www.webcompare.com/server-main.html.* Unless you already have a full-time Net connection, you're probably better off finding or renting space on someone else's server.

BOOKS

Internet Power Toolkit

GARETH BRANWYN AND SEAN CARTON
VENTANA PRESS, 1996, 1174 PAGES, $49.95 *(includes CD-ROM)*

Written by me and pal Sean Carton, the *Internet Power Toolkit* is a Net bible for the intermediate user. This massive book (which can also be used for weight lifting and a high-chair booster seat) covers everything from email and newsgroups to VRML plug-ins, streaming audio and video, and Net telephones. We tried to provide answers to "everything you always wanted to know about the Internet, but were afraid to ask." We delve into the very guts of the Internet and explain how it works and what happens when things go wrong. We also look at security, privacy, local area networks, traveling with computers, and lots more. The CD-ROM includes a number of essential programs, plug-ins (that extend the functionality of your Web browser), and utilities that can make your Net life easier.

Net Chick*:
A Smart-Girl Guide to the Wired World

CARLA SINCLAIR
HENRY HOLT, 1996, 244 PAGES, $19.95

In this ultra-cool book, Carla Sinclair maps out cyberspace for a young, hip female audience. There are lots of interviews with cyber-pioneers St. Jude, Stacy Horn, Lisa Palac, Reva Basch, Tiffany Lee Brown, and Trina Roberts, and profiles of many others. There's jargon-free technical how-to, tons of reviews of girl- friendly Net sites, and lots of Carla's tips, observations, and smart insights.

Teach Yourself Web Publishing with
HTML in 14 Days, the Premier Edition*

LAURA LEMAY
SAMS.NET
800 PAGES, $39.99 *(plus CD-ROM)*

This book constitutes a starter course in HTML publishing broken up into four-teen daylong lessons. If you need a disciplined approach to learning something that appears as off-putting as HTML (it's really not that hard), this book might be the way to go. It covers a significant range of material. If you actually take the course, you'll be a Webmaster by the time you're finished.

The Virtual Community*:
Homesteading on the Electronic Frontier

HOWARD RHEINGOLD
HARPERPERENNIAL, 1994, 316 PAGES, $13

Internet old-timer Howard Rheingold has always had an uncanny ability to be at the right place at the right time and to be able to record the experience in simple and potent language. He was there when virtual reality hit the wires (which he recorded in *Virtual Reality*) and soon after the houselights went on at The Well, his (and my) virtual home and the centerpiece of this book. Howard is smart enough to never let the technology of the Internet overshadow the people who make it live. In *The Virtual Community*, besides The Well, he looks at the accidental history of the Net, Usenet, fantasy worlds online (MUDs), IRC, virtual communities in Japan and France, the birth of the Electronic Frontier Foundation, online activism in general, and the negative impact of the Internet.

(MAGA)ZINES

The Net

IMAGE PUBLISHING, INC.
150 NORTH HILL DRIVE, BRISBANE, CA 94005
415-468-4869
WEB: www.thenet-us.com
$24.95 FOR 12 PRINT ISSUES WITH CD-ROMS

This monthly magazine and CD-ROM covers all facets of the Internet, with special emphasis (not surprisingly) on the World Wide Web. A large portion of the magazine is rated site reviews with accompanying screen shots. The CD-ROM contains Mac and Windows Net programs and plug-ins (the usual mix of freeware, shareware, and demos). One of the great things about the Internet is that you really don't have to read books and magazines to stay on top of it. All of the information (and most of the software) you need is available online. That said, there's still something attractive about print. And although *The Net* is a slick commercial publication, it has a slight fringe slant as evidenced by writers such R. U. Sirius, Carla Sinclair, Andrew Hultkrans, David Pescovitz, and Drue Miller. The CD-ROMs are handy, too, saving you the time downloading all that new Internet software.

Web Developer

20 KETCHUM STREET, WESTPORT, CT 06880
203-226-6967 FAX: 203-454-5840
WEB: www.webdeveloper.com
$29/6 ISSUES

This Mecklermedia publication is not for the faint at heart, but if you start taking this Web stuff seriously, *Web Developer* can provide you with breaking news on Web technology, industry news, and profiles of successful Web developers. Back issues are available at their Web site.

THE WEB PUBLISHER'S TOOLKIT

The following charts contain a sampling of the kinds of software you'll need to do a webzine. All of these programs are available for downloading over the Internet and many are freeware or low-cost shareware. Also, check out the Net Sites section for a listing of online software libraries where you can keep up with the latest releases and news of Net software.

MACINTOSH

SOFTWARE	DESCRIPTION	TYPE	WEB ADDRESS http://
Netscape Navigator Gold	Web browser with built-in HTML editor	Crippleware	home.netscape.com/ comdownload.html
RealAudio player	Streaming audio player	Freeware	www.realaudio.com
RealAudio server	Streaming audio server (you need a directly connected Internet machine to serve streaming audio on your site)	Commercial (30-day demo available)	www.realaudio.com
Shockwave	Viewer for Macromedia Director files. To create Director multimedia files, you'll need to buy the (very expensive) Director program	Freeware	www.macromedia.com/ index.html
QuickTime player	QuickTime movie player	Freeware	www.apple.com
QuickEditor	QuickTime movie editor	Shareware	hyperarchive.lcs.mit.edu
Adobe Acrobat	PDF publisher ("distiller") and viewer ("reader")	Reader-Freeware Distiller-commercial software	www.adobe.com
BBEdit Lite	Text editor	Freeware	www.barebones.com/
PageSpinner	HTML editor	Shareware	www.algonet.se/~optima
Graphic Converter	Converts graphics between many common (and many uncommon) formats. Also has many painting and graphics manipulation tools	Shareware	www.tucows.com

SOFTWARE	DESCRIPTION	TYPE	WEB ADDRESS http://
Myrmidon	Converts many Mac document formats to HTML	Crippleware (30 days)	www.terrymorse.com
Smart Dubbing	GIF Animator	Freeware	www.xs4all.nl/~polder
GIFBuilder	GIF Animator	Freeware	iawww.epfl.ch/Staff/ Yves.Piguet/clip2gifhome/ GIFBuilder.html
D-SoundPRO	Sound editor	Shareware	hyperarchive.lcs.mit.edu

WINDOWS

SOFTWARE	DESCRIPTION	TYPE	WEB ADDRESS http://
Netscape Navigator Gold	Web browser with built-in HTML editor	Crippleware	home.netscape.com/ comdownload.html
RealAudio player	Streaming audio player	Freeware	www.realaudio.com
RealAudio server	Streaming audio server (you need a directly connected Internet machine to serve streaming audio on your site)	Commercial (30-day cripple-ware available)	www.realaudio.com
Shockwave	Viewer for Director files. To create Director multimedia files, you'll need to buy (the very expensive) Director program	Freeware	www.macromedia.com/ index.html
QuickTime player	QuickTime movie player. To actually create QuickTime movies you'll need a commercial package such as Premier	Freeware	www.apple.com
Adobe Acrobat	PDF publisher ("distiller") and viewer ("reader")	Reader-Freeware Distiller-commercial software	www.adobe.com
SuperPad	Text editor	Freeware	www.tucows.com
HotDog	HTML editor	Crippleware (30 days)	www.sausage.com
Paint Shop Pro	Painting and graphics conversion software	Shareware	www.pspro.ml.org
GIF Construction Set	GIF animator	Shareware	www.mindwork shop.com/alchemy/ gifcon.html
Cool Edit	Sound editor	Shareware	www.syntrillium.com/ cool.htm

NET SITES
[Publishing Tools

BrowserWatch

WEB: browserwatch.iworld.com/index.shtml

BrowserWatch, the leading site for information about browsers and plug-ins, offers breaking news in the browser and plug-ins industry, as well as one of the most complete lists on development of different plug-ins and browsers. A quick check allows you to find the plug-ins or browsers you want.

Cool Tool of the Day

WEB: www.cooltool.com

Cool Tool is an ambitious project run by software fanatic and keyboard comedian Sean Carton (bless his pointy little head). Every stinkin' day, Sean evaluates a new Net tool and writes a description of it. He spends most of the time talking about himself (what he had to eat, how hung over he is, how much coffee he's slugged) and playfully berating his readers. Eventually he gets around to reviewing the warez. As I write this, Sean's Cool Tool of the Day is being shown as a favorite on MSNBC's *The Site* show. A simple noncommercial Web site that was created as a way of sharing Sean's passion for software tool gathering has just gotten airtime on a national TV program. Imagine how much it would have cost him for a 60-second ad spot on MSNBC. The power and reach of the Net never ceases to amaze me.

Doctor HTML

WEB: www.imagiware.com/RxHTML

Doctor HTML lets you input the URL for your Web pages and then it runs a bunch of checks on it to see if it's in shape. It checks Spelling, Image Syntax, Image Analysis, Form Structure, Table Structure, Commands, Hyperlinks, and Overall Document Structure.

Electronic Frontier Foundation*

WEB: www.eff.org

The EFF has been called the ACLU of cyberspace. They offer the latest information on proposed legislation, legal cases, and other activities related to such things as online privacy, security, encryption, and intellectual property. They also offer legal counsel in select cases. Their Web site contains action alerts, press releases, legal briefs, articles, and papers related to online freedom.

HyperMac Archive*

WEB: hyperarchive.lcs.mit.edu/HyperArchive.html

> HyperMac has long been a featured software library for Macintosh. If you're looking for any type of Mac software (not just Internet related), this is the place to try first.

HTML Workshop

WEB: www.mcp.com/general/workshop

> This site from Macmillan provides HTML training for beginning, intermediate, and advanced Web makers. There are workshop, tips, examples, and links to other HTML-related Web sites and newsgroups.

Internet Mailing List Providers FAQ

WEB: www.cs.ubc.ca/spider/edmonds/usenet/ml-providers.txt
EMAIL: majordomo@edmonds.home.cs.ubc.ca with "get faq ml-providers.txt" in the body of the message.

> This is a list of individuals, organizations, and companies on the Net who offer mailing list services, either for a fee or as a service to the Net community. If you wish to start a mailing list, you can contact one or more of these services for more information.

L-Soft International

WEB: www.lsoft.com

> The Web site for the makers of ListServ, the popular Internet email server program. They offer commercial versions of ListServ and a Windows shareware version.

Shareware.Com

WEB: www.shareware.com

> Part of the CNet computer and TV network, Shareware.Com is a massive shareware software library for both Mac and Windows.

Stroud's*

WEB: www.stroud.com

> Stroud's is a one-stop shop for Windows Internet software. The site contains links to hundreds of programs along with reviews and ratings of each.

Submit It!*

WEB: 204.57.42.244/submit.htm

Submit It! registers your Web site with fifteen of the main search engines and Internet directories. Creating a webzine is not difficult, getting people to it is. This one form will quickly put you on the map.

Webmonkey

WEB: www.webmonkey.com

Run by Wired Ventures (who publish the print magazine *Wired* and the Web pub *HotWired*), Webmonkey offers advice and tutorials to Web publishers. It covers HTML, Java, and other deep geek aspects of the Web. One of the coolest things at Webmonkey is a tune-up page that checks your browser and plug-ins and makes sure that you have all the latest versions and that everything is configured correctly.

Windows95.Com

WEB: www.windows95.com

This site also specializes in Windows Internet software, but it also includes an online magazine about Windows 95 and excellent step-by-step instructions for setting up Dial-Up Networking.

ZINE–RELATED RESOURCES

The Extext Archive

WEB: www.etext.org:80

E-zines, mailing lists, e-books, legal texts, religious texts, and Dorian Kim's Baseball Archives.

E-Zine FAQ

FTP: ftp.etext.org/pub/Zines/WhateverRamblings/publish.txt
GOPHER: gopher.locust.cic.net/Zines/WhateverRamblings/publish.txt

A great introduction to electronic zines maintained by Alex Swain. It covers everything from the basic concept of an e-zine to formats (text, multimedia, Web, and PDF), to content, distribution, the DIY ethic, and more. It includes a listing of zine-related newsgroups, Web sites, mailing lists, and other resources. Updated versions of the E-Zine FAQ are also posted periodically to the *alt.zines newsgroup*.

Factsheet Five-Electric*

WEB: www.well.com/conf/f5/f5index2.html
GOPHER: gopher.well.sf.ca.us:70/11/Publications/F5/Reviews
EMAIL: jerod23@well.com

> *Factsheet Five*'s central clearinghouse for print and e-zines. Some content from the print version of *Factsheet Five* is here, along with reviews from other zines and *F5-Electric* readers. There's also lots of links to other zine sites on the Net. *F5*'s Seth Friedman will soon have the new *F5* Web site up at *www.factsheet5.com.*

John Labovitz's E-Zine-List*

WEB: www.meer.net/~johnl/e-zine-list/index.html

> This is a directory of electronic zines around the world, accessible via the Web, Gopher, FTP, email, and other services. The list is updated approximately monthly and contains some 1,400 zines.

Zines, Zines, Everywhere*

WEB: www.thetransom.com/chip/zines

> Chip Rowe, editor of the ultra-cool print and e-zine *Chip's Closet Cleaner* and *The Zine Reader*, maintains this awesome zine and e-zine resource site. There are several useful articles on e-zine publishing and oodles of links to essential zine resources. Linked information covers: creating an e-zine, authoring software, publishing, and distribution. It includes a link to Submit It!, a one-stop form page that allows you to register your Web zine with a number of the top Web indexes. If you're just venturing into the world of e-zines, check this page out.

E-ZINES

BUST

www.bust.com

> The online version of my vote for one of the coolest zines on the planet. It's the postfeminist riot grrrly magazine.

Chip's Closet Cleaner

thetransom.com/chip/main.html

The Circular File

www.interbridge.com/circfile/circfile.html

CyberWire Dispatch
cyberwerks.com/cyberwire/

8-Track Mind
www.pobox.com/~abbot/8track/

Fine Fishing
www.finefishing.com

Gearhead
gearheads.wirewd.com

geekgirl
www.geekgirl.com.au/geekgirl

Gremlins in the Garage
www.gremlins.com

Gutter Voice
www.io.org/~gutter/voice.html

Minerva
www.maths.tcd.ie/%7Ethomas/minerva/

Proust Said That
www.well.com/user/vision/proust/

Star Facts
www.ccnet.com/odyssey/

Vagabond Monthly
www2.globaldialog.com/~tpatmaho/

The Wednesday Archives
www.tezcat.com/~wednsday, www.hallucinet.com/wednesday

Usenet Newsgroups:

alt.zines*

> The main Usenet hangout for both print and electronic zine publishers. Participants post solicitations for material, announcements of new issue releases, tips, hard knocks, and zine gossip.

alt.ezines

> Similar to the *alt.zines* group, but specifically focused on e-zines. It gets a lot less traffic than *alt.zines*.

alt.binaries.zines

> A newsgroup for e-zine publishers who want to post PDF and multimedia zines for Internet downloading. The zines are posted in a binary-encoded format. Users need unencoding software to view the zines. Free encoding and unencoding software is readily available on the Net and in the software libraries of commercial services such as AOL.

Keep on
JAMMING!

If you don't like what you're PLAYING, you can always PICK UP your needle and move it to another GROOVE.

—Timothy Leary

WHAT DOES *the* FUTURE HOLD *for* DIY MEDIA?) Good question. Certainly the Internet will continue to play a large role and get a lot of attention from media makers wanting to be where the action is. But with all our enthusiasm over the Net, it's easy to forget the other media options available and their unique strengths. The Net offers unprecedented power and reach for the money—and it's an exciting opportunity for the ambidextrous media hacker wanting to try his or her hand at several different media—but it has its limitations. As the common observation goes, you can't read Net content on the toilet, or curled up in bed, the way you can with a print publication. Reading large amounts of text on-screen is not popular with most people, either, limiting how you can use words online. It's also easy, in our enthusiasm over the potential of the Internet, to overrate the current reality of it. It'll be a long time before the quality of a QuickTime movie or a RealAudio cybercast can compete with more established means of presentation. The distribution of music over the Net seems inevitable, but it'll have to wait until lots of people have higher speed connections—something that's years away. And let's face it, artifacts—a tape, a CD, a zine, a video that you can hold in your hand—still have an undeniable allure you can't get by staring at a computer screen. With the advent of computers and the Internet, many people predicted the death of the book, the magazine, and the paper-strewn office. So far, this has proven not to be the case. Printed materials continue to sell right alongside their electronic counterparts. The Internet is great at delivering certain kinds of content to a select group of people, but it will be a while (if ever) before it becomes the home of all media.

There's also the question of the Internet's future. If the government and big media have their way, the Internet will soon become a broadcast medium, much like radio and television, with little room for the many-to-many communication that has so far made the Net unique. There are clearly two competing models now struggling against each other: one of the Net as a frontier territory with no central authority, people making up the rules as they go along and pitching in to help build the frontier towns, pitted against a government/corporate model that views the Net as basically a library, a shopping mall, and a TV. Or as John Perry Barlow of the Electronic Frontier Foundation puts it: "They want to give you just enough back bandwidth to operate the button on your clicker so that you can make purchases or play videogames." If the Net is to stay vital, interesting, and democratic, it must remain out of control and at least partially noncommercial. One hopes that the way it is structured (as a globally distributed system) will help to ensure its wildness, at least in some quarters. One sticky problem that government legislators fail to address head-on when discussing the imposition of controls over the Net is the fact that it's a global medium. If a new form of copyright policing, or a stringent decency law, or a ban on certain types of information is imposed, how can the United States get the entire technosphere to comply? If the United States could

Keep on

[AFTERWORD]
JAMMING!

convince other nations to comply, data havens—islands in the Net beyond the reach of the United States—would pop up to feed the demand. There are no borders in cyberspace. But let's not get too complacent. It's going to take a lot of activism on the part of netizens to make sure that the Net stays open and democratic, and that the best interests of the public (and not just big business and big media) are served.

IS ALTERNATIVE MEDIA DEAD?)

In discussing amateur media among fellow media hackers, the question of "selling out" inevitably arises. Within the fringe media community there are immediate aspersions cast upon fellow media makers who "go commercial." If you have a zine, for instance, that begins to attract advertising and that ad revenue allows you to add full-color covers, pay writers, and (God forbid) pay yourself, people will start talking. If your zine gets bought by a magazine publisher, or you get a contract to write a book based on your zine, you can expect a backlash within the zine community. A similar reaction occurs in music, video and film, webzines, and all the rest. Success equals sellout. I've always found this absurd. If, in going commercial, you lose your edge and alter your content to suit your advertisers (which is unfortunately common), then I can understand the criticism, but not if it's simply a knee-jerk reaction. If what you do is good, if it attracts an audience, it's also likely to attract commercial interest. And the truth is, most of us, when offered the opportunity to pay our bills while doing what we love, will jump at the chance. Given that this commercialization is happening more frequently, as zines, indie music and films, and hip webzines are becoming mainstream fare, a lot of people in these respective scenes have declared alternative media passé, absorbed into the mainstream.

The more important question, it seems to me, is not whether the current wave of alternative media has crashed, but whether the next wave is there to be caught. Even if current alternative media gets boring and co-opted by the mainstream, the tools that made it alternative are still available for the next generation of adventuresome media makers. As long as there are desktop computers, home studios, camcorders, cable-access programs, and radio transmitters, a free Internet, and something that needs to be expressed, there will be enterprising individuals who'll want to jam the media.

So, dear reader, the instruments are at hand, the inspiration is swirling all around you, and your audience is waiting. Ready to jam?

Credits

Acknowledgments

Forever topping my list of thanks must be my infinitely patient, supportive wife, Pam, and my son, Blake. Sean Carton was his usual ace datasurfing self, helping with research, editing, feedback, and encouragement. The bOING bOING posse: Mark Frauenfelder, Carla Sinclair, Jim Leftwich, Bill Barker, David Pescovitz, Jon Lebkowsky, Bruce Sterling, Richard Kadrey, RU Sirius, et al. You are a constant source of inspiration and high weirdness. Thanks to all my pals: Peter Sugarman, Patch Adams, Julia Pelosi (who contributed immensely to the film section of chapter 4), Mikki Halpin (who profiled geekgirl, BLO, Eric Saks, L.A. Freewaves, and contributed several sidebars), John Bergin, Darick Chamberlin, Alberto Gaitan, and my bartender, Joe Nickell. The Well's Wired, Media, and bOING bOING conferences were very helpful, especially Steve Rhodes, George Mokray, Rob Campanell, Richard Kadrey, Brian Goldberg, and the FringeWare list, especially Michael Townsend. Holly Willis and Brad Wieners contributed several profiles as well.

A tip of the propeller beanie also goes to (in no particular order): Monte McCarter, Paco Xander Nathan, Dany Drennan, Seth Friedman, Jerod Pore, Jim Romenesko, Chip Rowe, Greg Ruggiero, Micah Solomon, Joel Smith, J. D. Considine, Darby Romeo, Ron Anteroinen, Chase, Ram Samudrala, Kristin Thomson, Greg Werckman, Mark Hosler, Jeff Soldau, Webster Lewin, Robert Carr, Abbe Don, Andrew Yoder, Joop ter Zee, Shawn Wolfe, Anne Bray, Eric Saks, Craig Baldwin, Jon Rubin, James Stewart, Scott Huffines, Lloyd Dunn, Mark Dery, Mark Achbar, and Stuart Mangrum.

To all the media hackers in this book and in my life: You make the bizarre, wacked-out reality of life in the late twentieth century infinitely more bearable, relevant, and fun. Keep on jamming.

And last but not least, I'd like to thank my agent, Matt Wagner, and my editor, Jeff Schulte.